chicago

Masculine / Feminine

Masculine

Edited by BETTY ROSZAK
and THEODORE ROSZAK

/Feminine

*Readings in Sexual Mythology
and the Liberation of Women*

HARPER COLOPHON BOOKS
Harper & Row, Publishers
New York, Evanston, and London

The editors are indebted to the Women's History Research Center in Berkeley, California, for the use of its extensive periodicals files and catalogs on women's liberation.

FIRST EDITION: Harper Colophon Books
LIBRARY OF CONGRESS CATALOG CARD NUMBER: 74–133277

Contents

Foreword

He is playing masculine. She is playing feminine.

He is playing masculine *because* she is playing feminine. She is playing feminine *because* he is playing masculine.

He is playing the kind of man that she thinks the kind of woman she is playing ought to admire. She is playing the kind of woman that he thinks the kind of man he is playing ought to desire.

If he were not playing masculine, he might well be more feminine than she is—except when she is playing very feminine. If she were not playing feminine, she might well be more masculine than he is—except when he is playing very masculine.

So he plays harder. And she plays . . . softer.

He wants to make sure that she could never be more masculine than he. She wants to make sure that he could never be more feminine than she. He therefore seeks to destroy the femininity in himself. She therefore seeks to destroy the masculinity in herself.

She is supposed to admire him for the masculinity in him that she fears in herself. He is supposed to desire her for the femininity in her that he despises in himself.

He desires her for her femininity which is *his* femininity, but which he can never lay claim to. She admires him for his masculinity which is *her* masculinity, but which she can never lay claim to. Since he may only love his own femininity in her, he envies her her femininity. Since she may only love her own masculinity in him, she envies him his masculinity.

The envy poisons their love.

He, coveting her unattainable femininity, decides to punish

her. She, coveting his unattainable masculinity, decides to punish
him. He denigrates her femininity—which he is supposed to desire
and which he really envies—and becomes more aggressively masculine. She feigns disgust at his masculinity—which she is supposed to admire and which she really envies—and becomes more
fastidiously feminine. He is becoming less and less what he wants
to be. She is becoming less and less what she wants to be. But
now he is more manly than ever, and she is more womanly than
ever.

Her femininity, growing more dependently supine, becomes
contemptible. His masculinity, growing more oppressively domineering, becomes intolerable. At last she loathes what she has
helped his masculinity to become. At last he loathes what he has
helped her femininity to become.

So far, it has all been very symmetrical. But we have left one
thing out.

The world belongs to what his masculinity has become.
The reward for what his masculinity has become is power. The
reward for what her femininity has become is only the security
which his power can bestow upon her. If he were to yield to
what her femininity has become, he would be yielding to contemptible incompetence. If she were to acquire what his masculinity has become, she would participate in intolerable coer-
civeness.

She is stifling under the triviality of her femininity. The world
is groaning beneath the terrors of his masculinity.

He is playing masculine. She is playing feminine.

How do we call off the game?

If there is justification for an anthology like this, it lies in the
fact that, off the college campuses and outside small, intense
circles of metropolitan militancy, the home truths of women's
liberation continue to seem alien, quaint, and absurd. The apolo-
getics and metaphysics of sexism lie thick upon the public consciousness. Masculine privilege, ponderously rationalized, profoundly entrenched, dies hard; female self-assertion sleeps as deep
as Beauty in her tower surrounded by thickets of mystification,
dreaming the old and treacherous dream: that woman must wait

till the man comes seeking, that she cannot awaken till the man finds her pleasing and bestows on her a respectably dependent identity. Obviously enough, there are yet many men and women who require the well-spiced food for thought this collection of readings means to provide; for the movement has far to go.

How far? Take a rough measure.

Since the advent of black power militancy, Americans have gotten used to thinking about problems of racial justice in terms of quotas—not the best way to deal with the issue, for one should not need statistics to "prove" blatant inhumanity. But the approach can be used to dramatize the obvious. When we discover that the black tenth of America makes up less than 1 percent of our society's leadership and prestige categories, but far more than 10 percent of our menial, unemployed, and prison populations, we conclude that some form of direct or indirect, *de jure* or *de facto* discrimination must be at work. Now suppose we apply the same rule of thumb to social relations between the sexes. How many female politicians, union leaders, publicists, business executives, athletic stars, university professors, diplomats, scientists, artists . . . ? How many male housekeepers, child-minders, kindergarten teachers, stenographers . . . ? How many women holding positions of power, prestige, and initiative? How many men adapting their lives to the demands of their wives' careers?

Of course, all the ratios turn out to be so far from fifty-fifty that it is ludicrous to apply the test. But even more telling than the lopsided statistical imbalance is that hardly anyone, outside militant feminist circles, seriously anticipates that the sexual mix in the many callings of life will ever be half and half. Try to imagine it: half our congressmen become congresswomen; half our housewives become househusbands; half the mothering done by fathers; half the breadwinning done by women . . . *as if sex made no difference* to the way of the world.

An unthinkable prospect. Even the mass circulation magazines that have granted women's liberation access to their front covers hardly expect to see the day; for the male-favored ratio dominates their own editorial staffs and sex-stereotyped advertising fills their pages. And it is precisely in this widely sensed unthinkability of true man-woman equality that we find the burden of women's liberation. So it is that all the fatuities and slanders that have become nonnegotiable in the discussion of race remain current in the discussion of sex. As if they were doing more than confessing their own self-serving obtuseness, men—even educated, politically radical men—continue to recite the ancient litany of lies. Namely, that:

1. Women really are born cooks and bottle washers. That's why all the advertisements say so.

2. Women really do find their whole fulfillment in the joys of child rearing and diaper changing. Those who don't are obviously abnormal.

3. Women really prefer to be social subordinates. Ask them; see how many of them admit they like to be dominated.

4. Women have already been allowed more than enough opportunities to get ahead. If they don't use them, it's *their* fault.

5. Women are making steady progress as it is. Doesn't Margaret Mead get invited to every conference of the American Association for the Advancement of Science?

6. Women are actually lucky to be women. They've got it soft. After all, it's a dog-eat-dog world, and (honest to God!) it's no fun being boss big shot.

7. True, there is a "woman problem"—but as if by magic it will be solved as part of the class problem, the race problem, the national problem. Women must wait in attendance upon these far more urgent man-made revolutions. Impatience is a sign of selfishness and divides the movement.

And, it should be admitted, outside the radical feminist community, the majority of women continue to endorse the bankrupt arguments, prop up the male ego, and play for small and secret gains. The analogous phase of race relations, when much the same caliber of nonsense could still be publicly intoned to aid and abet a racist social system, was back in the days of Amos and Andy, Stepinfetchit, and Joe Louis. Back, that is, in the days when racial justice was conveniently interpreted (by whites) to be a matter of legal reform, tokenism, and cheerful self-improvement, rather than a matter of power and the overcoming of slave psychology.

Perhaps this is the most damaging of all the male chauvinist lies: that women who dare to grow restive for being thwarted in their growth are only so many exceptional, scattered cases of inexplicably underdeveloped talent and initiative. As long as that lie stands, there can be no movement for women's liberation, but only futile gestures of personal therapy. For the truth is that women are members of a caste, socially dispersed by the family system, but collectively victimized by a lifelong process of sexual stereotyping contrived to make the world safe for male supremacy. That is the plain fact of life which emerges clearly to every woman who once penetrates beyond our society's sexual mythology and begins to take herself seriously as a whole human being. With that recognition, the isolation of women has given way to the solidarity of the movement, and the long-lost cause of feminism becomes once again an inseparable part of radical politics.

The selections gathered together here view the subjugation of women from several perspectives. Some are unabashed projections of male chauvinism, a grim catalog of the calumnies men have unloaded upon women. Others are unrestrained cries of anguish and outrage from women who have had their fill of subserving the privileges of their husbands and lovers. Some explore the psychological contours of male dominance and female submission. Others trace the social and historical repercussions of male supremacy. The hope of the editors is that each essay will serve to illuminate still another facet of the oldest and most mythologized form of enslavement in human history.

This book makes no attempt to trace the sexual stereotypes and their ideological uses beyond their influence in modern times—since the beginning of militant feminist agitation. One could easily compile a book of documents twice this size expressing male vanity and contempt for women over the ages. Those who wish to trace the misogynist vein further may turn to anthologies such as Aileen Kraditor's *Up from the Pedestal* or *The Anti-Sex* by R. E. L. Masters and Eduard Lea.

We begin here with a brief survey of the invidious use of sexual stereotyping over the last century. Here are the many voices of male arrogance—angry vituperation, objective science, lyrical obfuscation—that have sought to explain or explain away the so-called woman problem over the last four generations. None of these attitudes have passed from the scene. Rather, they have been smoothly integrated into the pedagogy, the psychotherapy, and the mass media imagery of our day.

But just to keep the historical record clear, it must be noted that feminism has had at least a handful of male allies over the last half-century. A few of these are presented in the second section of the book as encouraging examples of men's capacity to be fair-minded in confronting the privileges of their caste.

The third section presents essays by women whose writing stems from the long lull between the old feminism and the new. These are selections from the thirties, forties, and fifties, the period during which feminism seemed like a defunct social movement. Here are women who clearly saw how little the first wave of feminist crusading had done to change the discriminatory relations between men and women. Yet, at the time, they were voices crying in the wilderness of what Betty Friedan was to call the "feminine mystique": the glossy, affluent housewifery and cult of suburban motherhood that has turned out to be one of the subtler strategies of masculine dominance.

The fourth section of the book is given over to the new feminism which appeared in the late sixties. The issues are contemporary, the tone militant, the style of thought far shrewder and more sophisticated than the feminism of our great-grandmothers. The discussions of sexuality are frank and wised-up; the sexual liberation of women is carefully distinguished from the phony (and male exploitive) freedom of *Playboy* permissiveness; the bitter recognition of sexist discrimination within the various radical political movements is a ubiquitous motif; above all, the critique of home, motherhood, and marriage is carried further than ever. In a sense in which it was never meant before, we now hear talk of "a community of women" as a necessary stage in the politics of feminism.

Finally, there is a collection of manifestoes which may serve as collective self-portraits of women in search of their liberation.

The Man Problem

Friedrich Nietzsche / *Woman De-Feminized*

The late nineteenth century was the great age of women haters. For many *lumpen* intellectuals of the day—men like Otto Weininger in Germany or Sir Almroth Wright in Great Britain—antifeminism easily became a total ideology worked up from the fragile assumption that all the criminality, cowardice, and folly of the human race was concentrated in the female psyche, where the naturally dominant male must make sure it remained carefully confined and patrolled.

Friedrich Nietzsche (1844–1900) is a sad example of how inane even a gifted mind could become when it turned to "the woman problem." In this shrill and bitter passage from *Beyond Good and Evil,* Nietzsche manages to summarize almost all the misogynist slanders and idiocies that came most readily to the lips of the manly men of his era. His outburst is especially typical in its propensity for mingling the petty with the cosmic: from domestic pique over burned toast at the breakfast table to sweeping world-historical and anthropological generalizations. This section of Nietzsche's book is typical, too, in associating feminism with socialism, pacifism, and with democratic values generally. Thus we have a broadside rejection of everything on the social scene that challenged the privileges of Europe's militaristic elites.

Note the heavy use of phallic metaphors in the section following the "Seven Epigrams on Woman." One might interpret these as so many Freudian slips that reveal what it was that really worried the author about these aggressive females. But surely Nietzsche was too clever a stylist not to have introduced this little nuance deliberately.

WOMAN WANTS to become self-reliant—and for that reason she is beginning to enlighten men about "woman as such": *this* is one of the worst developments of the general *uglification* of Europe. For what must these clumsy attempts of women at scientific self-exposure bring to light! Woman has much reason for shame; so much pedantry, superficiality, schoolmarmishness, petty presumption, petty licentiousness and immodesty lies concealed in woman —one only needs to study her behavior with children!—and so far all this was at bottom best repressed and kept under control by *fear* of man. Woe when "the eternally boring in woman"—she is rich in that!—is permitted to venture forth! When she begins to unlearn thoroughly and on principle her prudence and art—of grace, of play, of chasing away worries, of lightening burdens and taking things lightly—and her subtle aptitude for agreeable desires!

Even now female voices are heard which—holy Aristophanes! —are frightening: they threaten with medical explicitness what woman *wants* from man, first and last. Is it not in the worst taste when woman sets about becoming scientific that way? So far enlightenment of this sort was fortunately man's affair, man's lot— we remained "among ourselves" in this; and whatever women write about "woman," we may in the end reserve a healthy suspicion whether woman really *wants* enlightenment about herself —whether she *can* will it—

Unless a woman seeks a new adornment for herself that way —I do think adorning herself is part of the Eternal-Feminine? —she surely wants to inspire fear of herself—perhaps she seeks mastery. But she does not *want* truth: what is truth to woman? From the beginning, nothing has been more alien, repugnant, and hostile to woman than truth—her great art is the lie, her highest concern is mere appearance and beauty. Let us men confess it:

we honor and love precisely *this* art and *this* instinct in woman—
we who have a hard time and for our relief like to associate with
beings under whose hands, eyes, and tender follies our serious-
ness, our gravity and profundity almost appear to us like folly.

Finally I pose the question: has ever a woman conceded profundity to a woman's head, or justice to a woman's heart? And is
it not true that on the whole "woman" has so far been despised
most by woman herself—and by no means by us?

We men wish that woman should not go on compromising herself through enlightenment—just as it was man's thoughtfulness
and consideration for woman that found expression in the church
decree: *mulier taceat in ecclesia!* It was for woman's good when
Napoleon gave the all too eloquent Madame de Staël to understand: *mulier taceat in politicis!* And I think it is a real friend of
women that counsels them today: *mulier taceat de muliere!*[1]

It betrays a corruption of the instincts—quite apart from the
fact that it betrays bad taste—when a woman adduces Madame
Roland or Madame de Staël or Monsieur George Sand, of all people, as if they proved anything in *favor* of "woman as such."
Among men these three are the three *comical* women as such—
nothing more!—and precisely the best involuntary *counterargu-
ments* against emancipation and feminine vainglory.

Stupidity in the kitchen; woman as cook: the gruesome thought-
lessness to which the feeding of the family and of the master of
the house is abandoned! Woman does not understand what food
means—and wants to be cook. If woman were a thinking creature,
she, as cook for millennia, would surely have had to discover the
greatest physiological facts, and she would have had to gain possession of the art of healing. Bad cooks—and the utter lack of reason in the kitchen—have delayed human development longest
and impaired it most: nor have things improved much even today.
A lecture for finishing-school girls. . . .

1. The Latin is: Woman, shut up in church! Woman, shut up about matters of state! Woman, shut up about women!

What Dante and Goethe believed about woman—the former when he sang, *"ella guardava suso, ed io in lei,"* and the latter when he translated this, "the Eternal-Feminine attracts us *higher"* —I do not doubt that every nobler woman will resist this faith, for she believes the same thing about the Eternal-Masculine—

SEVEN EPIGRAMS ON WOMAN

How the longest boredom flees, when a man comes on his knees!

Science and old age at length give weak virtue, too, some strength.

Black dress and a silent part make every woman appear—smart.

Whom I thank for my success? God!—and my dear tailoress.

Young: flower-covered den. Old: a dragon denizen.

Noble name, the legs are fine, man as well: that he were mine!

Ample meaning, speech concise—she-ass, watch for slippery ice!

Men have so far treated women like birds who had strayed to them from some height: as something more refined and vulnerable, wilder, stranger, sweeter, and more soulful—but as something one has to lock up lest it fly away.

To go wrong on the fundamental problem of "man and woman," to deny the most abysmal antagonism between them and the necessity of an eternally hostile tension, to dream perhaps of equal rights, equal education, equal claims and obligations—that is a *typical* sign of shallowness, and a thinker who has proved shallow in this dangerous place—shallow in his instinct—may be considered altogether suspicious, even more—betrayed, exposed: probably he will be too "short" for all fundamental problems of life, of the life yet to come, too, and incapable of attaining *any* depth. A man, on the other hand, who has depth, in his spirit as well as in his desires, including that depth of benevolence which is capable of severity and hardness and easily mistaken for them, must always think about woman as *Orientals* do: he must conceive of woman as a possession, as property that can be locked, as something predestined for service and achieving her perfection in that. Here he must base himself on the tremendous reason of Asia, on Asia's superiority in the instincts, as the Greeks did formerly, who were Asia's best heirs and students: as is well known, from Homer's time to the age of Pericles, as their culture *increased* along with the range of their powers, they also gradually became *more severe,* in brief, more Oriental, against woman. *How* necessary, *how* logical, *how* humanely desirable even, this was—is worth pondering.

In no age has the weaker sex been treated with as much respect by men as in ours: that belongs to the democratic inclination and basic taste, just like disrespectfulness for old age. No wonder that this respect is immediately abused. One wants more, one learns to demand, finally one almost finds this tribute of respect insulting, one would prefer competition for rights, indeed even a genuine fight: enough, woman loses her modesty. Let us immediately add that she also loses taste. She unlearns her *fear* of man: but the woman who "unlearns fear" surrenders her most womanly instincts.

That woman ventures forth when the aspect of man that inspires fear—let us say more precisely, when the *man* in man is no longer desired and cultivated—that is fair enough, also comprehensible enough. What is harder to comprehend is that, by the same token—woman degenerates. This is what is happening today: let us not deceive ourselves about that.

Wherever the industrial spirit has triumphed over the military and aristocratic spirit, woman now aspires to the economic and legal self-reliance of a clerk: "woman as clerk" is inscribed on the gate to the modern society that is taking shape now. As she thus takes possession of new rights, aspires to become "master" and

writes the "progress" of woman upon her standards and banners,
the opposite development is taking place with terrible clarity:
woman is retrogressing.

Since the French Revolution, woman's influence in Europe has
decreased proportionately as her rights and claims have increased;
and the "emancipation of woman," insofar as that is demanded
and promoted by women themselves (and not merely by shallow
males) is thus seen to be an odd symptom of the increasing
weakening and dulling of the most feminine instincts. There is
stupidity in this movement, an almost masculine stupidity of
which a woman who had turned out well—and such women are
always prudent—would have to be thoroughly ashamed.

To lose the sense for the ground on which one is most certain
of victory; to neglect practice with one's proper weapons; to let
oneself go before men, perhaps even "to the point of writing a
book," when formerly one disciplined oneself to subtle and cunning humility; to work with virtuous audacity against men's faith
in a basically different ideal that he takes to be *concealed* in
woman, something Eternally-and-Necessarily-Feminine—to talk
men emphatically and loquaciously out of their notion that woman
must be maintained, taken care of, protected, and indulged like
a more delicate, strangely wild, and often pleasant domestic animal; the awkward and indignant search for everything slavelike
and serflike that has characterized woman's position in the order
of society so far, and still does (as if slavery were a counterargu-
ment and not instead a condition of every higher culture, every
enhancement of culture)—what is the meaning of all this if not
a crumbling of feminine instincts, a defeminization?

To be sure, there are enough imbecilic friends and corrupters
of woman among the scholarly asses of the male sex who advise
woman to defeminize herself in this way and to imitate all the
stupidities with which "man" in Europe, European "manliness,"
is sick: they would like to reduce woman to the level of "general
education," probably even of reading the newspapers and talking
about politics. Here and there they even want to turn women into
freethinkers and scribblers—as if a woman without piety would
not seem utterly obnoxious and ridiculous to a profound and
godless man.

Almost everywhere one ruins her nerves with the most pathological and dangerous kind of music (our most recent German music) and makes her more hysterical by the day and more incapable of her first and last profession—to give birth to strong children. Altogether one wants to make her more "cultivated" and, as is said, make the weaker sex *strong* through culture—as if history did not teach us as impressively as possible that making men "cultivated" and making them weak—weakening, splintering, and sicklying over the *force of the will*—have always kept pace, and that the most powerful and influential women of the world (most recently Napoleon's mother) owed their power and ascendancy over men to the force of their will—and not to schoolmasters!

What inspires respect for woman, and often enough even fear, is her *nature*, which is more "natural" than man's, the genuine, cunning suppleness of a beast of prey, the tiger's claw under the glove, the naïveté of her egoism, her uneducability and inner wildness, the incomprehensibility, scope, and movement of her desires and virtues—

What, in spite of all fear, elicits pity for this dangerous and beautiful cat "woman" is that she appears to suffer more, to be more vulnerable, more in need of love, and more condemned to disappointment than any other animal. Fear and pity: with these feelings man has so far confronted woman, always with one foot in tragedy which tears to pieces as it enchants.

What? And this should be the end? And the breaking of woman's magic spell is at work? The "borification" of woman is slowly dawning? O Europe! Europe! We know the horned animal you always found most attractive; it still threatens you! Your old fable could yet become "history"—once more an immense stupidity might become master over you and carry you off. And this time no god would hide in it; no, only an "idea," a "modern idea"!

August Strindberg / *The Vampire Wife*

The playwright August Strindberg (1849–1912) is the most pathetic of the nineteenth-century male chauvinists; certainly no man of his time paid a dearer price for his obsessive masculinity. The casualty of three disastrous marriages, he more than once sacrificed his sanity to the love-hate traumas of the sex war. In each of his marriages, he found himself linked to a woman of ambition and independence: twice to actresses and once to a journalist. Clearly, a woman of talent and self-possession was the only sort that Strindberg could love; and yet, in each case, his male egotism poisoned the love and turned it to spiteful loathing.

Strindberg's futile domestic struggles to dominate the assertive women in his life are reflected—often in embarrassingly autobiographical detail—in any number of his literary works, including several of his most powerful dramas. The plays *Comrades, The Bond, The Father, The Dance of Death,* along with the collection of short stories, *Married,* are prime documents on sex relations at the turn of the century. While the women in his plays emerge, for the most part, as vampires and ruthless moral pygmies, Strindberg's dramatic instincts could never allow his dramas to become one-dimensional. His men frequently reveal a telltale defensiveness, instability, and arrogance that make them far less than heroic. In fact, many of them are pathetic figures, as responsible for their marital anguish as the wives they despise. For this reason, Strindberg's work is an excellent insight into the private married life of the nineteenth century.

The same remarkable honesty characterizes Strindberg's thinly disguised memoirs, *A Madman's Defense,* from which the following excerpt comes. The book recounts the disintegration of his marriage to the actress Siri von Essen. Despite the heavy vilification the wife suffers in the story, Strindberg self-consciously confesses to many nasty truths about himself: his oppressive male vanity, his brutal possessiveness, his capacity to bully and resort to violence, his childlike dependence on the woman he hates. An especially interesting aspect of the story is the husband's jealous fantasy that his wife is enjoying a lesbian love-life. (This fantasy still appears as a common male reaction to the phenomenon of feminism.)

Where this excerpt begins, the marriage is in an advanced state of decay. As the miserable couple trek back and forth across Europe, the husband experiences continual fits of paranoia. Meanwhile, Marie, the wife, seeks to lead her own life among friends who include some militant feminists.

WE FOLDED our tents, and made our way to Switzerland . . . and no sooner had we installed ourselves in a pension, which we did to avoid all quarrels on the subject of housekeeping, than she began making up for lost time. Being alone now and without friends, I was again in her power.

From the very beginning she posed as the keeper of a harmless lunatic. She got to know the doctor, warned the proprietor and proprietess, and informed the waitresses, the servants, and other guests. I was shut off from association with intelligent people of my own kind who might understand me. At meals she revenged herself for the silence to which she had been condemned in Paris. She missed no opportunity of joining in the conversation and literally inundated us with a never-ending stream of the foolish twaddle. . . . And since the uncultured, commonplace crowd among whom we lived always very politely agreed with her, all I had to do was be silent, and *voilà*, she was completely convinced of her superiority. . . .

Everything I loved, she detested. She sniffed at the Alps because I admired them; she scorned the beautiful walks; she avoided being alone with me; she made a practice of anticipating my wishes so as to thwart them; . . . she hated me to the point of absolute loathing. . . .

When her pregnancy was a fact I no longer felt it necessary to be quite so careful in our most intimate relations. Since there was no excuse for turning me away, she thought of ways of stimulating me and provoking me, but when she saw my happiness and contentment after our uninhibited lovemaking, she was angry for having given me so much wholesome joy.

It was too much of a good thing. My nervous symptoms were the result of sexual abstinence, first, last, and always! . . .

Trained by long study, my well-developed brain was thrown into confusion by contact with an inferior brain, and every attempt to bring it into tune with my wife's gave me spasms. . . .

Marie triumphed. I was on the verge of getting soft in the head, and the first symptoms of a persecution mania showed themselves.

Mania? Did I say "mania"? But I *was* being persecuted, and consequently it was altogether logical that I thought I was being persecuted!

It was as if I were becoming a child again. Extremely feeble, I lay for hours on the sofa, my head in her lap, my arms around her waist, like Michelangelo's *Pietà*. I pressed my forehead against her bosom, she called me her child, and I chimed in, "Your child, yes." I forgot my sex in the arms of the mother who was no longer female but sexless. Sometimes she regarded me with the eyes of the conqueror, sometimes she looked at me kindly, seized with the sudden tenderness the hangman is said to feel sometimes for his victim. She was like the female spider that devours her mate immediately after having been impregnated. . . .

A Scandinavian lady appeared on the scene, full of that nonsense called woman's emancipation. When she and Marie became friends, what chance did I stand?

She brought with her the pitiable book of a castrated writer, who, rejected and disavowed by all parties, became a traitor to his own sex by embracing the cause of all the bluestockings in the civilized world. After having read "Man and Woman" by Émile de Girardin, I, for my part, could foresee all the results of this woman's movement.

To depose man and put woman in his place and return to the matriarchy, to dethrone the true lord of the world who created civilization, spread the blessings of culture, who fathered all the great thoughts, the arts, the professions, all that is great and beautiful in the world, and crown woman, who, with few exceptions and those insignificant ones, has not shared in the great work of civilization, was in my mind a direct challenge to my sex. The very thought of having to witness the recognition and apotheosis of these intelligences of the Bronze Age, these anthropoids, these semi-apes, this pack of pestilent animals, roused my manhood. And a strange fact worth noting was that I was cured of my illness, cured through my intense repugnance to any enemy, who, though intellectually inferior, was more than a match because she totally lacked any moral code.

I take this very seriously, since in a tribal war the less honorable, the more degenerate comes out on top. Man's prospects of winning the battle are very dubious, considering his inborn respect for woman—to say nothing of the privileges he bestows on her by being the breadwinner and giving her the leisure time to prepare her battle plans. I armed myself for this new war and planned a book that in my mind would be a gauntlet flung right in the face of the emancipated women, those fools who demanded freedom at the price of man's bondage. . . .

In three months' time the book was ready for publication. It was a collection of stories of matrimonial life,[1] with an introduction in which I voiced a great number of disagreeable home truths along this line:

Woman is not a slave by any stretch of the imagination, for she and her children are supported by her husband's work. She is not oppressed, for nature has ordained that she should live

---

1. *Married: Stories of Married Life* (1884).

under the protection of her husband while she fulfills <u>her mission</u> <u>in life as a mother.</u> Woman is not man's equal in the realm of intellect, and man is not her equal when it comes to bearing children. She is not essential to the great work of civilization, since man understands its tasks and purposes better than she does. Evolution teaches us that the greater the difference between the sexes, the stronger and more fit will be the resulting off-spring. Consequently "masculinism" in woman, the equality of the sexes, is a retrogression and an utter absurdity, the last dream of romantic and idealistic socialism.[2]

Woman, man's necessary appendage, the spiritual creation of man, has no right to the privileges of her husband, since she constitutes "the other half" only by virtue of her numbers; comparatively, she is merely the sixth part of a sixth. <u>She should</u> <u>not, therefore, invade the labor market, and man for his part</u> <u>must be responsible for the support of his wife and family.</u> And the fact should be stressed that every time a woman wrests a job from a man, there is inevitably one more old maid or prostitute. . . .

The result of my attack on the strongholds of the feminists soon made itself felt. The Swiss press attacked me in such a manner that my life in Switzerland became unbearable. The sale of my books was prohibited, and I fled, hunted from town to town, to France. . . .

Almost without means I at last found neutral territory in a colony of artists in the neighborhood of Paris. . . . The society I found myself in consisted of young Scandinavian artists, recruited from professions as various as they were strange. But, worse still, there were numerous female artists—women utterly free from prejudices, completely emancipated and wildly enamored of hermaphroditic literature that convinced them that they were the equals of men. They tried to conceal their sex as

2. Strindberg lost his socialist and democratic sympathies during 1886–87, mainly because of the controversy surrounding his position on woman's emancipation. The young advanced thinkers of the time usually believed in both democracy and feminism. When Strindberg came out strongly against feminism and Ibsenism, many of his admirers deserted him. Then the aristocratic side of his nature came to the fore. He had already abandoned his socialist views—for the time being—when he first read Nietzsche in the summer of 1888.

far as possible by adopting certain masculine manners and habits. They smoked, drank, played billiards . . . and made love to each other.

The crowning touch!

As an alternative to utter isolation, I made friends with two of those monstrous women. One of them was a so-called literary woman, the other a dauber. The writer called on me first, as is customary when one happens to be a well-known author. My wife was jealous at once. She was anxious to win for herself this new ally of mine, who seemed sufficiently enlightened to appreciate my arguments against half-women. . . .

Meanwhile, a fresh complication confronted me, worse, if possible than any of the previous ones. The authoress who had pretended to be in love with me made a conquest of Marie, and Marie became so devoted to her that people began to talk. Simultaneously, the jealousy of the authoress' former "inseparable" was aroused, which did not exactly lessen the ugly rumors.

One evening in bed, hot and excited from our embraces, Marie asked me whether I was in love with her friend. . . .

"Don't be crazy! She's disgusting—a lush! You're joking."

"I'm mad about her!" she replied. "Strange, isn't it? . . . I'm afraid to be alone with her!"

"Why?"

"I don't know! She's so delicious. . . . A wonderful body . . . "

"Really? . . ."

The following week we invited some of our Paris friends, artists without moral scruples or prejudices, and their wives.

The men came, but alone. The wives sent apologies so transparent that they amounted to insults.

Dinner degenerated into a perfect orgy. The scandalous conduct of the men nauseated me.

They treated Marie's two friends as if they were prostitutes, and when everyone was more or less intoxicated I saw my wife letting herself be kissed repeatedly by a lieutenant.

I waved my billiard cue above their heads and demanded an explanation. "He's a childhood friend, a relative! Don't make yourself ridiculous, my poor darling," she riposted. "Besides, it's an old Russian custom to kiss in public, and we Finns are Russian subjects."

"Rubbish!" exclaimed one of the guests. "Those two relatives! Never on your life!"

I nearly committed murder. I—

The thought of leaving my children without father and mother arrested my arm.

When I was alone with Marie, I let her have it. "Whore!"

"Why?"

"Because you let yourself be treated like one."

"Don't tell me you're jealous?"

"That's right. I'm jealous. Jealous of my honor, the dignity of my family, the reputation of my wife, the future of my children! Because of your disgusting conduct, we're ostracized by all decent women. Letting yourself be kissed like that in public by a stranger! You know what you are? A slut. You don't see, don't hear, don't understand what you're doing! You're completely lacking a sense of duty! If you don't change for the better, darling, I'll have you put in a cage. And to begin with, I forbid you to have anything more to do with those two women!"

"It's all your fault! You egged me on!"

"I wanted to see how far you would go! A trap to catch you red-handed."

"See how far I would go! I know what you suspect about me and my friends, but do you have any proof?"

"Proof, no! But I've heard your cynical confessions. And didn't one of your friends admit that in her own country she would fall into the hands of the law?"

"I thought you denied the existence of vice!"

"I don't care how your friends amuse themselves so long as their games don't interfere with the welfare of my family. However, from the moment that their 'peculiarities,' if you prefer this word, threaten to injure us, they are, as far as we are concerned, criminal acts. True, as a philosopher, I don't admit the existence of vice but only of physical and moral defects. And when this unnatural 'vice' was discussed only recently in the French Parliament, all the French physicians of note were of the opinion that it was not the province of the law to interfere in these matters, except in cases where citizens incurred some harm."

I might as well have preached to a stone wall. How could I hope to make this woman, who acknowledged no other law than her animal instincts, grasp a philosophical distinction! . . .

In Germany, the land of militarism, where the patriarchal system is still in full force, Marie felt completely lost. No one would listen to her silly talk about alleged women's rights. Here young girls had been forbidden to attend the university; here the dowry of a woman who marries an officer of the army has to be deposited with the War Office as the inalienable property of the family; here all government appointments are reserved for the man, the breadwinner of the family.

Marie struggled and fought as if she were caught in an ambush. On her first attempt to hoodwink me she was severely taken to task by the women in the group. For the first time I found the fair sex entirely on my side, and poor little Marie had to lick the dust. Friendly chats with the officers braced me. Their manner and behavior influenced mine in accordance with the law of adaptation and after ten years of spiritual emasculation my manhood reasserted itself.

I let my hair grow as it liked and combed away the bangs on which Marie had insisted. My voice, which had grown thin and reedy from everlastingly baby-talking to an hysterical woman, regained its former resonance. The hollows in my cheeks filled out, and although I was now beginning my fortieth year, my whole physique gained in strength and vigor. . . .

I was on friendly terms with all the women in the house and soon fell into the habit of taking a very active part in the conversation, while Marie, poor, unpopular Marie, had to play second fiddle.

She began to be afraid of me. One morning, for the first time in the six years of our marriage, she appeared fully dressed in my bedroom before I was up. I could not understand this sudden change. We had a stormy scene, during which she let it out of the bag that she was jealous of the girl who came into my room every morning to light the fire in my stove.

"And I detest your new ways!" she exclaimed. "I hate this so-called manliness and I loathe you when you put on airs."

Well, I knew that it had always been the page, the lapdog, the weakling, "her child," that she loved. The married woman never loves the man in her husband, however much she may admire it elsewhere.

I became more and more popular with the women. I sought their society. My whole nature was expanding in the friendly warmth that radiated from women, real women who inspired respectful love, the unconscious surrender of the man by which he pays tribute to the womanly woman. . . .

I hated her now with a hatred more fatal than indifference because it was the other side of love. It grew there in hiding to such an extent that I am tempted to formulate an axiom: I hated her because I loved her. It was on a Sunday, while we were dining in the summer arbor, that the electric force that had gathered during the last ten years discharged itself. I don't know what caused it. No matter! I struck her, for the first time in my life. I slapped her face repeatedly, and when she tried to defend herself I seized her wrists and forced her on her knees. She uttered a terrified scream. The temporary satisfaction I had felt at my action gave way to dismay. The children, frightened to death, cried out with fear. It was the worst moment of my miserable life! It is a crime, a most unnatural crime, to strike a woman, a mother! And in the presence of her children. . . . It seemed to me that the sun ought to hide its face . . . I felt sick to death.

And yet there was peace in my soul, like the calm after a storm, a satisfaction such as is only derived from duty done. I regretted my action but I felt no remorse. It was merely a matter of cause and effect.

In the evening I saw her walking in the moonlit garden. I joined her; I kissed her. She did not repulse me; she burst into tears. We walked for a few minutes, then she accompanied me to my room and stayed with me, making love until midnight.

Strange marriage! In the afternoon I struck her; at night we held each other in our arms.

Strange woman who kisses her executioner with hot and willing lips!

Why had I not known it before? If I had struck her ten years ago I should now have been the happiest of husbands.

There's a piece of advice!
Remember it, fellow members of the league of deceived husbands!

Sigmund Freud / *Anatomy Is Destiny*

Of all the major minds that addressed themselves to "the woman problem," Sigmund Freud (1856–1939) made the most enduring and perhaps cruelest anti-feminist contribution. His famous theory of penis envy is surely the definitive formulation of the notion that woman's anatomy dictates her whole destiny —and all the more intimidating since Freud, as founder and *pontifex maximus* of psychoanalysis, could disguise his well-developed contempt for women as impeccable science. To be sure, the theory has been soundly challenged by many psychiatrists. Clara Thompson has, for example, explained that penis envy—insofar as it exists at all—is obviously the symbolic expression of women's thwarted aspirations in male-dominated society. (See her "Penis Envy in Women," in *Psychiatry*, 1943, pp. 123–125. Also see Karen Horney's essay in this anthology.) Nevertheless, this unlikely idea, for which there is about as much clinical evidence as one might expect to conjure up for breast envy or womb envy in men, lingers on in one modified form or another among many Freudian analysts today.

It is hardly difficult to account for Freud's unshakable belief in the innate inferiority of women. Raised in a conventionally

From "Femininity" in *New Introductory Lectures on Psychoanalysis*, Vol. 22, translated and edited by James Strachey (New York, Norton, 1965), pp. 112–135. Copyright 1933 by Sigmund Freud. Copyright renewed 1961 by W. J. H. Sprott. Copyright © 1965, 1964 by James Strachey. Reprinted by permission of W. W. Norton & Company, Inc.

patriarchal middle-class home, he easily transferred the classic
pattern of Victorian paternalism into his own marriage and
family life. Mrs. Freud, the most agreeably submissive of
wives, apparently never failed to corroborate her husband's
male supremacist convictions. (See Ronald V. Sampson's remarks on the relations between Dr. and Mrs. Freud in this
anthology.) Moreover, most of the other women in Freud's
life were—with few exceptions—female hysterics who came to
him as patients and, in the process of therapy, displayed all the
symptoms of neurotic dependence. Freud was, in short, heir
to all the sexual mythology of his age, and his own limited
range of experience did little to call his preconceptions into
question.

The selection that follows is from a lecture delivered late in
Freud's career (1932). The argument that precedes this excerpt is as follows: male and female sexuality becomes radically
different following the "Oedipal" or "phallic" phase of childhood development. Prior to this phase, girls and boys alike
focus all their eroticism on their mothers. Also, girls freely enjoy
masturbating by way of the clitoris—which Freud refers to
quaintly as their "penis-equivalent." During the phallic phase,
however, Freud insists that the girl must carry off two very
tricky bits of psychological acrobatics. She must transfer her
erotic sensitivity from clitoris to vagina (whence originates the
myth of the vaginal orgasm), and she must transfer her libidi-
nal attachments from mother to father (lest she fail to be
sexually straight). As Freud puts it: "a girl has to change her
erotogenic zone and her object—both of which a boy retains."
How is the girl to manage this? Freud's conclusion is that she
achieves her femininity by way of the female castration complex.
For women, the resolution of that complex is the lifelong burden of "penis envy," and from this, Freud argues, all the
feminine attributes follow: passivity, dependence, sexual frigidity, and general incompetence. Women, doomed to an unre-
lieved "genital deficiency" and lacking the strong male super-
ego, fail to develop any capacity to create culture. They are
natural-born homebodies, scatterbrains, and parasites.

It is interesting to note that Freud was but one of a long line of nineteenth-century male experts on female sexuality—all of whom came to the same conclusion; namely, that women are very close to being asexual animals. Dr. William Acton, the Victorian English sexologist, decided that "the best mothers, wives, and managers of households know little or nothing of sexual indulgences. Love of home, children, and domestic duties are the only passions they feel." (For a comment on this male denial of women's erotic rights, see Havelock Ellis's essay in this anthology.) Similarly, the German gynecologist Dr. Windscheid was absolutely certain that "in the normal woman, especially of the higher social classes, sexual instinct is acquired, not inborn. When it *is* inborn or awakens by itself, there is abnormality. Since women do not know this instinct before marriage, they do not miss it when they have no occasion in life to learn it."

As you hear, then, we ascribe a castration complex to women as well. And for good reasons, though its content cannot be the same as with boys. In the latter the castration complex arises after they have learnt from the sight of the female genitals that the organ which they value so highly need not necessarily accompany the body. At this the boy recalls to mind the threats he brought on himself by his doings with that organ, he begins to give credence to them and falls under the influence of fear of castration, which will be the most powerful motive force in his subsequent development. The castration complex of girls is also started by the sight of the genitals of the other sex. They at once notice the difference and, it must be admitted, its significance, too. They feel seriously wronged, often declare that they want to "have something like it, too," and fall a victim to "envy for the penis," which will leave ineradicable traces on their development and the formation of their character and which will not be surmounted in even the most favourable cases without a severe expenditure of psychical energy. The girl's recognition of the fact of her being without a penis does not by any means imply that she submits to the fact easily. On the contrary, she continues to hold on for a long time to the wish to get something like it

herself and she believes in that possibility for improbably long
years; and analysis can show that, at a period when knowledge
of reality has long since rejected the fulfilment of the wish as
unattainable, it persists in the unconscious and retains a considerable cathexis of energy. The wish to get the longed-for penis eventually in spite of everything may contribute to the motives that
drive a mature woman to analysis, and what she may reasonably expect from analysis—a capacity, for instance, to carry on
an intellectual profession—may often be recognized as a sub-
limated modification of this repressed wish.

One cannot very well doubt the importance of envy for the
penis. You may take it as an instance of male injustice if I assert that envy and jealousy play an even greater part in the
mental life of women than of men. It is not that I think these
characteristics are absent in men or that I think they have no
other roots in women than envy for the penis; but I am inclined
to attribute their greater amount in women to this latter influence.
Some analysts, however, have shown an inclination to depreciate
the importance of this first installment of penis-envy in the phallic
phase. They are of the opinion that what we find of this attitude
in women is in the main a secondary structure which has come
about on the occasion of later conflicts by regression to this early
infantile impulse. This, however, is a general problem of depth
psychology. In many pathological—or even unusual—instinctual
attitudes (for instance, in all sexual perversions) the question
arises of how much of their strength is to be attributed to early
infantile fixations and how much to the influence of later experiences and developments. . . . Both factors play a part in varying
amounts in the causation. . . . The infantile factor sets the pattern
in all cases but does not always determine the issue. . . . Precisely
in the case of penis-envy I should argue decidedly in favour of
the preponderance of the infantile factor.

The discovery that she is castrated is a turning-point in a girl's
growth. Three possible lines of development start from it: one
leads to sexual inhibition or to neurosis, the second to change of
character in the sense of a masculinity complex, the third, finally,
to normal femininity. We have learnt a fair amount, though not
everything, about all three.

The essential content of the first is as follows: the little girl has hitherto lived in a masculine way, has been able to get pleasure by the excitation of her clitoris, and has brought this activity into relation with her sexual wishes directed towards her mother, which are often active ones; now, owing to the influence of her penis-envy, she loses her enjoyment in her phallic sexuality. Her self-love is mortified by the comparison with the boy's far superior equipment, and in consequence she renounces her masturbatory satisfaction from her clitoris, repudiates her love for her mother and at the same time not infrequently represses a good part of her sexual trends in general. No doubt her turning away from her mother does not occur all at once, for to begin with the girl regards her castration as an individual misfortune, and only gradually extends it to other females and finally to her mother as well. Her love was directed to her *phallic* mother; with the discovery that her mother is castrated it becomes possible to drop her as an object, so that the motives for hostility, which have long been accumulating, gain the upper hand. This means, therefore, that as a result of the discovery of women's lack of a penis, they are debased in value for girls just as they are for boys and later perhaps for men.

You know the immense aetiological importance attributed by our neurotic patients to their masturbation. They make it responsible for all their troubles and we have the greatest difficulty in persuading them that they are mistaken. In fact, however, we ought to admit to them that they are right, for masturbation is the executive agent of infantile sexuality, from the faulty development of which they are indeed suffering. But what neurotics mostly blame is the masturbation of the period of puberty; they have mostly forgotten that of early infancy, which is what is really in question. . . . From the development of girls . . . I can give you the example of a child herself trying to get free from masturbating. She does not always succeed in this. If envy for the penis has provoked a powerful impulse against clitoridal masturbation but this nevertheless refuses to give way, a violent struggle for liberation ensues in which the girl, as it were, herself takes over the role of her deposed mother and gives expression to her entire dissatisfaction with her inferior clitoris in her efforts against ob-

taining satisfaction from it. Many years later, when her masturbatory activity has long since been suppressed, an interest still
persists which we must interpret as a defence against a temptation that is still dreaded. It manifests itself in the emergence of
sympathy for those to whom similar difficulties are attributed, it
plays a part as a motive in contracting a marriage and, indeed,
it may determine the choice of a husband or lover. Disposing of
early infantile masturbation is truly no easy or indifferent
business.

Along with the abandonment of clitoridal masturbation a certain
amount of activity is renounced. Passivity now has the upper
hand, and the girl's turning to her father is accomplished prin-
cipally with the help of passive instinctual impulses. You can see
that a wave of development like this, which clears the phallic
activity out of the way, smooths the ground for femininity. If too
much is not lost in the course of it through repression, this
femininity may turn out to be normal. The wish with which the
girl turns to her father is no doubt originally the wish for the
penis which her mother has refused her and which she now
expects from her father. The feminine situation is only established, however, if the wish for a penis is replaced by one for a
baby, if that is, a baby takes the place of a penis in accordance
with an ancient symbolic equivalence. It has not escaped us that
the girl has wished for a baby earlier, in the undisturbed phallic
phase; that, of course, was the meaning of her playing with dolls.
But that play was not in fact an expression of her femininity; it
served as an identification with her mother with the intention of
substituting activity for passivity. *She* was playing the part of
mother and the doll was herself: now she could do with the
baby everything her mother used to do with her. Not until the
emergence of the wish for a penis does the doll-baby become a
baby from the girl's father, and thereafter the aim of the most
powerful feminine wish. Her happiness is great if later on this
wish for a baby finds fulfilment in reality, and quite especially
so if the baby is a little boy who brings the longed-for penis
with him. Often enough in her combined picture of "a baby from
her father" the emphasis is laid on the baby and her father left
unstressed. In this way the ancient masculine wish for the posses-

sion of a penis is still faintly visible through the femininity now achieved. But perhaps we ought rather to recognize this wish for a penis as being *par excellence* a feminine one.

With the transference of the wish for a penis-baby on to her father, the girl has entered the situation of the Oedipus complex. Her hostility to her mother, which did not need to be freshly created, is now greatly intensified, for she becomes the girl's rival, who received from her father everything that she desires from him. . . . For girls the Oedipus situation is the outcome of a long and difficult development; it is a kind of preliminary solution, a position of rest which is not soon abandoned, especially as the beginning of the latency period is not far distant. And we are now struck by a difference between the two sexes, which is probably momentous, in regard to the relation of the Oedipus complex to the castration complex. In a boy the Oedipus complex, in which he desires his mother and would like to get rid of his father as being a rival, develops naturally from the phase of his phallic sexuality. The threat of castration compels him, however, to give up that attitude. Under the impression of the danger of losing his penis, the Oedipus complex is abandoned, repressed and, in the most normal cases, entirely destroyed and a severe super-ego is set up as its heir. What happens with a girl is almost the opposite. The castration complex prepares for the Oedipus complex instead of destroying it; the girl is driven out of her attachment to her mother through the influence of her envy for the penis and she enters the Oedipus situation as though into a haven of refuge. In the absence of fear of castration the chief motive is lacking which leads boys to surmount the Oedipus complex. Girls remain in it for an indeterminate length of time; they demolish it late and, even so, incompletely. In these circumstances the formation of the super-ego must suffer; it cannot attain the strength and independence which give it its cultural significance, and feminists are not pleased when we point out to them the effects of this factor upon the average feminine character.

To go back a little. We mentioned as the second possible reaction to the discovery of female castration the development of a powerful masculinity complex. By this we mean that the girl refuses, as it were, to recognize the unwelcome fact and, defiantly rebellious, even exaggerates her previous masculinity, clings to her clitoridal activity and takes refuge in an identification with her phallic mother or her father. What can it be that decides in favour of this outcome? We can only suppose that it is a constitutional factor, a greater amount of activity, such as is ordinarily characteristic of a male. However that may be, the essence of this process is that at this point in development the wave of passivity is avoided which opens the way to the turn towards femininity. The extreme achievement of such a masculinity complex would appear to be the influencing of the choice of an object in the sense of manifest homosexuality. Analytic experience teaches us, to be sure, that female homosexuality is seldom or never a direct continuation of infantile masculinity. Even for a girl of this kind it seems necessary that she should take her father as an object for some time and enter the Oedipus situation. But afterwards, as a result of her inevitable disappointments from her father, she is driven to regress into her early masculinity complex. The significance of these disappointments must not be exaggerated; a girl who is destined to become feminine is not spared them, though they do not have the same effect. The predominance of the constitutional factor seems indisputable; but the two phases in the development of female homosexuality are well mirrored in the practices of homosexuals, who play the parts of mother and baby with each other as often and as clearly as those of husband and wife. . . .

It is not my intention to pursue the further behaviour of femininity through puberty to the period of maturity. But I will bring a few features together in what follows. Taking its prehistory as a starting-point, I will only emphasize here that the development of femininity remains exposed to disturbance by the residual phenomena of the early masculine period. Regressions . . . frequently occur; in the course of some women's lives there is a repeated alternation between periods in which masculinity or femininity gains the upper hand. Some portion of what we men call "the enigma of women" may perhaps be derived from this expression of bisexuality in women's lives. But another question seems to have become ripe for judgement in the course of these researches. We have called the motive force of sexual life "the libido." Sexual life is dominated by the polarity of masculine-feminine; thus the notion suggests itself of considering the relation of the libido to this antithesis. It would not be surprising if it were to turn out that each sexuality had its own libido appropriated to it, so that one sort of libido would pursue the aims of a masculine sexual life and another sort those of a feminine one. But nothing of the kind is true. There is only one libido, which serves both the masculine and the feminine sexual functions. To it itself we cannot assign any sex; if, following the conventional equation of activity and masculinity, we are inclined to describe it as masculine, we must not forget that it also covers trends with a passive aim. Nevertheless, the juxtaposition "feminine libido" is without any justification. Furthermore, it is our impression that more constraint has been applied to the libido when it is pressed into the service of the feminine function, and that—to speak teleologically—Nature takes less careful account of its demands than in the case of masculinity. And the reason for this may lie—thinking once again teleologically—in the fact that the accomplishment of the aim of biology has been entrusted to the aggressiveness of men and has been made to some extent independent of women's consent.

The sexual frigidity of women, the frequency of which appears to confirm this disregard, is a phenomenon that is still insufficiently understood. Sometimes it is psychogenic and in that case accessible to influence; but in other cases it suggests the hypothesis of its being constitutionally determined and even of there being a contributory anatomical factor.

I have promised to tell you of a few more psychical peculiarities of mature femininity, as we come across them in analytic observation. We do not lay claim to more than an average validity for these assertions; nor is it always easy to distinguish what should be ascribed to the influence of the sexual function and what to social breeding. Thus, we attribute a larger amount of narcissism to femininity, which also affects women's choice of object, so that to be loved is a stronger need for them than to love. The effect of penis-envy has a share, further, in the physical vanity of women, since they are bound to value their charms more highly as a late compensation for their original sexual inferiority. Shame, which is considered to be a feminine characteristic *par excellence* but is far more a matter of convention than might be supposed, has as its purpose, we believe, concealment of genital deficiency. We are not forgetting that at a later time shame takes on other functions. It seems that women have made few contributions to the discoveries and inventions in the history of civilization; there is, however, one technique which they may have invented—that of plaiting and weaving. If that is so, we should be tempted to guess the unconscious motive for the achievement. Nature herself would seem to have given the model which this achievement imitates by causing the growth at maturity of the pubic hair that conceals the genitals. The step that remained to be taken lay in making the threads adhere to one another, while on the body they stick into the skin and are only matted together. If you reject this idea as fantastic and regard my belief in the influence of lack of a penis on the configuration of femininity as an *idée fixe*, I am of course defenceless.

The determinants of women's choice of an object are often made unrecognizable by social conditions. Where the choice is able to show itself freely, it is often made in accordance with the narcissistic ideal of the man whom the girl had wished to become. If the girl has remained in her attachment to her father . . . her choice is made according to the paternal type. Since, when she turned from her mother to her father, the hostility of her ambivalent relation remained with her mother, a choice of this kind should guarantee a happy marriage. But very often the outcome is of a kind that presents a general threat to such a settlement of the conflict due to ambivalence. The hostility that has been left behind follows in the train of the positive attachment and spreads over on to the new object. The woman's husband, who to begin with inherited from her father, becomes after a time her mother's heir as well. So it may easily happen that the second half of a woman's life may be filled by the struggle against her husband, just as the shorter first half was filled by her rebellion against her mother. When this reaction has been lived through, a second marriage may easily turn out very much more satisfying. Another alteration in a woman's nature, for which lovers are unprepared, may occur in a marriage after the first child is born. Under the influence of a woman's becoming a mother herself, an identification with her own mother may be revived, against which she had striven up till the time of her marriage, and this may attract all the available libido to itself, so that the compulsion to repeat reproduces an unhappy marriage between her parents. The difference in a mother's reaction to the birth of a son or a daughter shows that the old factor of a lack of a penis has even now not lost its strength. A mother is only brought unlimited satisfaction by her relation to a son; this is altogether the most perfect, the most free from ambivalence of all human relationships. A mother can transfer to her son the ambition which she has been obliged to suppress in herself, and she can expect from him the satisfaction of all that has been left over in her of her masculinity complex. Even a marriage is not made secure until the wife has succeeded in making her husband her child as well and in acting as a mother to him. . . .

The fact that women must be regarded as having little sense of justice is no doubt related to the predominance of envy in their mental life; for the demand for justice is a modification of envy and lays down the condition subject to which one can put envy aside. We also regard women as weaker in their social interests and as having less capacity for sublimating their instincts than men. The former is no doubt derived from the dissocial quality which unquestionably characterizes all sexual relations. Lovers find sufficiency in each other, and families too resist inclusion in more comprehensive associations. The aptitude for sublimation is subject to the greatest individual variations. On the other hand I cannot help mentioning an impression that we are constantly receiving during analytic practice. A man of about thirty strikes us as a youthful, somewhat unformed individual, whom we expect to make powerful use of the possibilities for development opened up to him by analysis. A woman of the same age, however, often frightens us by her psychical rigidity and unchangeability. Her libido has taken up final positions and seems incapable of exchanging them for others. There are no paths open to further development; it is as though the whole process had already run its course and remains thenceforward insusceptible to influence—as though, indeed, the difficult development to femininity had exhausted the possibilities of the person concerned. . . .

Robert Graves / *Real Women*

Robert Graves, famous English poet and novelist, begins his essay with a historical analysis of the confused and deteriorating roles of the sexes. Here is a man who assumes the posture of reverence before his own fiction of the primitive, idealized woman, the figure he has so well popularized as the White Goddess of prehistoric Europe. But, woman, beware of ever descending from the high place he has assigned to you! Woman is holy, she is the poet's muse: her job is to bring inspiration and solace to the harassed and overintellectualized male—but nothing more.

This viewpoint is, in fact, the most insidious (and the least obvious) aspect of the male put-down because of its very flattery. Graves, who makes every effort in this artful essay to be sympathetic to the injustices of woman's place and role and who appears to be on the side of woman's freedom, like many other males, is still placing woman outside of the real, male world—the place where all the decisions get made. He thus insists, even though history began with female rule and though *man*kind now sorely needs a return to her "guiding force," that the *main concern* of the real woman is still her beauty. She contemptuously eschews "feminism" as mere intellectual distraction. As Graves defines her, the real woman comes very close indeed to the official or orthodox view of women put forth by the fashion magazines. Possibly the only difference between the orthodoxy and Graves is that for Graves

From *Mammon and the Black Goddess* (New York, Doubleday, 1965), pp. 101–114. First published in *Ladies' Home Journal*, 1964. Copyright © 1964 by Robert Graves. Reprinted by permission of Collins-Knowlton-Wing, Inc.

the real woman is not happy with money and her stupid husband alone, but is <u>continually seeking her counterpart, that also mythical creature: the real man.</u>

THE MOST important historical study of all, utterly dwarfing all economic and political ones, is for me the changing relationship between men and women down the centuries—from prehistoric times to the present moral chaos in which both sexes have become equally confused about their roles. But I am a poet by calling, and have lived outside ordinary civilization for so many years that anything I write about real women must read oddly. Except perhaps to real women themselves, or the occasional man whom some accident of birth or experience tempts to agree with me.

A real woman, <u>by my definition, neither despises nor worships</u> *real ♀* <u>men, but is proud not to have been born a man, does everything she can to avoid thinking or acting like one, knows the full extent of her powers, and feels free to reject all arbitrary man-made obligations.</u> She is her own oracle of right and wrong, firmly believing in her five sound senses and intuitive sixth. Once a real woman has been warned by her nose that those apples are tasteless, or assured by her fingertips that this material is shoddy, no salesman in the world can persuade her to the contrary. Nor, once she has met some personage in private, and summed him up with a single keen glance as weak, vain, or crooked, will his mounting public reputation convince her otherwise. She takes pleasure in the company of simple, happy, undemanding women; but seldom or never finds a friend worthy of her full confidence. Since she never settles for the second best in love, <u>what most troubles her is the rareness of real men</u>. Wherever she goes, her singularity will arouse strong feelings: adulation, jealousy, resentment, but never pity for her loneliness. Real women are royal women; the words once had the same meaning. Democracy has no welcome for queens.

It would be wrong to identify the real woman with the typical wild one who, after a difficult childhood, has left home early to live by her wits at the expense of men. <u>The wild woman is in</u> *wild ♀* <u>capable either of friendship for other women, whom she cannot</u>

fail to regard as rivals, or of love for a man, her declared enemy.
But at least she keeps her eyes open and ridicules the view that
women must enthusiastically accept this glorious modern world
of plenty bestowed on them by their hard-working menfolk, and
that they enjoy being passionately swept off their feet and afterwards treated with amused indulgence. There was never, of
course, any truth in the comic-strip legend of a primitive he-man
who would grab his woman by the hair, threaten her with a
knobbed club if she refused his advances, and haul her off pant-
ing ecstatically to his cave. . . .

To reach some understanding of real women, one must think
back to a primitive age, when men invariably treated women as
the holier sex, since they alone perpetuated the race. Women
were the sole agriculturists, guardians of springs, fruit trees, and
the sacred hearth fire, and lived unaffected by any notions of progress. Tribal queens never thought in terms of historical time,
but only of seasons; judged each case on its own merits, not by
a legal code, as real women still do; and showed little regard
for trade or mechanical inventions. Chance discoveries or new
techniques in arts and crafts were welcome, so long as these
neither upset tribal economy nor enhanced the importance of
individuals. It was the queen's task to restrain men from letting
their ambition or intellectual curiosity over-ride practical common sense, as it is still woman's task to ask her husband: "Must
you kill yourself making money? Haven't we enough for the next
five years at least, even if you stopped working altogether? Surely
you don't enjoy your martyrdom?" But even if he cares to listen,
social pressures compel him to provide for his family until he
drops dead.

History begins with the emergence of men from female rule.
They had at last discovered that a woman cannot conceive without male assistance—and brooded over the implications of this
surprising fact. After long whispered conferences it was agreed
that men ought to claim their freedom. They asked, "Why should
descent be reckoned in the female line, not the male? Why
should a man when he marries go to the woman's home, not
contrariwise? Why should a woman, not a man, sow the seed
corn? Why should women control the tribe? Surely men are the

true creators, sowers of seed, and therefore the holier sex, as well as being physically stronger?" Thus the male habit of reasoning from irrelevant facts, rather than relying on woman's practical wisdom, began the war between the sexes that has been raging ever since.

Men gradually usurped women's prerogatives in farming, magic, handicrafts, war—the Amazons are no mere figment—and government. The story is epitomized in a classical Greek myth: how the goddess Hera pitied a poor, bedraggled cuckoo and warmed him at her breast. This cuckoo was her brother Zeus in disguise, who ravished and humiliated her by seizing throne and sceptre. Later, when Hera and her kinsfolk rebelled against Zeus, he hung her from the vault of heaven with an anvil tied to each foot. . . .

Men consolidated their victory. They reckoned descent in the male line, brought wives to their own homes, invented historical annals, legal codes, weights and measures, standing armies, engineering, logic, and philosophy. On the excuse of protecting the weaker sex, they placed woman under male tutelage; henceforward she must serve her father's or husband's domestic needs as though not only spiritually but mentally inferior to him. . . .

It seems puzzling that the real women of those days let all this happen to them. The sole reason I can suggest is that they thought far ahead. Since man had a certain undeveloped intellectual capacity, of which it would have been wrong to deny him full use, the real women sat back patiently, prepared to give him a free hand for some hundreds or thousands of years. Only a long series of disastrous experiments could make him realize the error of his headstrong ways. Eventually he must return to them in willing and chastened dependence. . . .

Financial pressures of men's own making brought about the recent so-called emancipation of women. Grown daughters could no longer stay idling at home, a burden to their parents and to themselves until married off. Industry was booming and, with appropriate moral safeguards, they might fill the widening gaps in man-power. Women, who can now earn and keep their own money, even when wives, and have been granted the franchise— "franchise" originally meant "freedom from being a serf"—need show men no gratitude for this liberality. Their freedom is still limited. They remain citizens of the second degree, auxiliary male personnel barred from all the highest offices; and would never have got where they are so quickly had it not been for two world wars and such loveless male inventions as machine guns, submarines, bombing planes and universal conscription.

Strangely enough, it is easier to be a real woman in backwaters of Christianity or Islam or Hinduism, where codes of behaviour have not changed for centuries, than in urbanized Europe or America. There she knows what part she must play, and can guard her inborn dignity. Although the husband, as head of the family, makes all decisions, he will never dare overrule even her unspoken protests. . . .

Among us Westerners, because of man's jealous insistence on marital privacy, *home* has shrunk from settlement to farmhouse, thence to the cottage, thence to the ten-roomed apartment, thence to three rooms and a kitchenette with the usual labour-saving devices, in a huge residential block full of utter strangers. The housewife has her washing machine, telephone, television, refrigerator, electric cooker, car and door keys, to pay for which a husband must be out working all the week. She cannot regret (because she never knew) the easy companionship of her great-grandmother's day: quilting bees and husking bees, taking the cousins to do a week's washing down at the creek, lending a hand with the shearing and harvest, making jams and pickles, getting up round dances, singing and playing practical jokes. But no real woman can ever accept the present situation.

Man's logic has defeated itself. Boredom often drives the married woman back to a job as soon as she can leave her children at a nursery school; or to infidelity; or to an analyst. Home is home for only two days of the week. Which is why some paternally-minded industrialists take advice from professors of sociology and plant their employees all together in a wholesome suburban neighbourhood, where the company's standards of taste and respectability must rule their lives. . . . Spouses are thus shackled by a well-paid job to which the husband need no longer commute, by house, garden and swimming pool, by children, by hope of advancement and the prospect of a pension. Any sign of noncompliance is scored against both. No real woman can ever accept this situation either. . . .

Wild women take advantage of this artificial state of affairs by exploiting the dormant dissatisfactions of husbands. One of them told me the other day, "Yes, you may call me a mean, greedy, undependable, lazy, treacherous, spendthrift bitch. That's true enough a good part of the time; but it isn't the whole story. In fact, I've given myself to myself, and to no one else. My beauty is my own, and I take good care of it. If I choose a lover, I grant the lucky fellow no rights over me; and if he has sense, he won't claim any. As for breaking up a home, nobody can do that unless it's already cracked!" . . .

Marriage, like money, is still with us; and, like money, progressively devalued. The ties between these two male inventions get closer and closer. Originally marriage meant the sale of a woman by one man to another; now most women sell themselves, though they may have no intention of delivering the goods listed in the bill of sale. Not only is the wife, on an average, five years younger than her husband, but she lives statistically longer. So money power passes progressively into the hands of women. Also, divorce legislation (forced on guilt-ridden legislators by nagging spouses) grossly favours the wife. A youthful rival figures in most divorce suits, and though she and the wife seldom act collusively, they share an old-fashioned insistence on the honourable state of marriage, which enriches both. Wild women will commit matrimony when things go hard for them, without the least thought of keeping their obligations. The entranced husbands never know what has hit them, nor do they profit by the experience.

The United States, though often described as a matriarchy in all but name, remains patriarchal. Matriarchy, to be effective, needs real women. When women organize themselves intellectually on masculine lines, they merely stimulate the feminization of men, who for terror of husband-hunting viragoes, are apt to seek refuge in the cul-de-sac of homosexuality. . . .

A real woman's main concern is her beauty, which she cultivates for her own pleasure—not to ensnare men. Though she despises fashion as a male financial business, she will not make herself conspicuous by a defiance of conventions. The materials, colours, and cut of her clothes, her hair style and her jewels are all chosen to match a sense of personal uniqueness. She can dress in advance of fashion, yet seem to lead it; and to any irregular features she may have, she lends a lovely ugliness denied to common beauty queens. Perfect detachment from the artificial or second-hand keeps her face unclouded. She has no small talk on current topics, and will suddenly vanish from a party, however grand, as soon as it grows boring.

If she plays games, it will be for fun, not competition; and if up against a win-at-all-costs opponent in tennis or golf, she will take care to lose handsomely—as one who competes only against herself. If she drinks, it will be because she likes the taste; and if she smokes, it will be for the same reason, not to steady her nerves.

She misses real men—men who would recognize her potentiality and agree that our world, despite its appearance of rational organization, is a wholly haphazard one, clanking on noisily to its fate along a random course once defined as "progress." And that a calamitous collapse must come before a new start can be made—from the point where the sex war was first declared and woman's conservative instinct as the guiding force of humankind repudiated. Because womanhood remains incomplete without a child, most real women marry—preferring simple, affectionate husbands who cannot understand them. This is not a renunciation of real love, since they agree with the thirteenth-century Countess of Narbonne: "Conjugal affection has absolutely nothing in common with love. We say 'absolutely,' and with all consideration, that love cannot exist between husband and wife."

Man's biological function is to do; woman's is to be. This difference is not a contrast of mere activity with mere passivity. "To be" is indeed a full-time occupation. A real woman has no leisure in the modern economic sense—leisure as a consumer's relaxed insistence on commercial entertainment—but is always thinking, taking stock of herself, setting a stage on which actors can perform. If she paints or writes, this will be for her own private amusement, not to satisfy ambition; and if forced to earn her livelihood in this way, she repudiates the public personage forced on her by dealers and critics.

A real woman is content to dress with a difference, to make her home unmistakably her own, to illuminate any company she enters, to cook by instinct, not by the cookery book. This is her evidence of being, the proof of which lies in her sense of certitude. She is no feminist; feminism, like all "isms," implies an intellectual approach to a subject; and reality can be understood only by transcending the intellect.

Mental institutions on both sides of the Atlantic house hundreds of young, beautiful, silently brooding girls, victims of the sex war—defeated before they could come to terms with life. Their tragedy has been brilliantly described in *The Ha-Ha*, a novel by Jennifer Dawson, whose heroine is almost a real woman, because: "she never just plays a game with herself or other people, and refuses to learn the rules of society—meaning the worthy, useful ordinary women who are so busy finding husbands and houses and good income brackets that they just haven't time to be conscious of themselves, and who see the world as an inventory, a container of so many things, and other people as so many tin-openers to undo it for them." The friendly and intelligent staff of the mental institution cannot persuade her that she should realign herself with the orderly outside male world. Being not quite real enough to escape defeat by pretending conformity, she loses all pride in her appearance, ceases to concentrate on any self-imposed task; and when at last she desperately breaks out, the police, we foresee, cannot fail to fetch her back for sedation and still closer surveillance.

A real woman somehow avoids suicide, or virtual suicide, or the mental institution; but is always painfully aware of having been born out of her true epoch; considered as either the past, or as the long-distant future. A sense of humour saves her from defeat. "This is not worthy of me," she will remind herself ten times a day, "but to preserve my inner self I must once more act an alien part."

None of her women neighbours, idly content with money and what it will buy, feel any need for drastic change in the man-woman relationship; she treats them politely, and has patience. If she ever comes across a real man, the thin thread of human hope that eventually the world will make practical sense again —cannot yet have snapped.

Lionel Tiger / *Why Men Need a Boys' Night Out*

Lionel Tiger, who is a young Canadian anthropologist, takes as the main thesis of his recent book the biological need of men to form all-male groups that totally reject contact with females. Drawing upon studies of primate behavior and upon his own speculations about the evolution of society since the age of prehistoric hunting-and-gathering bands, he hypothesizes that the male specialization in hunting caused the evolutionary physical differentiation of the sexes. While disclaiming any antifemale prejudice and declaring himself to be only an objective scientist stating the facts, Tiger insists on the innate biological differences so dear to the hearts of nineteenth-century misogynists, such as the natural aggressiveness of men, their "greater spatial-geographical ability," and their superior talent for throwing spears. As he puts it:

> Males dominate females in occupational and political spheres. This is a species-specific pattern and is associated with my other proposition: that males bond in a variety of situations involving power, force, crucial or dangerous work. . . . They consciously and emotionally *exclude* females from these bonds. The significant notion here is that these broad patterns are biologically based. . . . To use Count's term, male dominance and bonding are features of the human "biogram."[1]

Thus, for Tiger, dominant groups which exist "for men only" are a necessary biological adjunct of our society. His "scien-

---

1. *Men in Groups*, p. 112.

tific" justification for masculine supremacy barely disguises an all-too-typical masculine arrogance. Like Robert Ardrey in *The Territorial Imperative,* Tiger seeks to explain all wars as expressions of the innate aggressive drive of man and concludes with Ardrey that keeping the peace is well-nigh impossible. What Tiger's pseudo-anthropology leaves unexplained is why the supposed naturalness of male dominance needs such elaborate institutional machinery to maintain itself. And further, why so many women (like blacks and other oppressed minorities) fail to abide by this "natural" caste system.

In the selection offered here, Tiger ponders the consequence of the exclusive male bond for "social policy," accepting a future of human inequality with a sanguineness born of his own male sense of superiority. Note that he seems unable to conceive of society without the dominance of some group or other. Note also his approval of sex segregation as a necessary part of male dominance in education, recreation, politics, and the professions.

I<small>F</small> [<small>MY</small>] <small>HYPOTHESIS</small> is true, and if understanding is encouraged to guide behaviour, what are the consequences for social policy? . . . These can range from the provision of facilities for male association in housing developments, to the diagnosis of psychological and psychiatric illnesses of men unable to enjoy or find bonds with other men, and paradoxically may help to solve the problems of those extreme effeminate homosexuals whose eagerness to attract other males may as clearly betray a craving for male bonds as a . . . desire to be female. But I will deal primarily with . . . education, politics, aggression and its control, and—briefly—architecture and town planning.

What is the relevance of male bonding—as a process—to the educational system? This is necessarily bound up with the general question of sexual differences. Boys and girls mature at different rates, develop different skills at different times, and may express different interests. But in many, if not most, schools . . . boys and girls attend the same schools and often compete against each other for teachers' attention, grades, and prizes.

School boards and teachers may find this administratively and morally easier, but the interests of individual students and the community at large may be poorly served. . . .

The evidence is only impressionistic, but there is some suggestion that males who attend all-male schools—particularly where these schools are also associated with high social status—develop mannerisms, traits of character, social and other skills, etc., which appear to advance the boys' adult careers in a marked way. . . . Obviously high initial status and attendance at a prestigious school provides advantages to females as well as to males. But in girls' schools much more emphasis is placed upon the graces, skills, and socio-sexual preoccupations appropriate to attracting and marrying high-status males. . . . In general, girls appear to prepare for high-status marriage while males prepare for high-status work. Of course these are not static patterns, and it is by no means universal that girls' schools are more concerned with marriage than work and hence with social rather than explicitly academic excellence. In one Canadian school of very high social standing, academic success has become as important, if not more important, than immediate social success. This is a change which has occurred over the past decade and is attributable chiefly to the fact that the men in the marital "catchment area" of this particular school must now demand university-trained wives because of changes in the occupational and political worlds. The school thus produces girls who can pass the difficult university entrance exams. The general status patterns have not changed; . . . what have changed are the criteria on the basis of which desirable males choose their mates. . . .

A realistic assessment of respective life chances of males and females is involved here; we must stress the social-functional differences in the all-male and all-female school. We must also suggest that [private] schools—unlike their coeducational counterparts—maintain the status of particularly the most elevated families in a direct and concrete way. Perhaps unisexual schools are particularly conservative in relation to social class and occupational achievement. . . . The argument is that a unisexual school system, coupled with high-status support for certain institutions within it, tends strongly in the direction of stratification rather than charisma. The males' stratification problem is linked to the world of work and power. The females' problem is tied to the crucial matter of whom it is possible to marry. Normally, females will seek males favoured in the stratification system, favoured in good part because of their school and possibly university attendance, and because of their links with other males who will provide, if not actual jobs, at least business propositions and clients and perhaps shared and reflected glory. Other social institutions frequently organize themselves on the basis of comparable social networks. But I am concerned to stress the particular importance of unisexual institutions in maintaining high social statuses for already dominant groups and persons in any community. . . .

If the high-status ideal is the male who has attended an all-male school, who is versed in the "manly arts" such as sports, hunting, possibly war, who is fond of all male activities such as clubbing, fishing, and hunting, then presumably the conception of masculinity in the community in question will depend in good measure upon this image arising out of all-male schooling.

I do not want to press too far the relationship between male bonding and the educational system. But given the importance of social learning in expressing and organizing any species-specific behavioural patterns, one would expect significant differences between all-male school systems and heterosexual ones, particularly in the kind and intensity of links formed between males. It is not by chance that this matter relates directly to the maintenance of privilege of high-status groups. It reflects the link between bonding, "equilibration," and superior positions in social hierarchies. Therefore, the compatibility of public-school systems with flexible democracy, for example, as in England, is perhaps a question even more perplexing than researchers, politicians, and educators have heretofore recognized. This is because the [English] public-school system is a generalized expression of core human patterns. The system is not only involved in training social and technical skills, but also with conceptions of maleness and of male loyalty. Change or retention of the schools must have wide-reaching effects extending well beyond the educational system itself to include such phenomena as conceptions of hierarchical propriety and the sexual division of labour, principles of colleague and mate selection, notions of societal firmness and flexibility, and the nature of the career.

A consequence of this particular emphasis on male groups and sexual differentiation for the content of educational programmes must be greater recognition of these sexual differences, in both individual and social-organizational behaviour. Obviously, much of the difficulty in this area results as much from prudery as from misinformation and ignorance. All the same, it is clearly to the advantage of both sexes for the males to learn not only about the physical events of the menstrual cycle but also about the behavioural and temperamental changes of its different phases. It is curiously anomalous that, while young males may be taught about the tax system, about the value of exercise, or the poetry of Browning, they are unlikely to receive systematic knowledge about the specialized patterns of behaviour of members of the sex with whom the great majority will spend a good deal of their adult lives. More realistic and analytic treatment of the different typical careers and life-chances of males and females might alleviate what appears to be frequent disharmony between what many females expect about their working and married lives and the extent to which communities help them to meet these expectations. In particular, some objective discussion of the anti-female tradition and the nature of male exclusion of females from various male groups could simplify or clarify the problems women may feel who seek careers in predominantly male organizations. This would be especially pertinent for females entering politics. To date there has been relatively little change in the political role of women. Understanding the resistance to females could lead to self-conscious changes in electoral and political practices to facilitate women's entry into the political world. Changes of such a kind would have to be introduced because of information about the nature of human society rather than as an admission of female inferiority or incapacity. There need be no element of condescension implied by an attempt to increase the representativeness of political bodies. The very recognition of the problem—if so it is defined—in this form could be an important step in its solution.

But it is simply prudent to point out that historical evidence weighs strongly against the optimistic feminists in this matter.

Particularly in terms of "access to a public forum," as Robert Murphy calls it, . . . females may suffer relatively inflexible disabilities; they may simply not provide the "releasers" or generally satisfactory images of power, discretion, foresight, etc., which induce communities to follow their leaders.

At times of war and national crisis this may be especially pertinent. If female involvement is to increase even in times of crisis more forceful measures than those which presently exist will have to be undertaken, if only because the inducements now available appear to produce relatively small effect. A more serious problem is whether or not it is "desirable" . . . for women to have high political office. I put this question in the same sense as the following question: is it desirable for men instead of women to rear children? Obviously considerable admixture of roles is possible in many spheres, but given cross-cultural data about the political role of females, it may constitute a revolutionary and perhaps hazardous social change with numerous latent consequences should women ever enter politics in great numbers. Even a but partly female-dominated policy may go beyond the parameters of "healthy" possibility, given the basic conservatism of the species. I am concerned less here with isolated women who achieve high office than with a major shift in the sexual composition of dominating bodies. Of course, the whole nature of political action could change were it defined as partly or largely female; certainly there would be major changes in relations between female-dominated states. But like disarmament, it is unlikely that any important nation would develop a female-biased or feminized political system unless other competing nations developed them also.

It appears to be widely believed that men are stronger and tougher, both physically and in terms of social action. To forego the exclusive or predominant use of men in international relations would involve considerable trust in the intentions and internal controls of other nations. Neither recent nor ancient political history stimulates the conclusion that this form of disengagement from effortful and hard international competition is imminent, or even possible in the foreseeable future. This may mean that female political activity would concentrate on domestic and local concerns. The complex contribution to political

change of which females are potentially the agents may have
to be made in a relatively limited sphere. My hunch is that any
such changes will be circumscribed and of minor import. While
the subject of female political participation may be more carefully and compassionately discussed than ever before, actual
socio-political changes will be influenced more extensively and
directly by other factors, such as technology, age-composition of
the population, the spread of armaments in the world, etc., than
by the efforts of females and their striving for political emancipation. . . .

Another broad but influential matter . . . to which attention
could be profitably turned, is the effect of male-female differences and the male bonding hypothesis on architecture and
town-planning. The layout of houses in new towns and suburban
developments may preclude the growth of male bonds in new
communities and so curtail the range of social experience available to men in their communities of residence. Succinctly stated,
men "need" some haunts and/or occasions which exclude females. Given the decreasing hours of work, and as potential time
at home increases, should not men's huts or their equivalent be
constructed? Obviously English pubs serve this function already.
On the other hand, all-male pubs tend to be restricted to old-
established working-class communities. In new developments,
planning is based on relatively middle-class norms; foreign to
these is the notion that males and females should even temporarily engage in sexually segregated drinking or discussion.
Sports facilities may satisfy part of the requirements I am projecting here; but there remains no place which is defined as
specifically and exclusively male, and which is not only exclusively male but also anti-female. No necessary hostility between
males and females is implied here, but rather an expression in
architecture and planning of a kind of social structuring which
may be both satisfying and "constructively" energizing for men.
From a planning point of view, it may be equally desirable to
provide similar facilities for females. Architects and planners
could have the responsibility to recognize formally in their
schemes the value of permitting men to enjoy forthright male
interaction in sanctioned situations. This would not replace voluntary organizations, hobby and sports groups, political activity,

and the host of other activities in which men alone, and men and women together engage. But proceeding from the observation that simple, pointless, unstructured conversation is a widely desired human activity, and that if friendship patterns, discussion groups at mixed parties, the existence of all-male dining and drinking clubs, etc., are an indication of a human propensity, then the provision of physical facilities for this male activity may be a responsibility of sophisticated planners of physical space.

This may seem to some a retrograde step—in a sense it would be. But some facilities for men, particularly in suburban areas, could provide a useful counter-balance for men to the heavy emotional and temporal demands of nuclear family life. It has been claimed often enough that suburban life is child-centered. In part, the reason must be that the institutional life of suburban communities reflects the strongly family-centered concepts of housing. Schools and churches—both family and/or child-centered—are typically the first public buildings to be constructed in new communities and a pattern is established which does not ultimately create a *formally* all-male environment for recreation. Even existing urban clubs are economically afflicted by the movement of their former clientele to suburbs where heterosexual country clubs usurp time men formerly spent in all-male establishments. . . . The trend of planning and prejudice of belief is in the direction of curtailing opportunities to establish male-only environments outside of work. Community views about familial activity, females' rights, and the assumed impropriety of all-male groups may deny men a relatively harmless and modest form of pleasure.

Though wives may fear their husbands' congregation in all-male groups because it is assumed they will collectively seek out other women, in fact they do not do this and prefer to drink, talk, or gamble. It is true that many females will regard their husbands' decision to spend time with men rather than their families as a threat to their own appeal and strength as women and wives. The weight of cultural expectations supports this. However, this does not mean the expectations are "desirable" or even biologically healthy. It is conceivable that—in the same way that children who are too rigorously supervised or women who are too dominated by men may be less likely to be lively and creative—so, also, men dominated by their wives and families may lose a certain constructive maleness of consequence to many of their activities. . . .

Numerous other implications of the male-bonding hypothesis must wait discussion after further work. I conclude with some comments about the efficacy of managing aggression through the male bond. . . .

There is a paradox. I have suggested that male associations and the exclusion of females are intimately linked with aggression, which, in turn, may be linked with unhappy social consequences. I have also proposed that failure to engage in male bonding may hinder the search for comprehensive and satisfactory male individual experience. The paradox is in fact a true one, and yet another expression of the dilemma any peacemaker faces who wishes to restrain the encounter of active hostile groups and yet not diminish the internal energy and productivity of the separate groups. . . .

For various reasons—chiefly military, historical, and the need for defence—notions of valid maleness are widely associated with the hard military virtues, with various activities such as hunting, speeding, fighting, and the extraction of substantial sums of money from either natural resources or people. The hard and "realistic" virtues created the dislocation of the Industrial Revolution in England, scarred the ground, polluted the air, and violently disrupted social life. Those who argued that this was wrong or intemperate were the idealists; they were soft. That later the realists would plant grass on the coal-mine tips, would replan slums and control air pollution, is a question of context; a change in the nature of social awareness has made welfare work in its varied forms tough, real, and partly manly. But none the less the control of goods, power, land, people remains more reputedly masculine than scholarship, art, or chemistry; the advertisements instruct us "Be a Man—Join the Army" not "Be a Man—Become a Fabric Designer."

There are two things to be said about this. Weapons, fast machines, complex and heavy structures, certain social activities such as war, decision-making and major social events, the maintenance of order—these may in fact elicit or stimulate "maleness" from men more directly and powerfully than designing jewelry, playing the harpsichord, or composing poetry. Maleness may be more forcefully released by certain hard and heavy phenomena in the same way that maternal feelings are better stimulated by a baby than by an aircraft, an elephant, or even an adult. Driving a racing car or leading a platoon are different from writing a good paragraph or having a pleasing idea or forming a friendship; there is a sense of moment, of manly drama. At a high speed any driving error can be dangerous or fatal; there are other drivers to watch and anticipate; there is the condition of the road, its curvature, and the line of vision; there is the car to understand and govern. It is this sense of moment, of the inevitability of decision, which may be manly, or at least a manliness of a different kind from what happens when a decision must be made about a patient, a lawyer's client, an inadequate student, or the sub-plot of a play. Perhaps it is this which underlies the war game and the great interest in armament which virtually all nations show. Perhaps for their leaders it is part of the masculine aesthetic. Involvement with guns confers validation, and decision-making about armaments elicits a sense of the rigour, providence, and virile realism of the decision-makers.

So the first point is that certain matters and things may be more successfully exciting stimuli for men than others. The second is that within whatever "natural" limits may exist, cultures define what is more or less masculine. Traditionally the masculine has been the hard and the militant. But traditions change; in the new atomic conditions of life war is not an ultimate test of power and skill but of self-destructive madness. This may conspire with other forces such as coeducation, increasing sexual freedom, the affluence of the young, the greater catholicism of more-travelled populations, and the very media of communication to promote changes in conceptions of maleness. The new conceptions will encourage the draft-card burner who argues that pacifism is more manly than using powerful weapons to fight Vietnamese peasants; it could allow the man who has his hair waved to disclose this fact in the company of men. Just as more women drive cars, wear trouser suits, and

independently enter the labour force, so more men can wear
colorful clothes, formerly the garb of homosexuals and deviants;
they can be flavoured with perfume and cosmetics; in a word
they can be dandies but men.

It is undeniable that changes in personal decor have occurred
—they always do—and in some ways these changes may minimize
sexual decorative differences. But also it may be premature to
see in this the reflection of large-scale and major shifts in sexual
roles and sexual balance of power and access to power. . . . The
sexual differentiation of role involves a highly charged human
core phenomenon, the importance of which is its adaptability to
different economic, ecological, and climatic circumstances. That
it should change its form and decor should not surprise us. The
content remains the same, and it is risky to surmise on the
vulgar basis of what is chic and sexy at any moment that basic
communal notions of maleness have changed.

Of course, they may have already changed, and it is the task
of human biologists to perceive and analyse these changes. But
I have argued throughout this book that the changes are slow
and possibly invisible to contemporaries of the changes. Though
the prestige of militarists may decline in some war-weary or
unbelieving communities, some other role or set of roles will be
given equivalent status and encouragement because the practitioners of the jobs in question help the community in its contest
with other communities for the world's goods and privileges.
These practitioners will also be seen as tough, manly, and quiet
masters of the momentous event. That they will often be successful at the expense of other communities . . . is a reiteration
of the aggressive pattern discussed earlier. . . . There will be
many, at the same time, who develop drugs, perfect inventions,
rescue lives, organize flood relief, who will be rewarded by the
community. It is these wholly "constructive" heroes who may
represent a guide for new ways for men to validate themselves,
for women to love and breed with validated males, and for boys
to learn how to become men and what men do. History is dis-
couraging about the prospects. But this is as much a spur to
greater and more careful effort as an invitation to cynicism or
despair.

Can women help? The Indian government decreed that Untouchables should have a proportion of seats in legislatures and special privileges to redress a historical deprivation. Perhaps women can be guaranteed a proportion of places, not only in legislatures, but also in the critical decision-making bodies dealing with finance, defence, and war. This could be effective only if the men involved in these female-populated groups were not permitted to treat the formal group as a largely irrelevant forum for decisions taken by smaller all-male groups possessing the conviction of higher patriotism and realism than any mixed group could boast. This would ensure some democratic representativeness; more important, it would insert a new element into the decision-making which has yielded us a phenomenally well-armed world—a world where, since the Second World War, whose ghastliness seemed final at the time, there have been scores of painful and costly military encounters. This new female element could turn out to be much the same thing again, so that there would be no change. But if the theory presented here is correct, modifying the dynamics and repercussions of the male bond may be a crucial feature of altered attitudes to power, to the value of destroying other communities' people and property, and to the concept that manliness is strength rather than flexibility and authority rather than attentiveness to others. . . .

At the same time, should women join in male enterprises, particularly enterprises which now have the sense of masculine moment, it may necessitate some recognition of the desirability of either permitting or prohibiting sexual relations between participants, or at least recognizing the fact that sexual attraction exists between them and may cause difficulty to the group. This may be less problematic for the older individuals involved. But the complex series of taboos, titillations, laws, and hedonistic influences surrounding male-female relationships in industrial societies . . . will have to be adjusted to take account of the introduction of the sexual tension into affairs already tense as a result of their importance to communities and their consequences for individual careers.

Equality will cause problems. Doctors and nurses, executives and secretaries, producers and actresses, can and do manage because there is a status and dominance difference between them. It is relatively "normal" for men to seek sexual access to

females who are their subordinates. Sexual access is not even
in itself necessary. . . . But where status dominance does not
exist it is possible that some effort at stabilizing the internal
sexual power system by coitus or flirtation may result from
placing men and women as equals in charged situations concerned with power in the first place. In my own sphere, I have
been struck at how predictably academics considering employing
a younger female will comment upon her attractiveness *qua*
female. It is possible to regard this as an anticipation of possible
conflict between woman-as-colleague and woman-as-sexual-ob-
ject. Nor are women unaware of the importance of attractiveness
in securing desirable employment in largely male organizations.
Currently there appear to be no solid prospects for significant
change in this matter, and it seems but sensible to continue to
regard it as a hazard in the search for ways of introducing female influence in the councils of power.

It may be unwise, therefore, to be optimistic or even sanguine
about the possibility that females will soon stimulate much
change in the social sub-systems and systems at the root of war
as well as of happier actions. Women stay around and support
murderers, thieves, usurers, frauds, and even failures. It is unlikely they will spurn warriors, and it is likely there will always
be enough—indeed a surplus—of women happy and willing to
play the general's or the corporal's lady, to raise their children,
and move from base to base living as income and expectations
permit. It is their husband's job to kill or declare war or defend
territory or condemn a traitor or imprison a pacifist; the men
must do their job if only because it is too late in life to find
another. Usually the job is justified because humans are immensely imaginative, and if indeed women are more realistic
than men about the world, they boast the tact to allow men to
maintain their own version of the *realpolitik*—it is still this version
which prevails where it matters. Nor has Lysistrata's sexual bargaining ever been the answer. Should it come to that, the sexual-
reproductive urgency claims more than enough strike-breakers
who close the bedroom door behind them; women do not form
bonds. Dependent as most women still are on the earnings and
genes of men, they break ranks very soon.

Some Male Allies

George Bernard Shaw / *The Womanly Woman*

Shaw (1856–1950) needs no introduction. For our purposes here one need only be reminded that he was the first to bring the "new woman" of his day to the English stage, especially in *Candida* and *Mrs. Warren's Profession*. But beyond these portrayals, he also attacked contemporary mores and institutions which deprived women of their human rights. The most notable example of G.B.S. taking on a venerable anti-female institution is his little-performed play, *Getting Married*, in which he shrewdly demolishes the institution of marriage with all of its quaint English legal excrescences. *The Quintessence of Ibsenism* (1891), from which the following essay was taken, champions Henrik Ibsen, whose own iconoclastic dramatic works assaulted the false idols of the age. The illusion Shaw attacks here is the "womanly woman" who sacrifices herself for the sake of home and family. Shaw urges that women repudiate the oppressive ideal set up by men to keep them in their place. His analysis of the development of a woman's life upon marriage, from the innocent young bride to the disillusioned matron, is today still one of the most damning accounts of marriage as bondage. Shaw must be the first (and last) to have used the "parrot analogy" to describe women's plight: "If we have come to think that the nursery and the kitchen are the natural sphere of woman, we have done so exactly as

From *Selected Non-dramatic Writings of Bernard Shaw*, edited by Dan H. Laurence (Boston, Houghton, Mifflin, n.d.), pp. 224–230. Reprinted by permission of the Society of Authors for the Bernard Shaw Estate.

English children come to think that a cage is the natural sphere
of a parrot—because they have never seen one anywhere else."
The extension of this analogy is not only delightfully clever
but enlightening as well.

EVERYBODY REMEMBERS the "Diary of Marie Bashkirtseff." An
outline of it, with a running commentary, was given in the *Review of Reviews* (June 1890) by the editor, Mr. William Stead,
a sort of modern Julian the Apostate, who, having gained an immense following by a public service in rendering which he had
to perform a realistic feat of a somewhat scandalous character,
entered upon a campaign with the object of establishing the ideal
of sexual "purity" as a condition of public life.[1] As he retains his
best qualities—faith in himself, wilfulness, conscientious unscru-
pulousness—he can always make himself heard. Prominent among
his ideals is an ideal of womanliness. In support of that ideal he
will, like all idealists, make and believe any statement, however
obviously and grotesquely unreal. When he found Marie Bashkirtseff's account of herself utterly incompatible with the account
of a woman's mind given to him by his ideal, he was confronted
with the dilemma that either Marie was not a woman or else his
ideal did not correspond to nature. He actually accepted the
former alternative. "Of the distinctively womanly," he says, "there
is in her but little trace. She was the very antithesis of a true
woman." Mr. Stead's next difficulty was, that self-control, being
a leading quality in his ideal, could not have been possessed by
Marie: otherwise she would have been more like his ideal. Nevertheless, he had to record that she, without any compulsion from
circumstances, made herself a highly skilled artist by working
ten hours a day for six years. Let anyone who thinks that this is

1. William Stead's "realistic feat" was a journalistic stunt meant to pub-
licize the laxity of the laws governing child prostitution. In 1885 he purchased
a thirteen-year-old girl from her mother and, with no difficulty at all, trotted
her about town and off to the Continent "for immoral purposes." At the time,
the female "age of consent" in England was thirteen years. As a result of
Stead's exposé, the gentlemen of Queen Victoria's Parliament charitably
raised the age to sixteen.

no evidence of self-control just try it for six months. Mr. Stead's verdict, nevertheless, was "No self-control." However, his fundamental quarrel with Marie came out in the following lines. "Marie," he said, "was artist, musician, wit, philosopher, student —anything you like but a natural woman with a heart to love, and a soul to find its supreme satisfaction in sacrifice for lover or for child." Now of all the idealist abominations that make society pestiferous, I doubt if there be any so mean as that of forcing self-sacrifice on a woman under pretence that she likes it; and, if she ventures to contradict the pretence, declaring her no true woman. In India they carried this piece of idealism to the length of declaring that a wife could not bear to survive her husband, but would be prompted by her own faithful, loving, beautiful nature to offer up her life on the pyre which consumed his dead body. The astonishing thing is that women, sooner than be branded as unsexed wretches, allowed themselves to be stupefied with drink, and in that unwomanly condition burnt alive. British Philistinism put down widow idealizing with the strong hand; and suttee is abolished in India. The English form of it still survives; and Mr. Stead, the rescuer of the children, is one of its high-priests. Imagine his feelings on coming across this entry in a woman's diary, "I love myself." Or this, "I swear solemnly—by the Gospels, by the passion of Christ, by MYSELF—that in four years I will be famous." The young woman was positively proposing to exercise for her own sake all the powers that were given her, in Mr. Stead's opinion, solely that she might sacrifice them for her lover or child! No wonder he is driven to exclaim again, "She was very clever, no doubt; but woman she was not." Now observe this notable result. Marie Bashkirtseff, instead of being a less agreeable person than the ordinary female conformer to the ideal of womanliness, was conspicuously the reverse. Mr. Stead himself wrote as one infatuated with her mere diary, and pleased himself by representing her as a person who fascinated everybody, and was a source of delight to all about her by the mere exhilaration and hope-giving atmosphere of her wilfulness. The truth is, that in real life a self-sacrificing woman, is not only taken advantage of, but disliked as well for her pains. No *man* pretends that his soul finds its supreme satisfaction in self-sacrifice; such an affectation would stamp him as a coward and weakling; the manly man is he who takes the Bashkirtseff view of himself. But men are not the less loved on this account. No one ever feels helpless by the side of the self-helper; whilst the self-sacrificer is always a drag, a responsibility, a reproach, an everlasting and unnatural trouble with whom no really strong soul can live. Only those who have helped themselves know how to help others, and to respect their right to help themselves.

Although romantic idealists generally insist on self-surrender as an indispensable element in true womanly love, its repulsive effect is well known and feared in practice by both sexes. The extreme instance is the reckless self-abandonment seen in the infatuation of passionate sexual desire. Everyone who becomes the object of that infatuation shrinks from it instinctively. Love loses its charm when it is not free; and whether the compulsion is that of custom and law, or of infatuation, the effect is the same: it becomes valueless. The desire to give inspires no affection unless there is also the power to withhold; and the successful wooer, in both sexes alike, is the one who can stand out for honourable conditions, and failing them, go without. Such conditions are evidently not offered to either sex by the legal marriage of today; for it is the intense repugnance inspired by the compulsory character of the legalized conjugal relation that leads, first to the idealization of marriage whilst it remains indispensable as a means of perpetuating society; then to its modification by divorce and by the abolition of penalties for refusal to comply with judicial orders for restitution of conjugal rights; and finally to its disuse and disappearance as the responsibility for the maintenance and education of the rising generation is shifted from the parent to the community. . . .

Although the growing repugnance to face the Church of England marriage service has led many celebrants to omit those passages which frankly explain the object of the institution, we are not likely to dispense with legal ties and obligations, and trust wholly to the permanence of love, until the continuity of society no longer depends on the private nursery. Love, as a practical factor in society, is still a mere appetite. That higher development of it which Ibsen shows us occurring in the case of

Rebecca West in *Rosmersholm* is only known to most of us by the descriptions of great poets, who themselves, as their biographies prove, have often known it, not by sustained experience, but only by brief glimpses. And it is never a first-fruit of their love affairs. Tannhäuser may die in the conviction that one moment of the emotion he felt with Saint Elizabeth was fuller and happier than all the hours of passion he spent with Venus; but that does not alter the fact that love began for him with Venus, and that its earlier tentatives towards the final goal were attended with relapses. Now Tannhäuser's passion for Venus is a development of the humdrum fondness of the bourgeois Jack for his Jill, a development at once higher and more dangerous, just as idealism is at once higher and more dangerous than Philistinism. The fondness is the germ of the passion: the passion is the germ of the more perfect love. When Blake told men that through excess they would learn moderation, he knew that the way for the present lay through the Venusberg, and that the race would assuredly not perish there as some individuals have, and as the Puritan fears we all shall unless we find a way round. Also he no doubt foresaw the time when our children would be born on the other side of it, and so be spared that fiery purgation.

But the very fact that Blake is still commonly regarded as a crazy visionary, and that the current criticism of *Rosmersholm* entirely fails even to notice the evolution of Rebecca's passion for Rosmer into her love for him, much more to credit the moral transfiguration which accompanies it, show how absurd it would be to pretend, for the sake of edification, that the ordinary marriage of today is a union between a William Blake and a Rebecca West, or that it would be possible, even if it were enlightened policy, to deny the satisfaction of the sexual appetite to persons who have not reached that stage. An overwhelming majority of such marriages as are not purely *de convenance,* are entered into for the gratification of that appetite either in its crudest form or veiled only by those idealistic illusions which the youthful imagination weaves so wonderfully under the stimulus of desire, and which older people indulgently laugh at. This being so, it is not surprising that our society, being directly dominated by men, comes to regard Woman, not as an end in herself like Man, but

solely as a means of ministering to his appetite. The ideal wife
is one who does everything that the ideal husband likes, and
nothing else. Now to treat a person as a means instead of an end
is to deny that person's right to live. And to be treated as a means
to such an end as sexual intercourse with those who deny one's
right to live is insufferable to any human being. Woman, if she
dares face the fact that she is being so treated, must either
loathe herself or else rebel. As a rule, when circumstances enable
her to rebel successfully—for instance, when the accident of
genius enables her to "lose her character" without losing her
employment or cutting herself off from the society she values—
she does rebel; but circumstances seldom do. Does she then
loathe herself? By no means: she deceives herself in the idealist
fashion by denying that the love which her suitor offers her is
tainted with sexual appetite at all. It is, she declares, a beautiful,
disinterested, pure, sublime devotion to another by which a man's
life is exalted and purified, and a woman's rendered blest. And
of all the cynics, the filthiest to her mind is the one who sees,
in the man making honourable proposals to his future wife,
nothing but the human male seeking his female. The man himself keeps her confirmed in her illusion; for the truth is unbearable to him too: he wants to form an affectionate tie, and not
to drive a degrading bargain. After all, the germ of the highest
love is in them both, though as yet it is no more than the appetite
they are disguising so carefully from themselves. Consequently
every stockbroker who has just brought his business up to marrying point woos in terms of the romantic illusion; and it is agreed
between the two that their marriage shall realize the romantic
ideal. Then comes the breakdown of the plan. The young wife
finds that her husband is neglecting her for his business; that his
interests, his activities, his whole life except that one part of it
to which only a cynic ever referred to before her marriage, lies
away from home; and that her business is to sit there and mope
until she is wanted. Then what can she do? If she complains, he,
the self-helper, can do without her; whilst she is dependent on
him for her position, her livelihood, her place in society, her
home, her name, her very bread. All this is brought home to her
by the first burst of displeasure her complaints provoke. For-

tunately, things do not remain forever at this point—perhaps the most wretched in a woman's life. The self-respect she has lost as a wife she regains as a mother, in which capacity her use and importance to the community compare favourably with those of most men of business. She is wanted in the house, wanted in the market, wanted by the children; and now, instead of weeping because her husband is away in the city, thinking of stocks and shares instead of his ideal woman, she would regard his presence in the house all day as an intolerable nuisance. And so, though she is completely disillusioned on the subject of ideal love, yet, since it has not turned out so badly after all, she countenances the illusion still from the point of view that it is a useful and harmless means of getting boys and girls to marry and settle down. And this conviction is the stronger in her because she feels that if she had known as much about marriage the day before her wedding as she did six months after, it would have been extremely hard to induce her to get married at all.

This prosaic solution is satisfactory only within certain limits. It depends altogether upon the accident of the woman having some natural vocation for domestic management and the care of children, as well as on the husband being fairly good-natured and livable-with. Hence arises the idealist illusion that a vocation for domestic management and the care of children is natural to women, and that women who lack them are not women at all, but members of the third, or Bashkirtseff sex. Even if this were true, it is obvious that if the Bashkirtseffs are to be allowed to live, they have a right to suitable institutions just as much as men and women. But it is not true. The domestic career is no more natural to all women than the military career is natural to all men; although it may be necessary that every able-bodied woman should be called upon to risk her life in child-bed just as it may be necessary that every man should be called on to risk his life in the battlefield. It is of course quite true that the majority of women are kind to children and prefer their own to other people's. But exactly the same thing is true of the majority of men, who nevertheless do not consider that their proper sphere is the nursery. The case may be illustrated more grotesquely by the fact that the majority of women who have dogs are kind to them, and prefer their own dogs to other people's; yet it is not proposed that women should restrict their activities to the rearing of puppies. If we have come to think that the nursery and the kitchen are the natural sphere of a woman, we have done so exactly as English children come to think that a cage is the natural sphere of a parrot—because they have never seen one anywhere else. No doubt there are Philistine parrots who agree with their owners that it is better to be in a cage than out, so long as there is plenty of hempseed and Indian corn there. There may even be idealist parrots who persuade themselves that the mission of a parrot is to minister to the happiness of a private family by whistling and saying "Pretty Polly," and that it is in the sacrifice of its liberty to this altruistic pursuit that a true parrot finds the supreme satisfaction of its soul. I will not go so far as to affirm that there are theological parrots who are convinced that imprisonment is the will of God because it is unpleasant; but I am confident that there are rationalist parrots who can demonstrate that it would be a cruel kindness to let a parrot out to fall a prey to cats, or at least to forget its accomplishments and coarsen its naturally delicate fibres in an unprotected struggle for existence. Still, the only parrot a free-souled person can sympathize with is the one that insists on being let out as the first condition of its making itself agreeable. A selfish bird, you may say: one that puts its own gratification before that of the family which is so fond of it—before even the greatest happiness of the greatest number: one that, in aping the independent spirit of a man, has unparroted itself and become a creature that has neither the home-loving nature of a bird nor the strength and enterprise of a mastiff. All the same, you respect that parrot in spite of your conclusive reasoning; and if it persists, you will have either to let it out or kill it.

The sum of the matter is that unless Woman repudiates her womanliness, her duty to her husband, to her children, to society, to the law, and to everyone but herself, she cannot emancipate herself. But her duty to herself is no duty at all, since a debt is cancelled when the debtor and creditor are the same person. Its payment is simply a fulfillment of the individual will, upon which all duty is a restriction, founded on the conception of the

repudiate duty

will as naturally malign and devilish. Therefore Woman has to repudiate duty altogether. In that repudiation lies her freedom; for it is false to say that Woman is now directly the slave of Man: she is the immediate slave of duty; and as man's path to freedom is strewn with the wreckage of the duties and ideals he has trampled on, so must hers be. She may indeed mask her iconoclasm by proving in rationalist fashion, as Man has often done for the sake of a quiet life, that all these discarded idealist conceptions will be fortified instead of shattered by her emancipation. To a person with a turn for logic, such proofs are as easy as playing the piano is to Paderewski. But it will not be true. A whole basketful of ideals of the most sacred quality will be smashed by the achievement of equality for women and men. Those who shrink from such a clatter and breakage may comfort themselves with the reflection that the replacement of broken goods will be prompt and certain. It is always a case of "The ideal is dead: long live the ideal!" And the advantage of the work of destruction is, that every new ideal is less of an illusion than the one it has supplanted; so that the destroyer of ideals, though denounced as an enemy of society, is in fact sweeping the world clear of lies. . . .

Havelock Ellis / *The Love Rights of Women*

Havelock Ellis (1859–1939), one of England's most famous psychologists and a prolific writer on the subject of sex, is perhaps best known for his philosophical work, *The Dance of Life,* and a pioneer sexological treatise, *Studies in the Psy-*

From *On Life and Sex; Essays of Love and Virtue* (Garden City, N.Y., Doubleday, 1937), pp. 102–15. Reprinted by permission of Françoise Delisle.

chology of Sex. The following essay deals with the right of women to enjoy their own sexuality. It was written in 1922 in response to the poisonous and still prevalent Victorian notion that women did not have any sexuality at all, and if they did, it was abnormal and impure. As Ellis puts it, "Women who wanted pleasure were not considered fit for the home." He deplores this unnatural and repressive heritage of male arrogance and urges a necessary change. Yet today, when women's right to erotic pleasure is not only acknowledged but encouraged (on male terms), real sexual liberation is still to come, as the essay by Susan Lydon amply demonstrates later in this anthology.

WHAT IS the part of woman, one is sometimes asked, in the sex act? Must it be the wife's concern in the marital embrace to sacrifice her own wishes from a sense of love and duty towards her husband? Or is the wife entitled to an equal mutual interest and joy in this act with her husband? It seems a simple problem. In so fundamental a relationship, which goes back to the beginning of sex in the dawn of life, it might appear that we could leave Nature to decide. Yet it is not so. Throughout the history of civilisation, wherever we can trace the feelings and ideas which have prevailed on this matter and the resultant conduct, the problem has existed, often to produce discord, conflict, and misery. . . .

In Nature, before the arrival of Man, it can scarcely be said indeed that any difficulty existed. It was taken for granted at that time that the female had both the right to her own body, and the right to a certain amount of enjoyment in the use of it. It often cost the male a serious amount of trouble—though he never failed to find it worthwhile—to explain to her the point where he may be allowed to come in, and to persuade her that he can contribute to her enjoyment. . . . We have here the great natural fact of courtship. Throughout Nature, every act of sexual union is preceded by a process of courtship. There is a sound physiological reason for this courtship, for in the act of wooing and being wooed the psychic excitement gradually generated in the

brains of the two partners acts as a stimulant to arouse into full
activity the mechanism which ensures sexual union and aids
ultimate impregnation. . . .

evolu-
tion
of
society

 The evolution of society, however, tended to overlay and sometimes even to suppress those fundamental natural tendencies. The
position of the man as the sole and uncontested head of the
family, the insistence on paternity and male descent, the accompanying economic developments, and the tendency to view
a woman as an object of barter belonging to her father, the consequent rigidity of the marriage bond, and the stern insistence
on wifely fidelity—all these conditions of developing civilisation,
while still leaving courtship possible, diminished its significance
and even abolished its necessity. Moreover, on the basis of the
social, economic, and legal developments thus established, new
moral, spiritual, and religious forces were slowly generated,
which worked on these rules of merely exterior order, and in-
teriorised them, thus giving them power over the souls as well
as over the bodies of women. The result was that, directly and
indirectly, the legal, economic, and erotic rights of women were
all diminished. It is with the erotic rights only that we are here
concerned. . . . Monogamy and the home, it was claimed, alike

mono-
gamy
&
home

existed for the benefit and protection of women. It was not so
often explained that they greatly benefited and protected men,
with moreover this additional advantage: that while women were
absolutely confined to the home, men were free to exercise their
activities outside the home, even on the erotic side.

 Whatever the real benefits of the sexual order thus established,
it becomes clear that in certain important respects it had an unnatural and repressive influence on the erotic aspect of woman's
sexual life. It fostered the reproductive side of woman's sexual
life, but it rendered difficult for her the satisfaction of the instinct
for that courtship which is the natural preliminary of reproductive activity, an instinct even more highly developed in the
female than in the male, and the more insistent because in the
order of Nature the burden of maternity is preceded by the reward of pleasure. But the marriage order which had become
established led to the indirect result of banning pleasure in
women, or at all events in wives. It was regarded as too danger-

ous, and even as degrading. The women who wanted pleasure
were not considered fit for the home, but more suited to be
devoted to an exclusive "life of pleasure," which soon turned out
to be not their own pleasure but men's. . . .

The practices and the ideals of this established morality were
both due to men, and both were so thoroughly fashioned that
they subjugated alike the actions and the feelings of women.
There is no sphere which we regard as so peculiarly women's
sphere as that of love. Yet there is no sphere which in civilisation
women have so far had so small a part in regulating. Their deepest impulses—their modesty, their maternity, their devotion, their
emotional receptivity—were used, with no conscious and deliberate Machiavellism, against themselves, to mould a moral world
for their habitation which they would not themselves have
moulded. It is not of modern creation, not by any means due, as
some have supposed, to the asceticism of Christianity, however
much Christianity may have reinforced it. . . . In ancient classic
days this moral order was even more severely established than
in the Middle Ages. Montaigne, in the sixteenth century, declared
that "marriage is a devout and religious relationship, the pleasures derived from it should be restrained and serious, mixed
with some severity." But in this matter he was not merely expressing the Christian standpoint but even more that of pagan-
ism, and he thoroughly agreed with the old Greek moralist that
a man should approach his wife "prudently and severely" for fear
of inciting her to lasciviousness; he thought that marriage was
best arranged by a third party, and was inclined to think, with
the ancients, that women are not fitted to make friends of. Montaigne has elsewhere spoken with insight of women's instinctive
knowledge of the art and discipline of love and has pointed out
how men have imposed their own ideals and rules of action on
women from whom they have demanded opposite and contradictory virtues; yet, we see, he approves of this state of things and
never suggests that women have any right to opinions of their
own or feelings of their own when the sacred institution of marriage is in question.

Montaigne represents the more exalted aspects of the Pagan-
Christian conception of morality in marriage which still largely

prevails. But that conception lent itself to deductions, frankly accepted even by Montaigne himself, which were by no means exalted. "I find," said Montaigne, "that Venus, after all, is nothing more than the pleasure of discharging our vessels, just as nature renders pleasurable the discharges from other parts." Sir Thomas More among Catholics, and Luther among Protestants, said exactly the same thing in other and even clearer words, while untold millions of husbands in Christendom down to today, whether or not they have had the wit to put their theory into a phrase, have regularly put it into practice, at all events within the consecrated pale of marriage, and treated their wives, "severely and prudently," as convenient utensils for the reception of a natural excretion.

Obviously, in this view of marriage, sexual activity was regarded as an exclusively masculine function, in the exercise of which women had merely a passive part to play. Any active participation on her side thus seemed unnecessary, and even unbefitting, finally, though only in comparatively modern times, disgusting and actually degrading. Thus Acton [Dr. William Acton, the noted Victorian sexologist], who was regarded half a century ago as the chief English authority on sexual matters, declared that, "happily for society," the supposition that women possess sexual feelings could be put aside as "a vile aspersion," while another medical authority of the same period stated in regard to the most simple physical sign of healthy sexual emotion that it "only happened in lascivious women." This final triumph of the masculine ideals and rule of life was, however, only achieved slowly. It was the culmination of an elaborate process of training. At the outset men had found it impossible to speak too strongly of the "wantonness" of women. This attitude was pronounced among the ancient Greeks and prominent in their dramatists. Christianity again, which ended by making women into the chief pillars of the Church, began by regarding them as the "Gate of Hell." Again, later, when in the Middle Ages this masculine moral order approached the task of subjugating the barbarians of Northern Europe, men were horrified at the licentiousness of those northern women at whose coldness they are now shocked.

That, indeed, was, as Montaigne had seen, the central core of conflict in the rule of life imposed by men on women. Men were perpetually striving, by ways the most methodical, the most subtle, the most far-reaching, to achieve a result in women, which, when achieved, men themselves viewed with dismay. They may be said to be moved in this sphere by two passions, the passion for virtue and the passion for vice. But it so happens that both these streams of passion have to be directed at the same fascinating object: Woman. No doubt nothing is more admirable than the skill with which women have acquired the duplicity necessary to play the two contradictory parts thus imposed upon them. . . . They were forbidden, except in a few carefully etiquetted forms, the free play of courtship, without which they could not perform their part in the erotic life with full satisfaction either to themselves or their partners. They were reduced to an artificial simulation of coldness or of warmth, according to the particular stage of the dominating masculine ideal of woman which their partner chanced to have reached. But that is an attitude equally unsatisfactory to themselves and to their lovers, even when the latter have not sufficient insight to see through its unreality. It is an attitude so unnatural and artificial that it inevitably tends to produce a real coldness which nothing can disguise. It is true that women whose instincts are not perverted at the roots do not desire to be cold. Far from it. But to dispel that coldness the right atmosphere is needed, and the insight and skill of the right man. In the erotic sphere a woman asks nothing better of a man than to be lifted above her coldness, to the higher plane where there is reciprocal interest and mutual joy in the act of love. Therein her silent demand is one with Nature's. For the biological order of the world involves those claims which, in the human range, are the erotic rights of women.

The social claims of women, their economic claims, their political claims, have long been before the world. Women themselves have actively asserted them, and they are all in process of realisation. The erotic claims of women, which are at least as fundamental, are not publicly voiced, and women themselves would be the last to assert them. It is easy to understand why that should be so. The natural and acquired qualities of women, even the qualities developed in the art of courtship, have all been utilized in building up the masculine ideal of sexual morality; it is on feminine characteristics that this masculine ideal has been based, so that women have been helpless to protest against it. Moreover, even if that were not so, to formulate such rights is to raise the question whether there so much as exists anything that can be called "erotic rights." The right to joy cannot be claimed in the same way as one claims the right to put a voting paper in a ballot box. A human being's erotic aptitudes can only be developed where the right atmosphere for them exists, and where the attitudes of both persons concerned are in harmonious sympathy. That is why the erotic rights of women have been the last of all to be attained.

erotic apti- tudes

Yet today we see a change here. The change required is a change of attitude and a resultant change in the atmosphere in which the sexual impulses are manifested. . . . As many competent observers have noted, the young men of today show a new attitude toward women and toward marriage, an attitude of simplicity and frankness, a desire for mutual confidence, a readiness to discuss difficulties, an appeal to understand and to be understood. Such an attitude, which had hitherto been hard to attain, at once creates the atmosphere in which alone the free, spontaneous erotic activities of women can breathe and live.

new atti- tude

This consummation, we have seen, may be regarded as the attainment of certain rights, the corollary of other rights in the social field which women are slowly achieving as human beings on the same human level as men. It opens to women, on whom is always laid the chief burden of sex, the right to the joy and exaltation of sex, to the uplifting of the soul which, when the right conditions are fulfilled, is the outcome of the intimate approach and union of two human beings.

9 burden of sex should have joys

Gunnar Myrdal / *Women, Servants, Mules,*
and Other Property

It is rare and remarkable enough that a foreign scholar should make a major contribution to the study of American life and politics. Gunnar Myrdal, the Swedish sociologist, certainly achieved that with the publication of his massive analysis of racism, *An American Dilemma: The Negro Problem and Modern Democracy* (1944). But he did more. Hidden away in one of the appendixes of the work is the first serious attempt by a sociologist to spell out the parallel between the position of blacks and the position of women. Since the "woman as nigger" analysis has now become part of the standard repertory of women's liberation, it is interesting to see how the comparison was first developed by Myrdal back in the early forties. In effect, he was only rediscovering an old, but forgotten link between abolitionism and women's rights. Both movements were an attack upon the social paternalism of white males, which Myrdal identifies as "a fundamental basis of our culture."

paternalism of W♂ — basis of culture
position of B // position of ♀

IN EVERY society there are at least two groups of people, besides the Negroes, who are characterized by high social visibility ex-

From Appendix 5, "A Parallel to the Negro Problem," *An American Dilemma* (New York, Harper, 1944), pp. 1073–1078. Copyright 1944, 1962 by Harper & Row, Publishers, Inc. Reprinted by permission of the publisher.

pressed in physical appearance, dress, and patterns of behavior, and who have been "suppressed." We refer to women and children. Their present status, as well as their history and their problems in society, reveal striking similarities to those of the Negroes. In studying a special problem like the Negro problem, there is always a danger that one will develop a quite incorrect idea of its uniqueness. It will, therefore, give perspective to the Negro problem and prevent faulty interpretations to sketch some of the important similarities between the Negro problem and the women's problem.

In the historical development of these problem groups in America there have been much closer relations than is now ordinarily recorded. In the earlier common law, women and children were placed under the jurisdiction of the paternal power. When a legal status had to be found for the imported Negro servants in the seventeenth century, the nearest and most natural analogy was the status of women and children. The ninth commandment —linking together women, servants, mules, and other property— could be invoked, as well as a great number of other passages of Holy Scripture. We do not intend to follow here the interesting developments of the institution of slavery in America through the centuries, but merely wish to point out the paternalistic idea which held the slave to be a sort of family member and in some way—in spite of all differences—placed him beside women and children under the power of the *paterfamilias.*

There was, of course, even in the beginning, a tremendous difference both in actual status of these different groups and in the tone of sentiment in the respective relations. In the decades before the Civil War, in the conservative and increasingly antiquarian ideology of the American South, woman was elevated as an ornament and looked upon with pride, while the Negro slave became increasingly a chattel and a ward. The paternalistic construction came, however, to good service when the South had to build up a moral defense for slavery, and it is found everywhere in the apologetic literature up to the beginning of the Civil War. For illustration, some passages from George Fitzhugh's *Sociology for the South*, published in 1854, may be quoted as typical:

The kind of slavery is adapted to the men enslaved. Wives and apprentices are slaves; not in theory only, but often in fact. Children are slaves to their parents, guardians and teachers. Imprisoned culprits are slaves. Lunatics and idiots are slaves also.

A beautiful example and illustration of this kind of communism, is found in the instance of the Patriarch Abraham. His wives and his children, his men servants and his maid servants, his camels and his cattle, were all equally his property. He could sacrifice Isaac or a ram, just as he pleased. He loved and protected all, and all shared, if not equally, at least fairly, in the products of their light labour. Who would not desire to have been a slave of that old Patriarch, stern and despotic as he was? . . . Pride, affection, self-interest, moved Abraham to protect, love and take care of his slaves. The same motives operate on all masters, and secure comfort, competency and protection to the slave. A man's wife and children are his slaves, and do they not enjoy, in common with himself, his property?

Other protagonists of slavery resort to the same argument:

In this country we believe that the general good requires us to deprive the whole female sex of the right of self-government. They have no voice in the formation of the laws which dispose of their persons and property. . . . We treat all minors much in the same way. . . . Our plea for all this is, that the good of the whole is thereby most effectually promoted. . . . [Charles Hodge, "The Bible Argument on Slavery" (1860).]

Significant manifestations of the result of this disposition [on the part of the Abolitionists] to consider their own light a surer guide than the word of God, are visible in the anarchical opinions about human governments, civil and ecclesiastical, and on the rights of women, which have found appropriate advocates in the abolition publications. . . . If our women are to be emancipated from subjection to the law which God has imposed upon them, if they are to quit the retirement of domestic life, where they preside in stillness over the character and destiny of society; . . . if, in studied insult to the authority of God, we are to renounce in the marriage contract all claim to obedience, we shall soon have a country over which the genius of Mary Wollstonecraft would delight to preside, but from which all order and all virtue would speedily be banished. There is no form of human excellence before which we bow with profounder deference than that which appears in a delicate woman, . . . and there is no deformity of human character from which we turn with deeper loathing than from a woman forgetful of her nature, and clamourous for the vocation and rights of men. [Albert T. Bledsoe, "An Essay on Liberty and Slavery" (1853).]

Hence her [Miss Martineau's] wild chapter about the "Rights of Women," her groans and invectives because of their exclusion from the offices of the state, the right of suffrage, the exercise of political authority. In all this, the error of the declaimer consists in the very first movement of the mind. "The Rights of *Women*" may all be conceded to the sex, yet the rights of *men* withheld from them. [W. Gilmore Simms, "The Morals of Slavery" (1853).]

The parallel goes, however, considerably deeper than being only a structural part in the defense ideology built up around slavery. Women at that time lacked a number of rights otherwise belonging to all free white citizens of full age.

So chivalrous, indeed, was the ante-bellum South that its women were granted scarcely any rights at all. Everywhere they were subjected to political, legal, educational, and social and economic restrictions. They took no part in governmental affairs, were without legal rights over their property or the guardianship of their children, were denied adequate educational facilities, and were excluded from business and the professions. [Virginius Dabney, *Liberalism in the South* (1932).]

The same was very much true of the rest of the country and of the rest of the world. But there was an especially close relation in the South between the subordination of women and that of Negroes. This is perhaps best expressed in a comment attributed to Dolly Madison, that the Southern wife was "the chief slave of the harem."

From the very beginning, the fight in America for the liberation of the Negro slaves was, therefore, closely coordinated with the fight for women's emancipation. It is interesting to note that the Southern states, in the early beginning of the political emancipation of women during the first decades of the nineteenth century, had led in the granting of legal rights to women. This was the time when the South was still the stronghold of liberal thinking in the period leading up to and following the Revolution. During the same period the South was also the region where

Abolitionist societies flourished, while the North was uninterested in the Negro problem. Thereafter the two movements developed in close interrelation and were both gradually driven out of the South.

The women suffragists received their political education from the Abolitionist movement. Women like Angelina Grimke, Sarah Grimke, and Abby Kelly began their public careers by speaking for Negro emancipation and only gradually came to fight for women's rights. The three great suffragists of the nineteenth century—Lucretia Mott, Elizabeth Cady Stanton, and Susan B. Anthony—first attracted attention as ardent campaigners for the emancipation of the Negro and the prohibition of liquor. The women's movement got much of its public support by reason of its affiliation with the Abolitionist movement: the leading male advocates of woman suffrage before the Civil War were such Abolitionists as William Lloyd Garrison, Henry Ward Beecher, Wendell Phillips, Horace Greeley, and Frederick Douglass. The women had nearly achieved their aims, when the Civil War induced them to suppress all tendencies distracting the federal government from the prosecution of the War. They were apparently fully convinced that victory would bring the suffrage to them as well as to the Negroes.

The Union's victory, however, brought disappointment to the women suffragists. The arguments "the Negro's hour" and "a political necessity" met and swept aside all their arguments for leaving the word "male" out of the Fourteenth Amendment and putting "sex" alongside "race" and "color" in the Fifteenth Amendment. Even their Abolitionist friends turned on them, and the Republican party shied away from them. A few Democrats, really not in favor of the extension of the suffrage to anyone, sought to make political capital out of the women's demands, and said with Senator Cowan of Pennsylvania, "If I have no reason to offer why a Negro man shall not vote, I have no reason why a white woman shall not vote." Charges of being Democrats and traitors were heaped on the women leaders. Even a few Negroes, invited to the women's convention of January 1869, denounced the women for jeopardizing the black man's chances for the vote. The War and Reconstruction Amendments had thus sharply divided the women's problem from the Negro problem in actual politics.[1] The deeper relation between the two will, however, be recognized up till this day. Du Bois' famous ideological manifesto *The Souls of Black Folk* is, to mention only one example, an ardent appeal on behalf of women's interests as well as those of the Negro.

This close relation is no accident. The ideological and economic forces behind the two movements—the emancipation of women and children and the emancipation of Negroes—have much in common and are closely interrelated. Paternalism was a preindustrial scheme of life, and was gradually becoming broken in the nineteenth century. Negroes and women, both of whom had been under the yoke of the paternalistic system, were both strongly and fatefully influenced by the Industrial Revolution. For neither group is the readjustment process yet consummated.

1. While there was a definite affinity between the Abolitionist movement and the woman suffrage movement, there was also competition and, perhaps, antipathy, between them that widened with the years. As early as 1833, when Oberlin College opened its doors to women—the first college to do so—the Negro men students joined other men students in protesting. The Anti-Slavery Convention held in London in 1840 refused to seat the women delegates from America, and it was on this instigation that the first women's rights convention was called. After the passage of the Thirteenth, Fourteenth, and Fifteenth Amendments, which gave legal rights to Negroes but not to women, the women's movement split off completely from the Negroes' movement, except for such a thing as the support of both movements by the rare old liberal, Frederick Douglass. An expression of how far the two movements had separated by 1903 was given by one of the leaders of the women's movement at that time, Anna Howard Shaw, in answer to a question posed to her at a convention in New Orleans:

"What is your purpose in bringing your convention to the South? Is it the desire of suffragists to force upon us the social equality of black and white women? Political equality lays the foundation for social equality. If you give the ballot to women, won't you make the black and white woman equal politically and therefore lay the foundation for a future claim of social equality?"

I read the question aloud. Then the audience called for the answer, and I gave it in these words, quoted as accurately as I can remember them:

"If political equality is the basis of social equality, and if by granting political equality you lay the foundation for a claim of social equality, I can only answer that you have already laid that claim. You did not wait for woman suffrage, but disfranchised both your black and white women, thus making them politically equal. But you have done more than that. You have put the ballot into the hands of your black men, thus making them the political superiors of your white women. Never before in the history of the world have men made former slaves the political masters of their former mistresses!" (*The Story of a Pioneer* [1915], pp. 311-312.)

74 *reorganize the family*   *Masculine/Feminine*

Both are still problem groups. The women's problem is the center of the whole complex of problems of how to reorganize the institution of the family to fit the new economic and ideological basis, a problem which is not solved in any part of the Western world unless it be in the Soviet Union or Palestine. The family problem in the Negro group, as we find when analyzing the Negro family, has its special complications, centering in the tension and conflict between the external patriarchal system in which the Negro was confined as a slave and his own family structure.

As in the Negro problem, most men have accepted as self-evident, until recently, the doctrine that women had inferior endowments in most of those respects which carry prestige, power, and advantages in society, but that they were, at the same time, superior in some other respects. The arguments, when arguments were used, have been about the same: smaller brains, scarcity of geniuses, and so on. The study of women's intelligence and personality has had broadly the same history as the one we record for Negroes. As in the case of the Negro, women themselves have often been brought to believe in their inferiority of endowment. As the Negro was awarded his "place" in society, so there was a "woman's place." In both cases the rationalization was strongly believed that men, in confining them to this place, did not act against the true interest of the subordinate groups. The myth of the "contented women," who did not want to have suffrage or other civil rights and equal opportunities, had the same social function as the myth of the "contented Negro." In both cases there was probably—in a static sense—often some truth behind the myth.

As to the character of the deprivations, upheld by law or by social conventions and the pressure of public opinion, no elaboration will here be made. As important and illustrative in the comparison, we shall, however, stress the conventions governing woman's education. There was a time when the most common idea was that she was better off with little education. Later the doctrine developed that she should not be denied education, but that her education should be of a special type, fitting her for her "place" in society and usually directed more on training her hands than her brains.

Political franchise was not granted to women until recently. Even now there are, in all countries, great difficulties for a woman to attain public office. The most important disabilities still affecting her status are those barring her attempt to earn a living and to attain promotion in her work. As in the Negro's case, there are certain "women's jobs," traditionally monopolized by women. They are regularly in the low salary bracket and do not offer much of a career. All over the world men have used the trade unions to keep women out of competition. Woman's competition has, like the Negro's, been particularly obnoxious and dreaded by men because of the low wages women, with their few earning outlets, are prepared to work for. Men often dislike the very idea of having women on an equal plane as co-workers and competitors, and usually they find it even more "unnatural" to work under women. White people generally hold similar attitudes toward Negroes. On the other hand, it is said about women that they prefer men as bosses and do not want to work under another woman. Negroes often feel the same way about working under other Negroes.

In personal relations with both women and Negroes, white men generally prefer a less professional and more human relation, actually a more paternalistic and protective position—somewhat in the nature of patron to client in Roman times, and like the corresponding strongly paternalistic relation of later feudalism. As in Germany it is said that every Gentile has his pet Jew, so it is said in the South that every white has his "pet nigger," or—in the upper strata—several of them. We sometimes marry the pet woman, carrying out the paternalistic scheme. But even if we do not, we tend to deal kindly with her as a client and a ward, not as a competitor and an equal.

In drawing a parallel between the position of, and feeling toward, women and Negroes we are uncovering a fundamental basis of our culture. Although it is changing, atavistic elements sometimes unexpectedly break through even in the most emancipated individuals. The similarities in the women's and the Ne-

groes' problems are not accidental. They were, as we have
pointed out, originally determined in a paternalistic order of
society. The problems remain, even though paternalism is gradually declining as an ideal and is losing its economic basis. In the
final analysis, women are still hindered in their competition by
the function of procreation; Negroes are laboring under the
yoke of the doctrine of unassimilability which has remained although slavery is abolished. The second barrier is actually much
stronger than the first in America today. But the first is more
eternally inexorable.

Ronald V. Sampson / *Power Corrupts . . .*

In his strong and original study, *The Psychology of Power*,
R. V. Sampson (who teaches politics at the University of Bris-
tol, England) undertakes to defend human equality as the ultimate ethical principle by which all political policy is to be
judged. He argues that an inequality of power between people
wholly distorts the life of both the dominant and submissive
partners, thereby making any form of justice or decency impossible.

> Even though the parties of the relationship may be quite un-
> aware of the effect of their dominance or subjection upon them-
> selves, the moral effect is nevertheless inescapable. A relationship
> is always vitiated in proportion to the degree of power present.

From *The Psychology of Power* (New York, Pantheon, 1966), pp. 45–50;
93–102. Copyright © 1965 by R. V. Sampson. Reprinted by permission of
Pantheon Books, a division of Random House, Inc.

Dominance is inseparable from pride or arogance, while deference or compliance indicates weakness, if not servility, and is accompanied by resentment, conscious or unconscious.

In order to demonstrate his thesis, Sampson examines the family life of nineteenth-century England, showing how the crushing paternalism of the day blasted the lives of men and women in a hundred unseen and unconscious ways. In the selection offered here, Sampson addresses himself to the sharply contrasting manner in which two major thinkers—Sigmund Freud and John Stuart Mill—dealt with the problem of sexual inequality and its political ramifications. The selection nicely suggests how Freud's obtuseness on the subject of women's rights forced his thinking into the service of authoritarian social ideology.

POLITICALLY UNCOMMITTED, Freud has in fact strengthened the intellectual forces of both the Left and the Right. The Left he encouraged by sharing their meliorist aspirations as well as by confirming their conviction that human behaviour, if not human nature, is capable of modification. But the Right also drew comfort from his prevailing mood of scepticism and pessimism with its insistence on the fact that aggressive impulses and the urge to dominance were inherent in man; and that accordingly egalitarian, anarchical aspirations to unseat the role of power in human affairs were foredoomed. On balance, it is Freud's pessimism which has been most influential in politics. . . . He believed that men could not achieve the self-discipline and co-operation for stable social life without recourse to an authoritarian father-substitute in the shape of a coercive Government. And further he doubted the very possibility of putting an end to war because of man's allegedly inherent aggressive impulse. . . . It will further be argued [here] that Freud's failure of insight at this point lay in his inability to challenge the accepted view of the relations which ought to obtain between man and woman.

Freud's view governing the nature of the ideal sexual relationship did not differ essentially from the prevailing view among people of his class and time. It was a view which rejected equality as undesirable, although this would rarely be stated quite so bluntly. Since the sexual relationship is the most important of all human relations, in that it is the source of life itself as well as of subsequent child nurture, an error at this point is bound to distort the total picture of man's psychic possibilities. The assumptions of masculine primacy are so deep-seated in our culture that the real point is frequently not taken even today. For example, the story, no doubt apocryphal, of Sylvia Pankhurst trying to console one of her fellow-suffragettes in Holloway Prison by urging her, "Put your faith in God. She will help you," is guaranteed to cause amusement in any audience. But people are rarely conscious that there is anything odd about a culture in which such a story does seem irresistibly funny. . . .

Freud's hostility to political egalitarianism had as its logical counterpart a cherished prejudice concerning the inequality of the sexes. Here again . . . the connection is plain between Freud's own unexamined prejudice and the error in his psychoanalytic theories concerning the specifically female emotions. "There must be inequality," Freud is reported to have remarked in a conversation with Dr. J. Worthis on the subject of the relations between the sexes. And since this inequality must prevail, "superiority of the man is the lesser of the two evils." There is no reason to doubt that this aptly summarized Freud's own relations with his wife. The adored Gretchen of courtship is wooed tenderly and ardently in order to be raised subsequently to the respected position of matriarchal *Hausfrau*. The husband remains devotedly loyal, but distantly so in terms of emotional involvement. Erich Fromm attributes Freud's inability to establish relations of genuine warmth and intimacy with the opposite sex to his own sexually inhibited feelings and a weakly developed sexual drive. This lack of closeness was the source of his failure to understand the nature of feminine psychology. His theories on this subject, Fromm goes so far as to assert, were no more than "naïve rationalizations of male prejudices, especially of the male who needs to dominate in order to hide his fear of women." [See Fromm's study, *Sigmund Freud's Mission* (1959).]

It is not my concern to explore Freud's psychoanalytic theories concerning women or the deficiencies in those theories. What is relevant is the connection between Freud's view of the relations between the sexes and his view of the relations between large groups such as social classes. Convinced affectively as well as intellectually of the inferior status of women, he could not attain an adequately tender or complete relationship with a woman. Given this emotional inadequacy, the ego drive to power, already strong in Freud, received further nourishment. In one of his intellectual bent, it found expression in an excessive worship of reason as the sole instrument of truth destined to liberate mankind from the crippling prejudices of "common sense." It was the source of Freud's outstanding quality, his immense courage and faith in himself; but it was dearly purchased. For it led him to a thinly veiled contempt for those, the vast majority of mankind, who allow their surface emotional preoccupations to prevent the sublimation of their creative energies. How otherwise could men hope to penetrate with their reason beneath the surface of things and bring under control the anarchical world of nature? In short, Freud at heart never was nor could be a democrat. A typical child of the European Enlightenment, he shared Voltaire's aristocratic faith in reason without Tom Paine's parallel faith in the potential capacities of the common man. This ambivalence in the Enlightenment tradition and in Freud personally is very evident in Freud's attitude to John Stuart Mill, the prototype of nineteenth-century rationalism. Freud greatly admired Mill . . . and expressed his admiration in terms of their common penchant for rationalism. J. S. Mill was, he said, "perhaps the man of the century who best managed to free himself from the domination of customary prejudices."

He first became familiar with Mill's writings in 1880 at the age of twenty-four, when he translated into German the twelfth volume of Theodore Gomperz's edition of J. S. Mill's collected works, containing essays dealing with the labour question, the enfranchisement of women, and socialism. Mill, like Freud, put great faith in the power of human reason untrammelled by emotion. . . . He suffered from only one serious defect in Freud's eyes. He lacked a sense of humour in his inability to put into proper perspective the relations between the sexes. The relevant passage in one of Freud's letters is worth quoting at length:

On the other hand, . . . he [Mill] lacked in many matters the sense
of the absurd; for example, in that of female emancipation and in the
woman's question altogether. I recollect that in the essay I translated,
a prominent argument was that a married woman could earn as much
as her husband. We surely agree that the management of a house,
the care and bringing up of children, demands the whole of a human
being and almost excludes any earning, even if a simplified household
relieve her of dusting, cleaning, cooking, etc. He had simply forgotten
all that, like everything else concerning the relationship between the
sexes. That is altogether a point with Mill where one simply cannot
find him human. His autobiography is so prudish or so ethereal that
one could never gather from it that human beings consist of men and
women and that this distinction is the most significant one that exists.
In his whole presentation it never emerges that women are different
beings—we will not say lesser, rather the opposite—from men. He
finds the suppression of women an analogy to that of negroes. Any
girl, even without a suffrage or legal competence, whose hand a man
kisses and for whose love he is prepared to dare all, could have set
him right. It is really a stillborn thought to send women into the
struggle for existence exactly as men. If, for instance, I imagined my
gentle sweet girl as a competitor it would only end in my telling her,
as I did seventeen months ago, that I am fond of her and that I
implore her to withdraw from the strife into the calm uncompetitive
activity of my home. It is possible that changes in upbringing may
suppress all a woman's tender attributes, needful of protection and
yet so victorious, and that she can then earn a livelihood like men.
It is also possible that in such an event one would not be justified
in mourning the passing away of the most delightful thing the world
can offer us—our ideal of womanhood. I believe that all reforming
action in law and education would break down in front of the fact
that, long before the age at which a man can earn a position in
society, Nature has determined woman's destiny through beauty,
charm and sweetness. Law and custom have much to give women
that has been withheld from them, but the position of women will
surely be what it is: in youth an adored darling and in mature years
a loved wife.[1]

The patronizing tone towards woman is quite unconscious; it
bespeaks the period. The irony could hardly be greater. Mill is

1. Ernest Jones, *Sigmund Freud: Life and Work* (3 vols., London, Hogarth Press, 1953–57), vol. I, pp. 192–193.

singled out as the man above all others of his epoch who succeeded in surmounting contemporary prejudices; and then rebuked for his supreme achievement in unmasking the most disastrous of prejudices to which Freud succeeded in clinging his
life long. It was Freud's intellectual insight and courage that so
clearly illuminated the influence of nurture upon character through
the genuinely original conception of the Oedipus complex. It was
his tragedy that he was prevented by endemic sexual prejudice
from being able to complement this insight by an understanding
of the importance of equality for the establishment of a sane
relationship as the basis for human nurture. This point has the
most far-reaching implications for adult social and class relations,
and is far from being generally conceded even today. . . .

[Mill's essay] "The Subjection of Women" (1869) was ahead
of its time, and to some extent is still so. It was bitterly assailed
by contemporaries; and of all his work of abiding value it has
suffered most neglect.

On its first appearance it was attacked by an anonymous reviewer in *Blackwood's Magazine,* of which the following extract
is a fair sample: "His intense arrogance, his incapacity to do justice to the feelings or motives of all from whom he differs, his
intolerance of all but his own disciples, and lastly, in natural
consequence of these qualities, his want of playfulness in himself and repugnance to it in others, all combine to create something like antipathy." . . . Twenty-three years after Mill's death,
Frederic Harrison, the distinguished positivist, in an appreciation
of Mill in *The Nineteenth Century* (1896), appeared to find difficulty in restraining himself on this painful subject: "The subjection of women is a mere hysterical sophism in itself. The rem-
edy proposed to cure it is rank moral and social anarchy."

Mill was obviously touching a hypersensitive nerve. Why was
this? At one level, the explanation is obvious enough. Much of
Mill's argument demonstrates the potential equality of women
with men in vocational and professional terms in order to open
the gates of employment to them on the same terms as men.
This side of the case led directly in the political field to the
whole suffragette campaign. The prolonged and frequently bitter
struggle finally overcame all resistance; and the main aims were

attained. The right of women to compete with men in virtually
every form of employment not exclusively dependent on physical
strength is no longer a matter of serious controversy. Nor is there
need to speculate what might be achieved by women given equality of opportunity in education. The facts are there for all to see.
Mill's book has dated by the very success of his arguments. This
part of the book, trite though it may now seem, remains an eloquent testimony to the climate of opinion in which Mill was required to argue. That he in no wise exaggerated the power and
prejudice of contemporary masculinity is evidenced by the anonymous *Blackwood's* reviewer:

In the world, as we and all mankind that has preceded us have
known it, women under no conceivable circumstances can have the
law on their side but by the permission of men; therefore they seem
to us to act wisely by owning a natural law of subordination, and
submitting to "subjection" as a Bible word. . . .

The *Blackwood's* reviewer clearly thought he had disposed of
the matter by observing: "He [Mill] exactly corresponds to the
lunatic who proved logically that all the rest of the world was
insane. It is nothing to him that mankind from the beginning has
seen the matter in another light."

The reviewer was right in grasping the extreme radicalism of
Mill's position. Doubtless there is also a strong *prima facie* case
of error where a man claims to be the only member of the regi-
ment who is in step; although, if the rule were infallible, no
advance in human knowledge or ethical understanding would
ever have been possible. Mill had in fact made a profound and
revolutionary discovery at the heart of our society. The force of
the resistance he touched off only confirms this. But the implications of what Mill had grasped went deeper than even he
realized. . . .

The book's strength lies in its awareness that the quality of
the marital relationship has effects which ramify into every aspect
of the life of society. The thesis is that the existing marital relationship is one of subordination of the female to the male; that
such a relationship is morally indefensible; that this moral defect
is the *fons et origo* of all the moral deficiencies of the greater

society; and that until it is remedied and put on a basis of complete equality, it will be vain to look for any appreciable measure of human advancement in other spheres. "We have had the morality of submission, and the morality of chivalry and generosity; the time is now come for the morality of justice." Existing sexual relations are an anachronistic survival in a society whose needs are no longer met. The consequences of this relationship are then traced for the male, the female, and the children of the union.

The portrait of the male in particular is exceptionally well done, wholly convincing, and the unflattering verisimilitude of the portrait so near the bone that few male readers could have failed to recognize something of themselves. This itself would explain some of the hostility the book aroused. Mill drew from life; the portrait is of the bourgeois Victorian male. The lot of women delivered over to that large number of men who are "little higher than brutes" is a conjecture that evokes in him a scarcely repressed shudder. This aspect of the question, touching on unplumbed depths of human misery, strikes him as so appalling as to require no further argument. He proceeds to dissect the more subtle effects of bourgeois marriage upon the males of the society in which he was himself nurtured. Here he could speak from firsthand knowledge.

No doubt there are families which exemplify the ideal to which the institution is supposed to conform. But such families, working by the light of sympathy and self-forgetfulness, are rare exceptions. Much oftener the pattern of family life stems from the fact that the husband is the linchpin of the institution. All other members derive such rights as they may enjoy from the fact that they are felt to reflect the man's own interests and become extensions of his own personality, so to speak. Under these conditions, the family, far from being a civilizing institution inculcating gentler *mores,* is a "school of wilfulness, overbearingness, unbounded self-indulgence, and a double-dyed and idealized selfishness, of which sacrifice itself is only a particular form, a school of despotism, in which the virtues of despotism, but also its vices, are largely nourished." The corrosive effect upon the character of the male of this universal assumption of his primacy over the female is brilliantly portrayed. Power and privilege corrupt heads of families as they corrupt all privileged groups or persons. . . .

Further, this egocentric assumption that the male is more important than those who are dependent upon him is self-perpetuating. The male child in the family subject to the *patria potestas* feels the brunt in his own person, but he is quick to detect that his subjection is temporary only. For one day he too will become eligible to join this privileged class of male adults. The seeds of superiority consciousness and consequent corruption are thus sown very early in the mind of the male child. Since his entire culture is saturated in assumptions of male superiority, he is permeated with its implications from his earliest days. If he does not quickly sense it for himself, he will be infected by his schoolmates with the idea that he is of greater consequence than his sisters, before long than his mother, and then by process of development than of the woman whom he will eventually honour by marriage.

"Is it imagined," says Mill rhetorically, "that all this does not pervert the whole manner of existence of the man, both as an individual and as a social being?" He is corrupted as any despot or hereditary monarch is by the heritage of absolute power over his subjects. The vassal may be abased by his servitude; but the lord's character is even more gravely affected in its moral wholeness by the power to hold in servitude. The harshness of this relation inside marriage is normally concealed by the emollient influence at work in our society and by the intimacy of the marriage tie. But the kind of emotion that is not based on freedom and equality is a spurious "love of freedom." However close the intimacy, when it is combined with overlordship it can only be productive of a sentiment that is not "the genuine or Christian love of freedom." Mill's insight into character is perspicacious enough to grasp that the love of freedom on the lips of many a libertarian is often a veiled expression of "an intense feeling of the dignity and importance of his own personality." This must be so, where the libertarian in his personal family life is a despotic father and husband. Nor is this a trite observation. It is still not the practice to submit the authenticity of the libertarian's public claims to this kind of test. But Mill did not push the analysis further to inquire in what way the assumption of greater right by one person in relation to another necessarily corrupts the wellsprings of spontaneous affection. That marital and paternal "love" are not compatible with the concept of *patria potestas* Mill grasped, though not very surely. But he was far from grasping its full consequence.

If marriage grounded on the principle of authority and subordination corrupts the male, what are its consequences for the female? . . . Women are also human beings; and as such must experience frustration and resentment by living in a permanent state of tutelage to men, a state in which the husband is the legal successor to the father, her first keeper. Mill admits that this resentment may not be visible on the surface. Women are schooled by convention, long discipline, and a sense of inevitability to suppressing and concealing such emotions. They may not even recognize them as such. Given the power of the existing ideal of woman's feminine role over the imagination, such emotions may well be rigorously repressed. Nevertheless, Mill insists, weakness, when deprived of liberty, cannot yield to power without psychic tension. The resentment is merely driven underground with harmful effects upon the character. As he puts it, "the internal principle remains, in a different outward form." The energies, dammed up in this way, will seek some other outlet. In the absence of freedom, that outlet will be the quest for power. "To allow to any human beings no existence of their own but what depends on others, is giving far too high a premium on bending others to their purposes. Where liberty cannot be hoped for, and power can, power becomes the grand object of human desire. . . ."

To have discerned the relation between woman's subordinate social role and the depth of the female craving for power was no mean analytic feat on Mill's part. The question then arises: what form does the urge to power take? Mill unfortunately does not realize how important this question is. . . .

What Mill did not see, indeed *could* not see (since had he done so, he would have been a different person), was that one of the commonest channels for a married woman's appetite for power is to be found in her relations with her children. This is

the most obvious source of relief and compensation for a mother
who is disappointed of self-realization, and whose energies cannot flow freely outward on equal terms with others. This is the
relationship which is the obvious target for corruption by emotions soured and starved in the marital and social roles by the
principle of female subordination. The children can so easily
become living objects for the receipt of "affections" compounded
of disappointed pride or crushed self-respect or rejected love.
Under what more innocent cloak than maternal love could such
bruised and thwarted emotions find a seemingly more legitimate
release? . . .

When healthy and sound emotions are denied a valid outlet,
it is not normally the case that they continue to beat against the
barrier impeding them until they have overcome it. Thwarted in
one direction, they seek to find substitute expression through
whatever outlets are available. As Mill correctly sees, the female
who is denied by birth the normal freedom permitted to persons
born as males will seek power as a surrogate. The fact that this
form of object identification is incompatible with psychic health,
genuine human affection and development to full maturity, can
only be revealed by deep and prolonged analysis. Because power
has developed as a necessary compensation in maintaining the
balance of the existing psychic structure, the individual feels a
threat to her ability to express her desire for power as a threat
to her fundamental emotional stability. In other words, women,
denied the rewards of psychic freedom, develop a strong interest
in preserving such opportunities for psychic power as they have
been able to forge for themselves.

Theodore Roszak / *The Hard and the Soft:*
The Force of Feminism in Modern Times

Rarely have historians granted feminism the dimensions of a major social movement. Rather, most textbook accounts and general histories deftly diminish the scale and import of the controversy which the demand for women's rights generated in the late nineteenth and early twentieth centuries. Our history, it seems, is also a man-made thing. In this essay, Theodore Roszak argues that, if one but views the matter with a bit of psychological sophistication, the great sex war emerges as the foremost influence upon the cultural character and political style of the Western world during the era of *realpolitik*.

SEARCH ANY standard history text and you will be lucky to find more than two or three scattered and pedestrian passages dealing with man-woman relations during the nineteenth and twentieth centuries—the critical period of feminist agitation. The emphasis is likely to be on America and England, limited for the most part to the bare legal and social facts and heavily weighted toward the later phases of the suffrage movement. So narrow a focus succeeds marvelously in making the suffragettes seem like a transient and freakish phenomenon, for it screens out the gathering momentum of the woman's rights movement through the course of the nineteenth century. A fair survey of feminism would see the pressure for woman's emancipation building from the 1830's and 1840's and reaching out well beyond the issue of the ballot. The militant suffrage campaign emerges only at a late stage of the movement and its bitterness derives from the fact that the vote had by the turn of the century become a symbol—both to men and women—of very much more than electoral equality.

What the normally perfunctory presentation of feminism ignores is that a major shift in sex relations, let alone so rapid and revolutionary a transformation as industrialism has caused in the West, is bound to produce a severe cultural trauma. What touches on conventions of manliness and womanliness risks igniting the most combustible human situation of all: the one social relationship men and women take to bed with them every night and there mingle with the strongest passions they know. One might almost suspect, from their consistent neglect of feminism's psychic impact, that the historians are a peculiarly undersexed breed.

In any event, it surely requires remarkable obtuseness to ignore the fact that by the late nineteenth century—in the wake of at least two generations of feminist organization and crusading—this supposedly marginal curiosity called the "woman problem" had become one of the most earth-shaking debates in the Western world, fully as explosive an issue as the class or national conflicts of the day. Here, after all, was the world's largest oppressed "minority" threatening mutiny: something no man could ignore. And none did. Even in countries where feminist agitation was minor or nonexistent, the great question nevertheless provoked outraged concern. Tolstoy in a Russia nearly untouched by feminism had to be as worried about keeping women in their place as England's William Gladstone. The "woman problem" was argued about, shouted about, raved about, agonized about endlessly, endlessly. By the final decades of the century, it permeated everything. One would be hard pressed to find many major figures of the period in any cultural field who did not address themselves passionately to the rights of women. As for lesser figures . . . the amount of literature (newspapers, magazines, novels, dramas, scholarship, pamphlets) that emerged from the ranks of now forgotten feminists and antifeminists must surely outweigh the material we have on any other social issue of modern

times. For some—thinkers of the caliber of Comte, Strindberg,
Nietzsche, Ibsen, Shaw, Spengler, Schopenhauer, Jung, D. H.
Lawrence—the debate over the sexual roles became an ever-
recurring theme in their work, if not an obsession. There were
even *lumpen* intellectuals, like the widely translated and much
applauded Otto Weininger, for whom virulent antifeminism became a total world view.[1]

Sound and fury . . . but, to judge by all subsequent appearances, signifying nothing. For within a decade following the
First World War the issue that had generated such a quantity
of scorching controversy had sunk in our historical consciousness
to the level of a quaint human interest story . . . something having to do with the advent of bloomers, with hysterical females
chaining themselves to the railings of state houses, and with a
now obsolete demand for women's suffrage. And there no doubt
the episode would still lie, an antiquarian's curio good for a few
chuckles in undergraduate history surveys, had not a new wave

1. A few quotations from Weininger's *Sex and Character* (London, Heinemann, 1906) may suffice to show how vicious even the sexological "scholarship" of the day could become. Bear in mind, Weininger was regarded in his
time not as a vulgar polemicist but as a scientific authority on his subject.

> Women have no existence and no essence; they are not, they are nothing. Man-
> kind occurs as male or female, as something or nothing. Woman has no share
> in ontological reality, no relation to the thing-in-itself, which, in the deepest
> interpretation, is the absolute, is God. . . . Woman has no relation to the idea,
> she neither affirms nor denies it; she is neither moral nor anti-moral; mathe-
> matically speaking, she has no sign; she is purposeless, neither good nor bad
> . . . she is as non-moral as she is non-logical. But all existence is moral and
> logical existence. So woman has no existence. (p. 286)

> Untruthfulness, organic untruthfulness, characterizes . . . all women. It is quite
> wrong to say that women lie. That would imply that they sometimes speak
> the truth. Sincerity . . . is the virtue of all others of which women are absolutely
> incapable, which is impossible for them! (pp. 273–274)

Like Weininger himself, many of the overwrought male chauvinists of his
day (Nietzsche, Von Treitschke, Kipling, Cecil Rhodes . . .) cut rather pathetic figures: small of size, sickly or crippled, and painfully sex shy. But
poor little Weininger may have been the saddest case of all. He poured his
whole hate-filled heart into his misogynist bible . . . and then committed
suicide in Beethoven's house at the age of twenty-three. Oswald Spengler
commemorated the deed in *The Decline of the West* as "one of the noblest
spectacles" of the age.

of feminist militancy lately arisen to remind us of how little the winning of the ballot settled in the protracted war of the sexes. It is difficult not to see in this depreciation of feminism another example of the defensive male's classic response to the grievance of women: shrug it off . . . play it down . . . trivialize it. And the ploy continues to be used. In 1970, a sadly appropriate cartoon appeared in one of the slick national magazines: an overstuffed, cigar-smoking chairman of the board telling his overstuffed cigar-smoking colleagues, "O.K., boys . . . Women's Lib is this year's big schtick."

But once allow reticent scholarship or the mass media to screen out the full significance of the feminist cause, and there is very little sense to be made of the history of our age. For in no small measure the last hundred years stand as the historical crisis of masculine dominance. During this period, under the pressure of advancing industrialization, the sexual stereotypes have played into the political life of the modern West with a special force— and more decisively perhaps than even many of the most militant feminists have realized.

The critical moment in this psychic dimension of history we are here discussing covers the two or three generations that precede the outbreak of the First World War—the war that was not just *another* war, but an apocalyptic disaster: the cultural default that continues to burn on the brow of Western civilization like the mark of the beast. For all its humanitarian pretensions, since 1914 our society and all the world that has fallen under its influence have never for a moment been free of the curse of total, annihilating war.

No one who has studied the life of the West during the half-century before the war has failed to recognize the astonishingly hard-boiled, war-prone style of the period. It is a bleak intellectual landscape shadowed by ugly ideologies. By the end of the century one finds militarism, imperialism, and racism inflated to the dimensions of secular religions. Social Darwinism, *realpolitik,* and "the strenuous life" become the ethical orthodoxies of the day. The literary style called "realism" steels itself to confront a reality held to be universally crude, rapacious, and torn by bestial struggle. The most strident elements in Nietzsche's philosophy are bastardized into a cult of sadistic bullying. The radical Left ideologues of the day—the anarchists, nihilists, syndicalists, Bolsheviks—turn progressively more violence-minded and vituperative, more deeply sunk in grim materialism and intentions of unpitying vengeance. Above all, one finds on all sides the ceaseless celebration of war and warriors, the ceaseless denigration of peace. Seldom have the discontents of civilized life been so flamboyantly advertised. "Perpetual peace," said General von Moltke of proudly martial Prussia, "is a dream—and not even a beautiful dream—and war is an integral part of God's ordering of the universe." "Lasting peace," said Jacob Burckhardt of inveterately peaceful Switzerland, "permits the rise of a mass of precarious, fear-ridden, distressful lives which . . . thicken the air and as a whole degrade the nation's blood. War restores real ability to honor."

The age throngs with such spokesmen of violence, prophets of a new savagery that contemptuously sweeps aside all humanitarian values, as if men had grown bone-weary of their own civilized standards. Bismarck and Cavour, Spencer and Sorel, Lenin and Necheyev, Kipling and Von Treitschke, Carnegie and Bakunin, Teddy Roosevelt and Cecil Rhodes, Houston Stewart Chamberlain and Jack London . . . bully boys and great predators one and all, for whom the world is a jungle, a battleground, a gladiatorial arena. Their world view bristles with corner-of-the-mouth invocations of blood and iron, power and bellicosity . . . to the extent that brute force is raised to the status of a supreme metaphysical principle. Filippo Marinetti's "Futurist Manifesto" of 1909 nicely captures the fanatical belligerence of it all:

> We are out to glorify war:
> The only health-giver of the world!
> Militarism! Patriotism!
> The Destructive Arm of the Anarchist!
> Ideas that kill!
> Contempt for women!

It should require little psychological insight to see such hairy-chested bravado for what it is: the full and hideous flowering of the politics of masculine dominance finally become more can-

didly proclaimed than ever before in history. The period leading
up to 1914 reads in the history books like one long drunken stag
party where boys from every walk of life and every ideological
persuasion goad one another on to ever more bizarre professions
of toughness, daring, and counterphobic mania—until at last the
boasting turns suicidal and these would-be supermen plunge the
whole of Western society into the blood bath of world war. Compulsive masculinity is written all over the political style of the
period. It echoes constantly through the political rhetoric of the
day. Thus, Theodore Roosevelt: "The nation that has trained itself to a cancer of unwarlike and isolated ease is bound, in the
end, to go down before other nations which have not lost *the
manly and adventurous virtues.*" Thus, the American General
Homer Lea: "As *manhood* marks the height of physical vigor
among mankind, so the militant successes of a nation mark the
zenith of its physical greatness." Thus, the Irish poet-revolution-
ary Patrick Pearse: "Bloodshed is a cleansing and a sanctifying
thing, and the nation which regards it as a final horror has *lost
its manhood.*" Thus, most strikingly, the Spanish political philosopher Juan Donoso-Cortés: "When a nation shows a civilized
horror of war, it receives directly the punishment of its mistake.
God changes its sex, despoils it of its common mark of virility,
changes it into a feminine nation, and sends conquerors to ravish
it of its honor."

Such literary panache may be a thing of the past; but the
castration-haunted psychology underlying these revealing metaphors should be familiar enough to all of us. It survives in the
blood-and-guts aesthetics of a Hemingway, a Farrell, a Mailer:
the cult of the bullfight and prize ring, of battlefield heroics and
barroom brawling and the good red wine. At a more vulgar level,
it flourishes in the sadistic fantasies of Mickey Spillane and Ian
Fleming—but especially in myriad he-man pulps where an endless fascination with the atrocities of war and Nazism prevails.
It permeates the guerrilla-warrior mystique of the New Left and
the Black Panthers: the desert boots . . . the uncouth manners
. . . the rough talk . . . the gun-slinging . . . the blood in the
eye . . . the ceaseless need to prove how tough, how *really* tough

one is. And never far off, there is always that same "contempt for women" which reduces the female to servant, camp follower, helpless subordinate.

At higher levels of power, we have seen the same crude caricature of masculinity survive in the chauvinist metaphysics of Fascism and Nazism: the same bizarre attempt to ennoble violence and suffering, to cheapen compassion and tenderness. "War alone," Mussolini proclaimed, "keys up the energies of man to their greatest pitch and sets the mark of nobility on those nations which have the bravery to face it." In recent years, the language of violence may have shifted toward semimathematical jargon, but the tough-guy posturings of our nuclear strategists are an obvious extension of the same tradition. The war lords have become computerized, but they still pride themselves that they do not turn green to think the unthinkable nor flinch to tick off the carnage by the "megadeath." And what is the term they coyly use to speak of global annihilation? It is their *wargasm.* How much more transparent could things be? Our international political leadership may talk high politics and heady ideology. But its space rocket and ballistic missile rivalry is all too clearly a world-wide contest of insecure penises out to prove their size and potency. It is the sort of pathetic competition "real men" often come down to at the end of a long, boozy night out.[2]

Now it is obviously no mere coincidence that, at the turn of the century, this obsessive glorification of toughness should coincide with the quickening tempo of the women's rights movement as it comes down from the 1830's and 1840's. As the women struggled to haul themselves out from under, they inevitably set the entire superstructure of male supremacy to rocking. No institution in the society could escape the reverberations—and so the men were forced to cling to their endangered prerogatives all the more desperately. More than any other issue of the time,

2. For a recent—and approving—full-dress parody of all this warlike, masculine pomposity, see Lionel Tiger's anthropological fantasy *Men in Groups,* New York, Random House, 1969. Here is the old chauvinist song and dance still aspiring to the status of scholarly respectability. (An excerpt from this book is included elsewhere in this anthology.)

the "woman problem" laid the knife-edge of anxiety against every man's most exposed nerve: his domestic supremacy. It hit below the belt; it struck at the groin and the glands . . . as it still does today. Deeper down than we are rich or poor, black or white, we are he or she. That is the last ditch of our socially prescribed identity . . . the one line of psychic defense we dare not surrender.

One can hardly expect to document the million secret skirmishes of the sex war that were fought out in every bedroom of the Western world night after night for the two or three generations leading up to the First World War. But from time to time the memoirs and the literature of the day give us a glimpse of the domestic melees for which organized feminism was but the public and political voice. The warfare was constant, savage, and entrenched. There could have been few men who did not carry with them, as they walked out to take their place in the world, the nagging fear that their much-prized manhood might be slipping from their grasp. Their masculinity was, after all, predicated upon the submissiveness of women . . . and women, perhaps their own wives, were growing less and less servile. Some, the militant suffragettes, were resorting to outright force: the indisputable male prerogative. Others—notorious libertines of the day like Marie Bashkirtsev, Isadora Duncan, Victoria Woodhull, Emma Goldman, Annie Besant—were brazenly trespassing upon all the other masculine privileges: liquor, strong language, aggressive politics, free love, an independent life. Sylvia Pankhurst, in her book *The Great Scourge,* was openly calling for an end to marriage, and for a general sexual strike. The whole meaning of manhood was being put cruelly in jeopardy—and the challenge ranged the entire social hierarchy.

In Granville-Barker's *The Madras House,* the middle-class male chauvinist of the play (he has himself converted to Islam and keeps a harem) pontificates,

Every great public question . . . all politics, all religion, all economy is being brought down to the level of women's emotions. Admirable in its way . . . charming in its place! But softening, sentimentalizing,

enervating . . . lapping the world, if you let it, in the nursery cotton
wool of prettiness and pettiness. Men don't realize how far rotted by
the process they are. . . . Women haven't morals or intellect in our
sense of the words. . . . Shut them away from public life and public
exhibition. It's degrading to compete with them . . . it's as degrading
to compete *for* them. Perhaps we're too late already.

The same fears and resentments can be found from the top
to the bottom of society. Sometimes their expression could be
remarkably crude, as when General von Bernhardi, one of the
windiest of Prussian militarists, affected the habit of having his
wife walk three paces behind him in public. At the lowest social
level, D. H. Lawrence could recall from his own prewar youth
how the colliers of Nottingham despised and fled the increasingly undeferential company of their wives. Even among these
wretched of the earth Lawrence could sense a secret longing
for that Spartan fellowship of arms which has always served as
the ultimate vindication of manly pride.

The miners worked underground as a sort of intimate community,
they knew each other practically naked, and with curious close
intimacy, and the darkness and the underground remoteness of the
pit "stall," and the continual presence of danger, made the physical,
instinctive, and intuitional contact between men very highly developed. . . . My father loved the pit. . . . He loved the contact, the
intimacy, as men in the war loved the intense male comradeship of
the dark days.

When Mrs. Emmeline Pankhurst spoke at rallies, the scorning
Englishmen in her audience, seeing her as the foremost destroyer
of their domestic privileges, used to throw trousers at her. In public, it was as close as they could come to manifesting their fears
of emasculation. But in the homes that were their castles, their
manly anxieties could find something more gratifying than symbolic expression. By the late nineteenth century, English court
records (which would of course report only those few cases that
found their way into litigation) gave a daily average of four
cases of "aggravated assault" by husbands upon wives. "Aggravated assault": the phrase means beatings that resulted in per-

manent bodily harm—the putting out of an eye, or setting of one's wife afire.[3]

John Stuart Mill observed that "the quality of the marital relationship has facets which ramify into every aspect of the life of society." It is a great truth, though one that will always be too closeted to be documented more than haphazardly. For all the public debate on the subject, the "woman problem" was—and is—ultimately rooted in the most secret and obscure corners of daily life: household hatreds, marital mayhem, tormenting fits of frigidity and impotence, the subtle thrust and parry that can chill each touch, gesture, whisper during the act of would-be love: the power politics of the bedstead. Here was the emotional dynamite the Western world was storing away in every private life throughout the society. And once the explosives were laid up, any spark would do to ignite them and blast the whole civilization to bits . . . sooner or later . . . sooner or later. . . .

Surely it is this crisis of the sexual stereotypes that accounts for much of that extraordinary craving for violence which gathers so ominously in the last few decades before the war. *Der Tag,* long anticipated and prepared, might even begin to look to many men like welcome relief: the chance at last for embattled manhood to prevail in the one arena it could yet claim wholly to itself. The soldiers might call the bloodsoaked fields of France and Flanders "no man's land"—but this was decidedly *man's* place and no female would dare dispute it. So it was that the call to arms became irresistibly seductive—even to artists. The poet

---

3. Vera Brittain, *Lady into Woman* (New York, Macmillan, 1953), p. 24. Wife beating in modern times is worth study in its own right. W. L. Burn, writing on the mid Victorian period in England, characterizes it as a favorite masculine pastime—especially among the working class. He draws this picture of the far from exceptional laborer of the time: "The two recreations he assiduously cultivates are drinking and thrashing his wife and children. When he goes home now he will thrash his wife with the buckle end of his belt, knock her to the floor and kick her into insensibility. One day he will kill her and be hanged for it." (*Age of Equipoise* [New York, Norton, 1964], p. 35.) English law, it is interesting to note, refused to recognize such a thing as rape between husband and wife until well into the twentieth century, no matter how brutal a husband's attentions became. Woman's legal vulnerability to drunken manhandling makes it clear why so many feminists also crusaded for temperance: not out of prudishness, but for the sake of simple self-defense.

Valéry only confessed the sick desires of millions when he wrote
to André Gide in the 1890's: "Oh, to fire on all the world! . . .
I am haunted by a panorama of slaughter and blinded by ravaged
lights. I almost wish for a monstrous war in which to flee amid
the shock of a crazed and red Europe." Gide, who shared his
"warrior" correspondent's "dream of the impact of shuddering
weapons," pronounced the letter "beautiful." Or again to quote
Ireland's Patrick Pearse, whose exuberance for the war could
hardly be restrained: "The last sixteen months [he wrote in
1915] have been the most glorious in the history of Europe.
Heroism has come back to the Earth. . . . The old heart of the
earth needed to be warmed with the red wine of the battlefields."

How many anonymous others were there, similarly possessed
by martial longings, who found in the war a balm for frustrations they hardly dared to admit? We know of at least one: a
German youth who later rose out of obscurity to tell the world
that when the war broke out, "I am not ashamed to say that,
overwhelmed by impassionate enthusiasm, I had fallen on my
knees and thanked Heaven out of my overflowing heart that it
had granted me the good fortune of being allowed to live in
these times." His name was Adolf Hitler, later to turn the First
World War into the major cause of the Second World War, and
to create the most barbarically masculine ideological movement
of the twentieth century.

Historians have pressed their search for the origins of the First
World War down to the most atomistic diplomatic and military
minutiae—as if one might trace the cause of so apocalyptic an
event to some minor miscalculation or ill-conceived policy. The
forest that gets lost in this fastidious enumeration of the trees
is the truth that Christabel Pankhurst put with such authorita-
tive simplicity in *The Suffragette*, August 7, 1914.

This then is the World as men have made it, life as men have
ordered it.

A man-made civilization, hideous and cruel enough in time of
peace, is to be destroyed.

A civilization made by men only is a civilization which defies the
law of nature, which defies the law of right Government.

This great war . . . is Nature's vengeance—is God's vengeance

upon the people who held women in subjection, and by doing that
have destroyed the perfect, human balance. Just as when the laws
governing the human body are defied we have disease, so when the
law of right government is defied—the law that men and women shall
cooperate in managing their affairs—we have a civilization imperfect,
unjust, savage at its best and foredoomed to destruction. . . . That
which has made men for generations past sacrifice woman and the
race to their lusts, is now making them fly at each other's throats, and
bring ruin upon the world.

But few feminists were perceptive enough to see the war in
that light. Even Christabel Pankhurst herself, within one week
of writing the words, was to turn her newspaper into a fiercely
anti-German propaganda sheet. The vast majority of the movement tragically misread the meaning of the conflict. In America,
the National American Woman Suffrage Association was among
the first groups to press for United States entry into the war. In
England, Mrs. Pankhurst dutifully called off the suffragette campaign for the duration, threw in with the war effort, and even
summoned her followers into the streets to hand out the white
feather of cowardice to able-bodied men not yet in uniform.
Overnight, feminists of all countries became, with few exceptions,
patriots and war-boosters, blindly endorsing this cataclysmically
brutal assertion of masculine dominance, the final desperate outlet for all the pent-up fury of a stereotypic manliness which they
themselves had done so much to threaten and thwart.

So the first round in the struggle for women's liberation ended.
The women accepted the war, and with it the continued supremacy of the masculine stereotype in our political life. The
great fear so often expressed before the war—that the first nation
to grant women's suffrage would by the very act be "feminized"
and rendered impotent before its foes—was laid to rest. In America, England, and elsewhere, the vote could now be given . . .
for the women had proved themselves "reliable." They had
agreed to leave the political world a man's world: an armed camp.

The dismal prelude to the First World War throws into sharp
relief one of the enduring dilemmas of women's liberation. What

it reveals dramatically is that the oppression of women has been, simultaneously, a savage subordination of the stereotypic feminine virtues which supposedly reside exclusively in the female psyche. The act of oppression has therefore provided men with several advantages at once. (Though to be sure, they are only deceptively "advantages," for they are purchased at the expense of grotesquely crippling the emotional and moral life of men.) Most obviously, the exclusion of women from worldly affairs has cleared out of men's way the competitive challenge of half the human race. At the same time, it has given them an inexhaustible supply of unpaid domestic labor and sexual gratification. In these respects, the subjection of women is similar in its effects to racial exploitation—a parallel that cannot be too frequently emphasized. Women were indeed the first niggers in history—and are still apt to be the last liberated.

But the oppression of women has also served to legitimize the claims of stereotypic masculinity to social dominance. It has given men carte blanche to go about their public business as specialized boors and bullies. And at this point, the parallelism between women's oppression and that of other exploited classes or races breaks down in a significant way. The black who seeks human equality strives to throw off a white racist stereotype that includes nothing of human worth. For what is it to be a nigger? It is to be stupid, shiftless, incompetent, servile, dishonest, infantile. True, the feminine stereotype overlaps with these obnoxious characteristics; but it *also* includes qualities of compassion and sensitivity indispensable to cultural growth and human survival.

This is what gives the oppression of women its strikingly ambivalent aspect. On the one hand, women have been the objects of crushing masculine contempt; but at the same time their oppressors have seen fit to deify the attributes of femininity. Earth Mother, muse, love goddess, siren, nymph, angelic maiden . . . in one form or another, all the feminine qualities have been elevated to the highest cultural status. Granted, such idealization has been cynically used to thwart women's claim to equality and workaday dignity in a thousand ingenious ways. Mythologizing woman has been a standard method of gilding her cage. But for

all that, the fact remains: *only* women of all the world's exploited
groups have been placed on a pedestal by their exploiters. Of
all the niggers in human history, woman has been the only one
to be idealized.

Why? Because men—and especially the artists, the seers, the
saints—have always sensed the insufficiency of the stereotypic
masculine virtues that officially govern the world. They have
known from their own experience that creativity, intuition, love,
cooperation, even submissiveness—all the fluid, fertile qualities
that water and feed the roots of culture—stem from the so-called
feminine side of the human psyche. And knowing the irrepres-
sible necessity of the feminine in themselves, they have projected
it into a repertory of magnificent, life-affirming images. No doubt,
too, this has been man's way of expiating in some degree the
guilt he has known for degrading woman. The tortuous contradictions of such a schizophrenic strategy are all too obvious:
to celebrate the feminine virtues, and yet to oppress the supposed
bearer of those virtues . . . this is to bestow an exaggerated
dignity with one hand and to snatch it away with the other.
Quite as obviously, the strategy double-binds the woman to the
point of excruciation. For she is expected—and expects herself
—to remain lady, angel, goddess under conditions of repression
that can only bring out the cornered beast in any normal human
being.

But as sorry and absurd as all this is, we must not lose sight
of one critical fact: in large measure, men and women alike
resort to such madly intricate psychic maneuvers out of an abiding concern to save the feminine attributes. William O'Neill
identifies it as a major weakness of early feminism that so many
of the sisters could not make a clear break with "the cult of
domesticity" and the mystique of motherhood. "Feminism," he
comments, "was made respectable by accommodating it to the
Victorian ethos that had forced it into being."[4] True enough.

4. William L. O'Neill, "Feminism as a Radical Ideology," in Alfred Young,
ed., *Dissent: Exploration in the History of American Radicalism* (De Kalb,
Ill., Northern Illinois University Press, 1968), p. 284. This is also a conclusion
O'Neill draws in his *Everyone Was Brave: The Rise and Fall of Feminism in
America* (Chicago, Quadrangle Press, 1969).

But was it not the feminists' dilemma that many of them clearly recognized in the feminine mystique, though just barely keeping afloat upon the drivel and syrup, many of the most redeeming powers of the human personality? Indeed, can any of us even imagine our race surviving much longer if tenderness and pity, loving kindness and receptivity do not soon become the prime qualities of our private and public lives? How long can the awesome power we now possess be left in the trust of those who feel no obligation to honor the nurturing impulse within them?

Because feminist leaders like Jane Addams did feel that obligation, they could not let go of the mystique. For how was woman to be emancipated into a man's world without losing her womanly qualities in the transition? The real weakness of the movement lay in the conviction of leaders like Addams that they must keep the compassionate virtues to themselves, rather than sharing them with men. This would have meant nothing less than ending the sexual stereotypes and thereby transforming the feminine virtues into *human* virtues. It would have meant recognizing that the woman most desperately in need of liberation is the "woman" every man has locked up in the dungeons of his own psyche. *That* is the basic act of oppression that still waits to be undone, though the undoing might well produce the most cataclysmic reinterpretation of the sexual roles and of sexual "normalcy" in all human history.

The point we raise here deserves special emphasis lest it be disastrously misunderstood. Saving the compassionate virtues is *not* the peculiar duty of women. On the contrary; the sooner we have done with the treacherous nonsense of believing that the human personality must be forced into masculine and feminine molds, the better. No matter how lyrically intoned, the notion that women are innately "feminine" and therefore uniquely responsible for the fate of the softer human virtues is a lethal deception. To think this way is to play dumb to the fact that throughout civilized history men have unloaded the nurturing talents on women for base purposes of manipulation and exploitation. Worst of all: it is to continue giving the men of the world a solid-gold rationale for repressing those talents in

themselves and for thus stripping power of its humanitarian discipline.

There, then, is the heart of the matter: *There are no masculine
and feminine virtues. There are only human virtues.* Courage,
daring, decisiveness, resourcefulness are good qualities, in women
as much so as in men. So, too, are charity, mercy, tenderness.
But ruthlessness, callousness, power lust, domineering self-assertion . . . these are destructive, whether in man or woman.
At this juncture in our history, it is the compassionate virtues
that need desperately to be given a new public dignity. But
what an act of hypocrisy it would be to pretend that these virtues are to be honored *in women!* Rather, they are to be given
reverence *in all of us,* for they *are* there.

If women's liberation in its latest phase means integrating
more women into positions of power and prestige within our
existing social order, there can of course be no way to fault the
movement by the conventional criteria of social justice. Full-
scale integration means equality, and against the egalitarian demand there can be no argument—least of all by those who
occupy the position of privilege. But the existing social order
has been fashioned by compulsively masculine men after *their*
image. If liberated women integrate with that society, what then
becomes of the compassionate virtues? Is the place of those
virtues still to be in the home, even after the women have de-
parted to pursue their careers? Will our political health be improved if half the politically irrelevant homemakers locked away
in those homes should be male . . . and half the power politicians female?

Here is the question that Simone de Beauvoir ignores when
in *The Second Sex* she equates human progress with the progressive masculinization of history. "The devaluation of femininity," she feels, "has been a necessary step in human evolution."
It represents the victory of "technique over magic, and reason
over superstition." Therefore, "the emancipated woman . . .
wants to be active, a taker, and refuses the passivity man means
to impose on her." She "accepts masculine values: she prides
herself on thinking, taking action, working, creating, on the
same terms as men."

Again, there is no disagreeing with De Beauvoir that all masculine privilege must be transformed into human right; that every personality be allowed to find its own destiny unburdened by the sexual stereotypes. But again, what becomes of the compassionate virtues if we endorse De Beauvoir's thesis? From her standpoint, it is only women who need to be liberated; they must be freed from their femininity . . . for femininity is the mark of a flawed and antiquated personality. She tells us that the world men have created, the world of "technique and reason," is good . . . excepting the fact that it excludes the poor, the nonwhite, the female. Man "makes the crops grow, he digs canals, he irrigates or drains the land, he lays out roads, he builds temples: he creates a new world." The "male principle" is that of "creative force, of light, of intelligence, of order. . . ." But what if this "male principle" is also the disease of our politics, the psychological source from which all the discontents of civilization flow: the tyranny of cerebral organization, the grinding obsession with productivity, the alienation that comes of the need to dominate? Then it will be no cure to have the whole human race infected with the virus, rather than only the pants-wearing half.

"We gotta get tough," says one of the slogans of women's liberation. And the more militant sisters advocate karate and celebrate the virtues of the Third World's sisters-in-arms. Well, no doubt, women's capacity for bone-breaking and gun-toting is every bit as great as men's. "Feminine" fragility comes no more naturally to females than military heroism does to males. So let there be no question about it: women can be every bit the brutes and bastards men have been . . . and they have as much right to cultivate the qualities.

Yet here is a great question: how shall this already too brutish and bastardly world be saved and made gentle by increasing the numbers of brutes and bastards among us?

Still, if that is the way things must go, then women's liberation is not, after all, the final revolution. Perhaps its historical purpose will be to shatter the sexual stereotypes *at the expense of the compassionate virtues*, leaving us all, men and women alike, with the nobler task still to achieve: Gandhi's hope: all

power renounced but that of love: the gentleness in all of us
redeemed and exalted: the peaceable kingdom.

From the Tao Te Ching

Humankind when living is soft and tender;
When dead, they are hard and tough.
The ten thousand creatures
And all plants and trees
While they live are supple and soft.
But when they die: hard and stiff.
So it is said: what is hard and stiff
Belongs to death;
The soft and tender belong to life.
Therefore, the weapon that is too rigid
Will shatter;
The tree made of hardest wood
Will break.
Truly: the hard and mighty are easily overthrown;
The soft and weak endure and rise up.

Toward Liberation

1. Between the Old Feminism and the New

Karen Horney / *Distrust Between the Sexes*

Karen Horney, noted German psychoanalyst, who in 1941 helped to found the New York Psychoanalytic Institute, here questions the primacy of Freud's libido theory. As a woman, Dr. Horney no doubt felt the injustice of Freud's sex-biased view that the development of the female is determined by envy of the male sex organ. While remaining firmly in the mainstream of the psychoanalytic school, Dr. Horney in the following essay (which was originally given as a speech in Berlin in 1930) exhibits a healthy criticism of Freudian thought. It is interesting not only for her attempt to revise male-oriented Freudian views, but also for the anthropological underpinnings of her analyses of other cultures.

THE RELATIONSHIP between men and women is quite similiar to that between children and parents, in that we prefer to focus on the positive aspects of these relationships. We prefer to assume that love is the fundamentally given factor and that hostility is an accidental and avoidable occurrence. Although we are familiar with slogans such as "the battle of the sexes" and "hostility between the sexes," we must admit that they do not mean a great deal. They make us overfocus on sexual relations between men and women, which can very easily lead us to a too one-sided view. Actually, from our recollection of numerous case his-

From *Feminine Psychology* (New York, Norton, 1967), pp. 107–118. Reprinted by the permission of the editor, Harold Kelman, M.D.

tories, we may conclude that love relationships are quite easily destroyed by overt or covert hostility. On the other hand we are only too ready to blame such difficulties on individual misfortune, on incompatibility of the partners, and on social or economic causes.

The individual factors, which we find causing poor relations between men and women, may be the pertinent ones. However, because of the great frequency, or better, the regular occurrence of disturbances in love relations, we have to ask ourselves whether the disturbances in the individual cases might not arise from a common background; whether there are common denominators for this easily and frequently arising suspiciousness between the sexes. . . .

I would like to start with something very commonplace—namely, that a good deal of this atmosphere of suspiciousness is understandable and even justifiable. It apparently has nothing to do with the individual partner, but rather with the intensity of the affects and with the difficulty of taming them.

We know, or may dimly sense, that these affects can lead to ecstasy, to being beside oneself, to surrendering oneself, which means a leap into the unlimited and the boundless. This is perhaps why real passion is so rare. For like a good businessman, we are loath to put all our eggs into one basket. We are inclined to be reserved and ever ready to retreat. Be that as it may, because of our instinct for self-preservation, we all have a natural fear of losing ourselves in another person. . . . One is inclined to overlook how little one gives of oneself, but one feels all the more this same deficiency in the partner, the feeling of "You never really loved me." . . . Even Strindberg [who was a misogynist] defensively managed to say on occasion that he was no woman hater, but that women hated and tortured him.

Here we are not dealing with pathological phenomena at all. . . . Anybody, to a certain extent, will be inclined to overlook his own hostile impulses, but under pressure of his own guilty conscience, may project them onto the partner. This process must, of necessity, cause some overt or covert distrust of the partner's love, fidelity, sincerity, or kindness. This is the reason why I prefer to speak of distrust between the sexes and not of hatred;

for in keeping with our own experience we are more familiar with the feeling of distrust.

A further, almost unavoidable, source of disappointment and distrust in our normal love life derives from the fact that the very intensity of our feelings of love stirs up all of our secret expectations and longings for happiness, which slumber deep inside us. All our unconscious wishes, contradictory in their nature and expanding boundlessly on all sides, are waiting here for their fulfillment. . . . As long as we assume that [the partner] could actually fulfill all these expectations, we invest him with the glitter of sexual overestimation. We take the magnitude of such overvaluation for the measure of our love, while in reality it merely expresses the magnitude of our expectations. The very nature of our claims makes their fulfillment impossible. Herein lies the origin of the disappointments with which we may cope in a more or less effective way. . . . Yet there remain traces of distrust in us, as in a child who discovers that his father cannot get him the stars from the sky after all. . . .

The analytical approach begins with the question: What special factors in human development lead to the discrepancy between expectations and fulfillment and what causes them to be of special significance in particular cases? Let us start with a general consideration. There is a basic difference between human and animal development—namely, the long period of the infant's helplessness and dependency. The paradise of childhood is most often an illusion with which adults like to deceive themselves. For the child, however, this paradise is inhabited by too many dangerous monsters. Unpleasant experiences with the opposite sex seem to be unavoidable. . . . Children are different in the aims of their drives, but above all, in the pristine integrity of their demands. They find it hard to express their desires directly, and where they do, they are not taken seriously. . . . In short, children will undergo painful and humiliating experiences of being rebuffed, being betrayed, and being told lies. They also may have to take second place to a parent or sibling, and they are threatened and intimidated when they seek, in playing with their own bodies, those pleasures that are denied them by adults. The child is relatively powerless in the face of all this. . . . Anger and

aggression are pent up within him in the form of extravagant
fantasies, . . . fantasies that are criminal when viewed from the
standpoint of the adult. . . . Since the child is vaguely aware of
these destructive forces within him, he feels, according to the
talion law, equally threatened by the adults. Here is the origin of
those infantile anxieties of which no child remains entirely
free. This already enables us to understand better the fear of
love of which I have spoken. . . . Just here, in this most irrational
of all areas, the old childhood fears of a threatening father or
mother are reawakened, putting us instinctively on the defensive.
In other words, the fear of love will always be mixed with the
fear of what we might do to the other person, or what the other
person might do to us. . . .

I would like to sketch briefly how childhood conflicts may
affect the relationship to the opposite sex in later life. Let us
take as an example a typical situation: The little girl who was
badly hurt through some great disappointment by her father,
will transform her innate instinctual wish to receive from the
man, into a vindictive one of taking from him by force. Thus
the foundation is laid for a direct line of development to a later
attitude, according to which she will not only deny her maternal
instincts, but will have only one drive, i.e., to harm the male,
to exploit him, and to suck him dry. She has become a vampire.
. . . We have here the fundamental constellation for the formation of a certain type of woman who is unable to relate to the
male because she fears that every male will suspect her of wanting something from him. This really means that she is afraid that
he might guess her repressed desires. . . . Or let us assume that
a reaction formation of excessive modesty will mask the repressed
drive for power. We then have the type of woman who shies
away from demanding or accepting anything from her husband.
Such a woman, however, due to the return of the repressed, will
react with depression to the nonfulfillment of her unexpressed,
and often unformulated wishes. . . . Quite often the repression
of aggression against the male drains all her vital energy. The
woman then feels helpless to meet life. She will shift the entire
responsibility for her helplessness onto the man, robbing him
of the very breath of life. Here you have the type of woman who,

under the guise of being helpless and childlike, dominates her man.

These are examples that demonstrate how the fundamental attitude of women toward men can be disturbed by childhood conflicts. . . . I shall now proceed to trace certain traits of male psychology. I do not wish to follow individual lines of development, though it might be very instructive to observe analytically how, for instance, even men who consciously have a very positive relationship with women and hold them in high esteem as human beings, harbor deep within themselves a secret distrust of them; and how this distrust relates back to feelings toward their mothers, which they experienced in their formative years. I shall focus rather on certain typical attitudes of men toward women and how they have appeared during various eras of history and in different cultures, not only as regards sexual relationships with women, but also, and often more so, in non-sexual situations, such as in their general evaluation of women.

I shall select some random examples, starting with Adam and Eve. Jewish culture, as recorded in the Old Testament, is outspokenly patriarchal. This fact reflects itself in their religion, which has no maternal goddesses; in their morals and customs, which allow the husband the right to dissolve the marital bond simply by dismissing his wife. Only by being aware of this background can we recognize the male bias in two incidents of Adam and Eve's history. First of all, woman's capacity to give birth is partly denied and partly devaluated: Eve was made of Adam's rib and a curse was put on her to bear children in sorrow. In the second place, by interpreting her tempting Adam to eat of the tree of knowledge as a sexual temptation, woman appears as the sexual temptress, who plunges man into misery. I believe that these two elements, one born out of resentment, the other out of anxiety, have damaged the relationship between the sexes from the earliest times to the present. Let us follow this up briefly. Man's fear of woman is deeply rooted in sex, as is shown by the simple fact that it is only the sexually attractive woman of whom he is afraid and who, although he strongly desires her, has to be kept in bondage. Old women, on the other hand, are held in high esteem, even by cultures in which the young woman

is dreaded and therefore suppressed. In some primitive cultures
the old woman may have the decisive voice in the affairs of the
tribe; among Asian nations also she enjoys great power and
prestige. On the other hand, in primitive tribes woman is surrounded by taboos during the entire period of her sexual maturity. . . . There is one basic thought at the bottom of all this:
Woman is a mysterious being who communicates with spirits
and thus has magic powers that she can use to hurt the male.
He must therefore protect himself against her powers by keeping
her subjugated. Thus the Miri in Bengal do not permit their
women to eat the flesh of the tiger, lest they become too strong.
The Watawela of East Africa keep the art of making fire a secret
from their women, lest women become their rulers. The Indians
of California have ceremonies to keep their women in submission; a man is disguised as a devil to intimidate the women. . . .
We find similar customs during the Middle Ages—the Cult of the
Virgin side by side with the burning of witches; the adoration of
"pure" motherliness, completely divested of sexuality, next to the
cruel destruction of the sexually seductive woman. Here again is
the implication of underlying anxiety, for the witch is in communication with the devil. Nowadays, with our more humane
forms of aggression, we burn women only figuratively, sometimes
with undisguised hatred, sometimes with apparent friendliness.
In any case, "The Jew must burn." [Translator's note: This is a
quote from *Nathan the Wise* by the eighteenth-century German
author Gotthold Ephraim Lessing, a humanist and a spokesman
for enlightenment and rationality. The expression became a col-
loquialism. It meant no matter how worthy and well-intentioned
his acts, by virtue of being a Jew, a man was guilty.] In friendly
and secret autos-da-fé, many nice things are said about women,
but it is just unfortunate that in her God-given natural state,
she is not the equal of the male. Moebius pointed out that the
female brain weighs less than the male one, but the point need
not be made in so crude a way. On the contrary, it can be
stressed that woman is not at all inferior, only different, but that
unfortunately she has fewer or none of those human or cultural
qualities that man holds in such high esteem. She is said to be
deeply rooted in the personal and emotional spheres, which is

wonderful; but unfortunately, this makes her incapable of exercising justice and objectivity, therefore disqualifying her for
positions in law and government and in the spiritual community.
She is said to be at home only in the realm of eros. Spiritual
matters are alien to her innermost being, and she is at odds with
cultural trends. She therefore is, as Asians frankly state, a second-
rate being. Woman may be industrious and useful but is, alas,
incapable of productive and independent work. She is, indeed,
prevented from real accomplishment by the deplorable, bloody
tragedies of menstruation and childbirth. And so every man
silently thanks his God, just as the pious Jew does in his prayers,
that he was not created a woman.

Man's attitude toward motherhood is a large and complicated chapter. One is generally inclined to see no problem in this
area. Even the misogynist is obviously willing to respect woman
as a mother and to venerate her motherliness under certain conditions, as mentioned above regarding the Cult of the Virgin. In
order to obtain a clearer picture, we have to distinguish between
two attitudes: men's attitudes toward motherliness, as represented in its purest form in the Cult of the Virgin, and their
attitude toward motherhood as such, as we encounter it in the
symbolism of the ancient mother goddesses. Males will always
be in favor of motherliness, as expressed in certain spiritual
qualities of women, i.e., the nurturing, selfless, self-sacrificing
mother; for she is the ideal embodiment of the woman who
could fulfill all his expectations and longings. In the ancient
mother goddesses, man did not venerate motherliness in the
spiritual sense, but rather motherhood in its most elemental
meaning. Mother goddesses are earthy goddesses, fertile like the
soil. They bring forth new life and they nurture it. It was this
life-creating power of woman, an elemental force, that filled
man with admiration. And this is exactly the point where problems arise. For it is contrary to human nature to sustain appprecia-
tion without resentment toward capabilities that one does not
possess. . . . Thus there has remained an obvious residue of
general resentment of men against women. This resentment expresses itself, also in our times, in men's distrustful defensive
maneuvers against the threat of women's invasion of their do-

mains; hence their tendency to devalue pregnancy and child-birth and to over-emphasize male genitality. This attitude does not express itself in scientific theories alone, but is also of far-reaching consequence for the entire relationship between the sexes, and for sexual morality in general. Motherhood, especially illegitimate motherhood, is very insufficiently protected by law—with the one exception of a recent attempt at improvement in Russia. Conversely, there is ample opportunity for the fulfillment of the male's sexual needs. Emphasis on irresponsible sexual indulgence, and devaluation of women to an object of purely physical needs, are further consequences of this masculine attitude.

From Bachofen's investigations we know that this state of the cultural supremacy of the male has not existed since the beginning of time, but that women once occupied a central position. This was the era of the so-called matriarchy, when law and custom were centered around the mother. Matricide was then, as Sophocles showed in the *Eumenides,* the unforgivable crime, while patricide, by comparison, was a minor offense. Only in recorded historical times have men begun, with minor variations, to play the leading role in the political, economical, and judicial fields, as well as in the area of sexual morality. At present we seem to be going through a period of struggle in which women once more dare to fight for their equality. . . .

I do not want to be misunderstood as having implied that all disaster results from male supremacy and that relations between the sexes would improve if women were given the ascendancy. However, we must ask ourselves why there should have to be any power struggle at all between the sexes. At any given time the more powerful side will create an ideology suitable to help maintain its position and to make this position acceptable to the weaker one. In this ideology the differentness of the weaker one will be interpreted as inferiority, and it will be proven that these differences are unchangeable, basic, or God's will. It is the function of such an ideology to deny or conceal the existence of a struggle. Here is one of the answers to the question raised initially as to why we have so little awareness of the fact that there is a struggle between the sexes. It is in the interest of men to obscure this fact; and the emphasis they place on their ideologies has caused women, also, to adopt these theories. Our attempt at resolving these rationalizations and at examining these ideologies as to their fundamental driving forces, is merely a step on the road taken by Freud.

I believe that my exposition shows more clearly the origin of resentment than the origin of dread, and I therefore want to discuss briefly the latter problem. We have seen that the male's dread of the female is directed against her as a sexual being. How is this to be understood? The clearest aspect of this dread is revealed by the Arunta tribe. They believe that the woman has the power to magically influence the male genital. This is what we mean by castration anxiety in analysis. It is an anxiety of psychogenic origin that goes back to feelings of guilt and old childhood fears. Its anatomical-psychological nucleus lies in the fact that during intercourse the male has to entrust his genitals to the female body, that he presents her with his semen, and interprets this as a surrender of vital strength to the woman, similar to his experiencing the subsiding of erection after intercourse as the evidence of having been weakened by the woman. . . . The great mother goddesses also brought death and destruction. It is as though we were possessed by the idea that the one who gives life is also capable of taking it away. There is a third aspect of the male's dread of the female that is more difficult to understand and to prove, but that can be demonstrated by observing certain recurrent phenomena in the animal world. We can see that the male is quite frequently equipped with certain specific stimulants for attracting the female, or with specific devices for seizing her during sexual union. Such arrangements would be incomprehensible if the female animal possessed equally urgent or abundant sexual needs as does the male. As a matter of fact, we see that the female rejects the male unconditionally, after fertilization has occurred. Although examples taken from the animal world may be applied to human beings only with the greatest of caution, it is permissible, in this context, to raise the following question: Is it possible that the male is sexually dependent on the female to a higher degree than the woman is on him, because in women part of the sexual energy

is linked to generative processes? Could it be that men, therefore, have a vital interest in keeping women dependent on them?
So much for the factors that seem to be at the root of the great
power struggle between men and women, insofar as they are of a
psychogenic nature and related to the male.

That many-faceted thing called love succeeds in building
bridges from the loneliness on this shore to the loneliness on the
other one. These bridges can be of great beauty, but they are
rarely built for eternity and frequently they cannot tolerate too
heavy a burden without collapsing. Here is the other answer to
the question posed initially of why we see love between the sexes
more distinctly than we see hate—because the union of the sexes
offers us the greatest possibilities for happiness. We therefore
are naturally inclined to overlook how powerful are the destructive forces that continually work to destroy our chances for
happiness.

Dorothy Sayers / *The Human-Not-Quite-Human*

Dorothy Sayers (1893–1957) combined in her writing the wit
and invention of the detective story writer and the devotion
of the committed Catholic. She is perhaps better known for
her Lord Peter Wimsey series of mystery novels than for her
studies and translations of Dante and her writings on Catholic theology. The following piquant, but essentially serious
essay turns the tables on the ubiquitous male Sunday-

From *Unpopular Opinions* (New York, Harcourt, Brace, 1947), pp. 142–
149. Copyright 1947 by Dorothy L. Sayers. Reprinted by permission of A.
Watkins, Inc.

supplement journalist who is forever writing up his patronizing interviews with "lady doctors," "lady engineers," "lady pilots," and so on. How would men feel if they were to be described in such terms? Sayers looks forward to the day when men stop treating women who dare to venture forth from the shelter of domesticity as freaks or "not-quite-human."

THE FIRST thing that strikes the careless observer is that women are unlike men. They are the "opposite sex"—(though why "opposite" I do not know; what is the "neighbouring sex"?). But the fundamental thing is that women are more like men than anything else in the world. They are human beings. *Vir* is male and *Femina* is female: but *Homo* is male and female.

This is the equality claimed and the fact that is persistently evaded and denied. No matter what arguments are used, the discussion is vitiated from the start, because Man is always dealt with as both *Homo* and *Vir,* but Woman only as *Femina.* . . .

Probably no man has ever troubled to imagine how strange his life would appear to himself if it were unrelentingly assessed in terms of his maleness; if everything he wore, said, or did had to be justified by reference to female approval; if he were compelled to regard himself, day in day out, not as a member of society, but merely . . . as a virile member of society. If the centre of his dress-consciousness were the cod-piece, his education directed to making him a spirited lover and meek paterfamilias; his interests held to be natural only insofar as they were sexual. If from school and lecture-room, press and pulpit, he heard the persistent outpouring of a shrill and scolding voice, bidding him remember his biological function. If he were vexed by continual advice how to add a rough male touch to his typing, how to be learned without losing his masculine appeal, how to combine chemical research with education, how to play bridge without incurring the suspicion of impotence. If, instead of allowing with a smile that "women prefer cavemen," he felt the unrelenting pressure of a whole social structure forcing him to order all his goings in conformity with that pronouncement.

He would hear (and would he like hearing?) the female counterpart of Dr. Peck [Dr. Peck had disclaimed adherence to the
Kinder, Kirche, Küche school of thought] informing him: "I
am no supporter of the Horseback Hall doctrine of 'gun-tail,
plough-tail and stud' as the only spheres for masculine action;
but we do need a more definite conception of the nature and
scope of man's life." In any book on sociology he would find,
after the main portion dealing with human needs and rights, a
supplementary chapter devoted to "The Position of the Male in
the Perfect State." His newspaper would assist him with a "Men's
Corner," telling him how, by the expenditure of a good deal of
money and a couple of hours a day, he could attract the girls
and retain his wife's affection; and when he had succeeded in
capturing a mate, his name would be taken from him, and society would present him with a special title to proclaim his
achievement. People would write books called, "History of the
Male," or "Males of the Bible," or "The Psychology of the Male,"
and he would be regaled daily with headlines, such as "Gentle-
men-Doctor's Discovery," "Male-Secretary Wins Calcutta Sweep,"
"Men-Artists at the Academy." If he gave an interview to a
reporter, or performed any unusual exploit, he would find it
recorded in such terms as these: "Professor Bract, although a distinguished botanist, is not in any way an unmanly man. He has,
in fact, a wife and seven children. Tall and burly, the hands
with which he handles his delicate specimens are as gnarled
and powerful as those of a Canadian lumberjack, and when I
swilled beer with him in his laboratory, he bawled his conclusions at me in a strong, gruff voice that implemented the promise
of his swaggering moustache." Or: "There is nothing in the least
feminine about the home surroundings of Mr. Focus, the famous
children's photographer. His 'den' is paneled in teak and deco-
rated with rude sculptures from Easter Island; over his austere
iron bedstead hangs a fine reproduction of the Rape of the
Sabines." Or: "I asked M. Sapristi, the renowned chef, whether
kitchen-cult was not a rather unusual occupation for a man. 'Not
a bit of it!' he replied, bluffly. 'It is the genius that counts, not
the sex. As they say in *la belle Écosse,* a man's a man for a' that'
—and his gusty, manly guffaw blew three small patty pans from
the dresser."

He would be edified by solemn discussions about "Should Men Serve in Drapery Establishments?" and acrimonious ones about "Tea-Drinking Men"; by cross-shots of public affairs, "From the Masculine Angle," and by irritable correspondence about men who expose their anatomy on beaches (so masculine of them), conceal it in dressing gowns (too feminine of them), think about nothing but women, pretend an unnatural indiffer- ence to women, exploit their sex to get jobs, lower the tone of the office by their sexless appearance, and generally fail to please a public opinion which demands the incompatible. And at dinner-parties he would hear the wheedling, unctuous, predatory female voice demand: "And why should you trouble your hand- some little head about politics?"

If, after a few centuries of this kind of treatment, the male was a little self-conscious, a little on the defensive, and a little bewildered about what was required of him, I should not blame him. If he traded a little upon his sex, I could forgive him. If he presented the world with a major social problem, I would scarcely be surprised. It would be more surprising if he retained any rag of sanity and self-respect.

"The rights of woman," says Dr. Peck, "considered in the economic sphere, seem to involve her in competition with men in the struggle for jobs." It does seem so indeed, and this is hardly to be wondered at; for the competition began to appear when the men took over the women's jobs by transferring them from the home to the factory. The medieval woman had effective power and a measure of real (though not political) equality, for she had control of many industries—spinning, weaving, baking, brewing, distilling, perfumery, preserving, pickling—in which she worked with head as well as hands, in command of her own domestic staff. But now the control and direction—all the intel- ligent part—of those industries have gone to the men, and the women have been left, not with their "proper" *work* but with *employment* in those occupations. And at the same time, they are exhorted to be feminine and return to the home from which all intelligent occupation has been steadily removed.

There has never been any question but that the women of the poor should toil alongside their men. No angry, and no compassionate, voice has been raised to say that women should not break their backs with harvest work, or soil their hands with blacking grates and peeling potatoes. The objection is only to work that is pleasant, exciting or profitable—the work that any human being might think it worth while to do. The boast, "My wife doesn't need to soil her hands with work," first became general when the commercial middle classes acquired the pluto-cratic and aristocratic notion that the keeping of an idle woman was a badge of superior social status. Man must work, and woman must exploit his labour. What else are they there for? And if the woman submits, she can be cursed for her exploita-tion; and if she rebels, she can be cursed for competing with the male: whatever she does will be wrong, and that is a great satisfaction.

The men who attribute all the ills of *Homo* to the industrial age yet accept it as the norm for the relations of the sexes. But the brain, that great and sole true Androgyne, that can mate indifferently with male or female and beget offspring upon itself, the cold brain laughs at their perversions of history. The period from which we are emerging was like no other: a period when empty head and idle hands were qualities for which a man prized his woman and despised her. When, by an odd, sadistic twist of morality, sexual intercourse was deemed to be a marital right to be religiously enforced upon a meek reluctance—as though the insatiable appetite of wives were not one of the oldest jokes in the world. . . . When to think of sex was consid-ered indelicate in a woman, and to think about anything else unfeminine. When to "manage" a husband by lying and the exploitation of sex was held to be honesty and virtue. When the education that Thomas More gave his daughters was de-nounced as a devilish indulgence, and could only be wrung from the outraged holder of the purse-strings by tears and martyrdom and desperate revolt, in the teeth of the world's mockery and the reprobation of a scandalised Church.

What is all this tenderness about women herded into factories? Is it much more than an excuse for acquiescing in the profitable herding of men? The wrong is inflicted upon *Homo*. There are temperaments suited to herding and temperaments that are not; but the dividing lines do not lie exactly along the sexual boundary. The Russians, it seems, have begun to realise this; but are revolution and blood the sole educational means for getting this plain fact into our heads?

Women are not human. They lie when they say they have human needs: warm and decent clothing; comfort in the bus; interests directed immediately to God and His universe, not intermediately through any child of man. They are far above men to inspire him, far beneath him to corrupt him; they have feminine minds and feminine natures, but their mind is not one with their nature like the minds of men; they have no human mind and no human nature. "Blessed be God," says the Jew, "that hath not made me a woman."

God, of course, may have His own opinion, but the Church is reluctant to endorse it. I think I have never heard a sermon preached on the story of Martha and Mary that did not attempt, somehow, somewhere, to explain away its text. Mary's, of course, was the better part—the Lord said so, and we must not precisely contradict Him. But we will be careful not to despise Martha. No doubt, He approved of her too. We could not get on without her, and indeed (having paid lip-service to God's opinion) we must admit that we greatly prefer her. For Martha was doing a really feminine job, whereas Mary was just behaving like any other disciple, male or female; and that is a hard pill to swallow.

Perhaps it is no wonder that the women were first at the Cradle and last at the Cross. They had never known a man like this Man—there never has been such another. A prophet and teacher who never nagged at them, never flattered or coaxed or patronised; who never made arch jokes about them, never treated them either as "The women, God help us!" or "The ladies, God bless them!"; who rebuked without querulousness and praised without condescension; who took their questions and arguments seriously; who never mapped out their sphere for them, never urged them to be feminine or jeered at them for being female; who had no axe to grind and no uneasy male dignity to defend; who took them as he found them, and was completely unself-conscious. There is no act, no sermon, no parable in the whole Gospel that borrows its pungency from female perversity; nobody could possibly guess from the words and deeds of Jesus that there was anything "funny" about woman's nature.

But we might easily deduce it from His contemporaries, and from His prophets before Him, and from His Church to this day. Women are not human; nobody shall persuade us that they are human; let them say what they like, we will not believe it, though One rose from the dead.

Ruth Herschberger / *Is Rape a Myth?*

In this perceptive essay, writer and poet Ruth Herschberger deals with the idea of rape as part of the masculine power mystique. Her goal is to examine the implications of rape as a "symbol with high emotional content"—a symbol of the innate physical superiority and aggressiveness of men. Viewed from this unusual standpoint, we can see the idea of rape as a male fantasy of domination over the weak, helpless woman—a very necessary part of the myth of male supremacy. The wish to dominate, to degrade, to compel physical intimacy and even to force enjoyment upon the unwilling female are all essential components of the myth. That rape crops up as the most common criminal sexual offense against females in our society is no coincidence, according to Herschberger, since it remains for many powerless, unfulfilled men the only way of proving their maleness. But whether the male supremacist commits the act in fact or fantasy, he still participates in and perpetuates the myth of rape.

From *Adam's Rib* (New York, Pellegrini & Cudahy, 1948), pp. 15–27. Reprinted by permission of the author.

RAPE AS criminal assault is widespread, and distressingly so. In pointing out the respects in which rape is a myth, we are not indifferent to the crime itself. Rather, is the crime being actively and invisibly supported by a legend of considerable glamour; the legend of man's natural sexual aggression toward women.

Rape is in this sense a mirror-image of our ordinary sex folkways. Two basic beliefs in these folkways are the natural sexual aggressiveness of man, and man's natural physical superiority over women. Put these two beliefs together, set up a competition for masculine prowess such as we have today, and no one should be surprised by the incidence of rape.

The typical description of man as aggressive, or *propulsive*, starts out amiably enough. In Karl Menninger's view, men have proportionately more of the death instinct, or the tendency to destroy. The dynamic essence of the masculine spirit is to make an impress upon something or someone.[1] This can lead to creativity or to death. (It is fair to say that it can also lead to rape.) The character of the result rests in the hands of woman. . . .

It means that women must view themselves as a bundle of instincts aimed at neutralizing man's hostility and his tendency to self-destruction. In this scheme the achievements of man are due in part to the little woman.

More important: so are his failures. Should anything go wrong, as in the production of a Hitler, a woman is said to be at the root of the trouble—in this case, Hitler's mother. For if a woman has a peculiar ability to interfere with the course of man's self-destructiveness,[2] it is her duty to devote her life to the mollification of this potential holocaust.

The so-called death instinct in men would seem to cover a multitude of sins. It is possible that society invented it expressly for this purpose. Anyone endowed with such an overdose of natural aggressiveness can scarcely be blamed for anything he may do, except for being too passive. Woman, gifted with a life

1. *Love Against Hate* (New York, Harcourt, Brace, 1942), p. 106.
2. *Ibid.*, p. 113. A woman's personality is predicated on that of her husband's, for by "protecting or building up the personality of her husband as lover by means of her receptivity, the woman builds her own personality." (p. 107)

instinct and the power of adaptability, is clearly the one to put
up with the propulsiveness of man.

How much of these instincts is innate and how much acquired?
If men can rape women, can women rape men? Can rape force
a woman to respond or to feel pleasure? How is rape distinguished from a marriage in which the sex act is forced upon
an unwilling woman? How does rape fit in with puritanism?

In exploring the ramifications of this subject, we may find we
are, in many cases, dealing less with a crime than with an ideal.
To study "rape" as a language symbol with high emotional content will be rather like traveling through an exotic country
filled with ventriloquists, trolls, and fair princes. It is certainly
not enough to leaf through a man-made dictionary and examine
the legal strait-jacket that has been given the term.

Nor need we be misled by the ease with which the forced and
unwilling woman of the rape myth becomes transformed into
the affectionate and grateful maiden. The legend of male aggressiveness must be traced through all its avatars, finally to be
comprehended as a faith which secretly enlists many educated
minds in one of the happiest of male fraternities. . . .

With the leverage provided by two words, *act* and *relationship*, the dichotomy of male and female sexuality is established
in the following description of rape.

No woman can force a man into the sex act for his participation in
it requires a physical preparation which can come only with some
degree of desire and willingness. . . . This is not so with a woman,
for she can be forced into a sexual relationship without the least
desire or preparedness.[3]

Act implies something done, the exercise of power, the accomplishment of a deed. Thus, the sex act for a man implies a
goal or climax which finds ultimate achievement. A relationship,
on the other hand, is a condition or a state of being. It does not
necessitate a goal or climax. An act is more impersonal than a
relationship; it has fewer psychological complications. In a
sexual relationship, a woman responds to the experience as a

3. Amram Scheinfeld, *Women and Men* (New York, Harcourt, Brace,
1943), p. 249.

whole, and does not consider completion or relief its *raison d'être*. To a woman a sexual relationship is a more spiritual rapport, and is its own reason for being. Long after the male sex act is completed, the woman's relationship to the man continues.

In this simple, unconscious antithesis of act and relationship, we begin to understand why it is that the raped woman should suffer a permanent stain on her honor. In some occult way, she has been *forced* into a state of psychological identification or relationship with the person who criminally assaulted her. . . .

Woman may resist, she may struggle, . . . but she is still forced to enter into a sexual *relationship,* provided her assailant is equipped with natural physical superiority—or a blackjack.

We are told that men, on the other hand, cannot be forced into a sexual relationship. In fact men's pride is as hurt by the thought that women might view sex as an "act," as that they themselves might enter into anything quite so confining, demanding, and sentimental as a "relationship."

The implications of the male act *vs.* the female relationship are as subtle as they are conclusive. The male act regards itself as single and indivisible, relatively unaffected by time, person, or place. It is therefore preceded by the definite article *the;* while a sexual relationship is feminine, diffuse, and employs the indefinite article.

Because it is so impossible for the masculine population to think of women in any connection except as responding to them, men are convinced that the raped victim, in spite of herself, responds in some degree to her assailant. No wonder a woman's purity is supposedly destroyed by a sex act forced upon her. She must enter into a sexual relationship with her aggressor; an intimacy with him is established for all time.

Rape is a form of violence involving the personal humiliation of the victim. The act of rape is not simply an expression of sexual instinct. Rape is not practiced among the lower animals, but only among industrialized primates. Sexual intercourse if actually forced on an unwilling woman is a sadistic perversion that could as well be called "intravaginal masturbation." This is a phrase which Menninger uses in connection with narcissism; it applies even more clearly to rape.

Murder is a form of violence forced upon an unwilling victim;

but murder does not humiliate its victim, unless sexual elements
are added. Not so with the raped woman. She is rendered passive, shamed, and dejected. . . . Her attitude toward the episode
remains conventionally one of despair, not resentment. Her
honor has been taken from her by force, and no recourse is
possible.

While a woman might "rape" a man in a highly mechanical
fashion, though no less mechanical than the male type of assault
(if we regard ordinary rape as a form of "intravaginal masturbation," woman's "rape" of man would be extravaginal masturbation), she could not humiliate him thereby. Society does not
permit the removal of a man's honor by force, lacking his consent
or participation. A man could be forced to submit to the indignity
of sexual exploitation, but no one could persuade him that he
had been forced into a permanent relationship with his aggressor.
He would emerge from the experience socially unscathed.

When we consider that a virtuous woman, resisting to the full
extent of her physical strength, is nevertheless robbed of her
honor by violence, we understand at least one respect in which
women are peculiarly at the mercy of higher powers in society.
With the extolling of woman's purity, men have purported to put
woman on a pedestal. What they have done is to take the
defense of her honor out of her own hands, discourage her
muscular reflexes, and virtually encourage various members of
their sex to wage war on the purity that woman holds dear.

When women are commended for sustaining constancy, tenderness, and sympathy during the sex act, it is because they are
taking care to concentrate on a psychological relationship, and
not to assist in the performance of an act. The thought of a
woman regarding the sex act as a means of finding sexual completion disturbs the soul. "It makes sex so mechanical!" exclaim
men, who have all this time stressed the "automatic" and "impersonal" nature of their own sex impulse.

Indeed, if the receptivity of women were put in doubt for a
moment, women might begin to think their own honor, as well
as man's, was defensible. The carnage that would almost immediately result in buses, streetcars, theatres, and other places of
public congregation would probably reduce the incidence of
rape to a whisper. . . .

The belief that aggression *per se* will iron out personality conflicts between human beings is equivalent to the belief that a sufficiently forceful war will eliminate the economic and social conflicts that caused the war. Much of the appeal of the rape myth stems from this worship of force.

When human beings, after much travail and tears, discover that force has not been particularly effective in solving a dilemma, nothing seems to prevent their hope that the next dilemma will be cured by a firmer application of the same nostrum. And there is always the possibility that the weaker factor in the conflict can be shut up for the time being.

In a polite way this has been happening in the conflicts between men and women. As women began to discover their own instincts and inclinations, husbands found their wives less and less amiable. The demands that were made in sensory matters alone contradicted everything a husband had been accustomed to expect from a wife. Soon there appeared on the market a succession of books, written by men, which asked eloquently that women be allowed to regain their ancient femininity, their receptivity of spirit; that they no longer be bothered with the chatter of emancipation.

The rape motif has made an interesting provision in its legend for this new development in the marriage mores. As women become more independent and recalcitrant in marriage, the vision of a woman who will actually, honestly, helplessly, and amiably submit to a man—because of applied force—cannot help appealing to the goaded and henpecked husband of the day. Here are the steps by which the rape myth wins over his mind.

Just as in the situation of rape, the man finds on his hands, secure within the bonds of marriage, an unwilling woman. It is true he picked her himself, but he may have done so at a time when all nice women were unwilling women, if they wished to remain members in good standing under the Purity Code. Let us use a bolder word, and call his unwilling woman frigid. . . . She is also vociferous, and gives her husband no peace. . . .

The unwilling woman submits to her husband's will, consistently and reluctantly, for twenty or thirty years. Meanwhile society permits her to express her unwillingness and resentment via the female institution of nagging. She may even acquire the

enviable reputation of someone who runs her husband. . . . He is
not unaware that his wife is sexually unwilling. After five or ten
years he may toss this realization into his subconscious, but
from the security of its new home the realization continues to
plague him. He finally tells himself that sexual aggression toward
women is the natural state of things, and he is only carrying out
nature's plan.

The rape rumor can offer him something further. It not only
agrees entirely that sexual aggression is the natural state, but it
rather suspects that the natural woman is unwilling. It promises
even more. For the rape myth conjures up an image of an unwilling stranger who, *unlike the unwilling wife,* instantly recognizes her assailant's right of sexual aggression—and loves him
for it.

When the man turns to the sensational image of rape, he
learns of a sex act which, if effected with any unwilling woman,
can force her to enter into a sexual relationship with him. She
can be forced into a psychological intimacy with him, as his wife
stubbornly is not. Thus in the dream world of gross aggression,
the husband finds the same unwilling woman of his marriage
situation. But in the rape victim the unwilling woman magically
becomes willing, her sensory nerves respond gratefully, stubborn
reflexes react obediently, and the beautiful stranger willy-nilly
enters into a state of sexual intimacy with her aggressor. . . .

The notion that a victim of sexual aggression is forced into
an experience of sensory delight should be relegated to the land
where candy grows on trees. . . . If any pressure applied to an
erogenous zone resulted in pleasure, there would be no frigidity
among women. If any pressure forced upon an erogenous zone
resulted in pleasure, there would be no impotence among men.

The actual result of forced stimulation can be anesthesia or
intense pain. This is true of the male if the stimulation is resisted
or unwelcome. Yet the assumption that women are totally recep-
tive has given rise to the belief that a rape victim cannot avoid
feeling pleasure.

Were sensory nerves really this naïve, or were men's sexual
apparatus as reflexive, automatic, and uncomplicated as some
writers maintain, the rape of men by sexually aggressive women

would be indeed possible. How could a man resist a woman who proved physically his superior? While the thought strikes us as ludicrous, it has never seemed particularly ludicrous to men that a woman should succumb with lightning speed to any force applied to her sensory centers. . . .

The true subscriber of the rape myth cannot relinquish the idea of the unwillingness of the woman because it is her unwillingness that makes his carnality so marvelously free and impersonal. If he permits the unwilling woman to be willing right from the start, it isn't long before he finds himself worrying about keeping her happy or wondering what she is thinking of. This looks too much like home. He insists that the overpowered stranger be strictly unwilling.

At the same time the man cannot bear to think that the woman is not *actually* enjoying herself. For the stern aggressor actually has a heart of gold, and would like to satisfy in the person of this unknown woman all the women he has failed to satisfy in the realm of the real. He wants an unwilling woman who later becomes willing—under his magic touch.

Lonely men, unrequited men, men who find love and sex difficult turn to the myth of rape in the belief that love, if it cannot be evoked, can at least be bullied into putting in an appearance. But force and aggression drive love away as often as they serve to capture it. . . .

An appropriate warning to those who contemplate a wide choice of subjects in this myth-image is that forcing the sex act on a resistant woman requires more physical strength than may at first be supposed. It is difficult to know how often the frantic resistance of an unwilling woman is merely an attempt to whet the vigor of a mutual experience. In general a woman must be predisposed, or dyspeptic enough to be overcome. Where a strong and beautiful subject is selected, it might be necessary to render her unconscious first, in which case it is difficult to presume that she is psychologically implicated in the act.

To regard the sex act as sexual aggression is a sop to the puritan conscience. This may be observed in a typical description of sexual intercourse. A man is said to be attracted to the opposite sex by a natural impulse which is beyond his will. He

performs an act in which a given reaction follows automatically.
The male cannot help himself, he is obeying the force of nature,
and has little psychological involvement in what he does. He
acts not through choice.

The man submits to the force of nature; the woman submits
to the man. Sex is an act of aggression with which she complies
only because she is physically the weaker. Her emphasis is on
the future bearing and rearing of children which, according to
Menninger, is woman's greatest achievement and the climax of
her erotic expression. . . .

> Then call them not the Authors of their ill,
>   No more than wax shall be accounted evil,
>   Wherein is stamped the semblance of the Devil.

So much for the *Rape of Lucrece*. It applies as well to the puritanical woman today who sincerely believes that it is only her
own helplessness that forces her to enter into a sexual relationship with a dominant member of the opposite sex.

Helen Mayer Hacker / *Women as a*
Minority Group

To recognize in 1951 that all was not sweetness and light in
the life of women, that there might be some discontent as a
result of the subordinate roles women were meant to play, and
that women might have some cause for dissatisfaction was to
go against the rising tide of the postwar "back to hearth and

From *Social Forces*, 30 (October, 1951), pp. 60–69. Reprinted by permission of the University of North Carolina Press.

home" movement. But Helen Mayer Hacker was one of the few sociologists who considered seriously the idea of viewing women as a minority group, with all the repercussions that this status implies. Taking her cue from Myrdal's concept of the Negro-Woman analogy, she here posits a sociological theory of the marginality of women's status in a masculine society. In spite of the jargon and professorial, impersonal tone (it was written, after all, for an academic journal), Hacker's paper is an important early recognition of the underlying resemblance of the oppressed, no matter to which group they belong. Her chart of feminine and Negro attributions is a neat compendium of the destructive stereotypes of race and sex.

ALTHOUGH SOCIOLOGICAL literature reveals scattered references to women as a minority group, comparable in certain respects to racial, ethnic, and national minorities, no systematic investigation has been undertaken as to what extent the term "minority group" is applicable to women. . . .

Yet it may well be that regarding women as a minority group may be productive of fresh insights and suggest leads for further research. The purpose of this paper is to apply to women some portion of that body of sociological theory and methodology customarily used for investigating such minority groups as Negroes, Jews, immigrants, etc. It may be anticipated that not only will principles already established in the field of intergroup relations contribute to our understanding of women, but that in the process of modifying traditional concepts and theories to fit the special case of women new viewpoints for the fruitful reexamination of other minority groups will emerge.

In defining the term "minority group," the presence of discrimination is the identifying factor. As Louis Wirth has pointed out, "minority group" is not a statistical concept, nor need it denote an alien group. Indeed for the present discussion I have adopted his definition: "A minority group is any group of people who because of their physical or cultural characteristics, are singled out from the others in the society in which they live for differential and unequal treatment, and who therefore regard themselves as objects of collective discrimination." It is apparent that this definition includes both objective and subjective characteristics of a minority group: the fact of discrimination and the awareness of discrimination, with attendant reactions to that awareness. A person who on the basis of his group affiliation is denied full participation in those opportunities which the value system of his culture extends to all members of the society satisfies the objective criterion, but there are various circumstances which may prevent him from fulfilling the subjective criterion.

In the first place, a person may be unaware of the extent to which his group membership influences the way others treat him. He may have formally dissolved all ties with the group in question and fondly imagine his identity is different from what others hold it to be. Consequently, he interprets their behavior toward him solely in terms of his individual characteristics. Or, less likely, he may be conscious of his membership in a certain group but not be aware of the general disesteem with which the group is regarded. A final possibility is that he may belong in a category which he does not realize has group significance. An example here might be a speech peculiarity which has come to have unpleasant connotations in the minds of others. Or a lower-class child with no conception of "class as culture" may not understand how his manners act as cues in eliciting the dislike of his middle-class teacher. The foregoing cases all assume that the person believes in equal opportunities for all in the sense that one's group affiliation should not affect his role in the larger society. We turn now to a consideration of situations in which this assumption is not made.

It is frequently the case that a person knows that because of his group affiliation he receives differential treatment, but feels that this treatment is warranted by the distinctive characteristics of his group. A Negro may believe that there are significant differences between whites and Negroes which justify a different role in life for the Negro. A child may accept the fact that physical differences between him and an adult require his going to bed earlier than they do. A Sudra knows that his lot in life has been cast by divine fiat, and he does not expect the perquisites of a Brahmin. A woman does not wish for the rights and duties of men. In all these situations, clearly, the person does not regard himself as an "object of collective discrimination."

For the two types presented above: (1) those who do not know that they are being discriminated against on a group basis; and (2) those who acknowledge the propriety of differential treatment on a group basis, the subjective attributes of a minority group member are lacking. They feel no minority group consciousness, harbor no resentment, and, hence, cannot properly be said to belong in a minority group. Although the term "minority group" is inapplicable to both types, the term "minority group status" may be substituted. This term is used to categorize persons who are denied rights to which they are entitled according to the value system of the observer. An observer, who is a firm adherent of the democratic ideology, will often consider persons to occupy a minority group status who are well accommodated to their subordinate roles.

No empirical study of the frequency of minority group feelings among women has yet been made, but common observation would suggest that, consciously at least, few women believe themselves to be members of a minority group in the way in which some Negroes, Jews, Italians, etc., may so conceive themselves. There are, of course, many sex-conscious women, known to a past generation as feminists, who are filled with resentment at the discriminations they fancy are directed against their sex. . . . Yet the number of women who participate in "women's affairs" even in the United States, the classic land of associations, is so small that one cannot easily say that the majority of women display minority group consciousness. . . .

Still, women often manifest many of the psychological characteristics which have been imputed to self-conscious minority groups. Kurt Lewin[1] has pointed to group self-hatred as a frequent reaction of the minority group member to his group affiliation. This feeling is exhibited in the person's tendency

1. Kurt Lewin, "Self-Hatred Among Jews," *Contemporary Jewish Record,* IV (1941), pp. 219–232.

to denigrate other members of the group, to accept the dominant group's stereotyped conception of them, and to indulge
in "mea culpa" breast-beating. He may seek to exclude himself
from the average of his group, or he may point the finger of
scorn at himself. Since a person's conception of himself is based
on the defining gestures of others, it is unlikely that members
of a minority group can wholly escape personality distortion.
Constant reiteration of one's inferiority must often lead to its
acceptance as a fact.

Certainly women have not been immune to the formulations
of the "female character" throughout the ages. From those, to
us, deluded creatures who confessed to witchcraft to modern
sophisticates who speak disparagingly of the cattiness and dis-
loyalty of women, women reveal their introjection of prevailing
attitudes toward them. Like those minority groups whose self-
castigation outdoes dominant group derision of them, women
frequently exceed men in the violence of their vituperations of
their sex. They are more severe in moral judgments, especially
in sexual matters. A line of self-criticism may be traced from
Hannah More, a blue-stocking herself, to Dr. Marynia Farnham,
who lays most of the world's ills at women's door. Women express themselves as disliking other women, as preferring to
work under men, and as finding exclusively female gatherings
repugnant. The *Fortune* polls conducted in 1946 show that
women, more than men, have misgivings concerning women's
participation in industry, the professions, and civic life. And
more than one-fourth of women wish they had been born in
the opposite sex.[2]

Militating against a feeling of group identification on the part
of women is a differential factor in their socialization. Members
of a minority group are frequently socialized within their own
group. Personality development is more largely a resultant of
intra- than inter-group interaction. The conception of his role
formed by a Negro or a Jew or a second-generation immigrant
is greatly dependent upon the definitions offered by members
of his own group, on their attitudes and behavior toward him.
Ignoring for the moment class differences within the group, the

2. *Fortune,* September, 1946, p. 5.

minority group person does not suffer discrimination from members of his own group. But only rarely does a woman experience this type of group belongingness. Her interactions with members of the opposite sex may be as frequent as her relationships with members of her own sex. Women's conceptions of themselves, therefore, spring as much from their intimate relationships with men as with women. . . .

Even though the sense of group identification is not so conspicuous in women as in racial and ethnic minorities, they, like these others, tend to develop a separate subculture. Women have their own language, comparable to the argot of the underworld and professional groups. It may not extend to a completely separate dialect as has been discovered in some preliterate groups, but there are words and idioms employed chiefly by women. Only the acculturated male can enter into the conversation of the beauty parlor, the exclusive shop, the bridge table, or the kitchen. In contrast to men's interest in physical health, safety, money, and sex, women attach greater importance to attractiveness, personality, home, family, and other people. . . .

We must return now to the original question of the aptness of the designation of minority group for women. . . . Formal discriminations against women are too well-known for any but the most summary description. In general they take the form of being barred from certain activities or, if admitted, being treated unequally. Discriminations against women may be viewed as arising from the generally ascribed status "female" and from the specially ascribed statuses of "wife," "mother," and "sister." . . .

As female, in the economic sphere, women are largely confined to sedentary, monotonous work under the supervision of men, and are treated unequally with regard to pay, promotion, and responsibility. With the exceptions of teaching, nursing, social service, and library work, in which they do not hold a proportionate number of supervisory positions and are often occupationally segregated from men, they make a poor showing in the professions. Although they own 80 percent of the nation's wealth, they do not sit on the boards of directors of great corporations. Educational opportunities are likewise unequal.

Professional schools, such as architecture and medicine, apply quotas. Women's colleges are frequently inferior to men's. In co-educational schools women's participation in campus activities is limited. As citizens, women are often barred from jury service and public office. Even when they are admitted to the apparatus of political parties, they are subordinated to men. Socially, women have less freedom of movement, and are permitted fewer deviations in the proprieties of dress, speech, manners. In social intercouse they are confined to a narrower range of personality expression.

In the specially ascribed status of wife, a woman—in several States—has no exclusive right to her earnings, is discriminated against in employment, must take the domicile of her husband, and in general must meet the social expectation of subordination to her husband's interests. As a mother, she may not have the guardianship of her children, bears the chief stigma in the case of an illegitimate child, is rarely given leave of absence for pregnancy. As a sister, she frequently suffers unequal distribution of domestic duties between herself and her brother, must yield preference to him in obtaining an education, and in such other psychic and material gratifications as cars, trips, and living away from home.

If it is conceded that women have a minority group status, what may be learned from applying to women various theoretical constructs in the field of intergroup relations?

One instrument of diagnostic value is the measurement of social distance between dominant and minority groups. But we have seen that one important difference between women and other minorities is that women's attitudes and self-conceptions are conditioned more largely by interaction with both minority and dominant group members. Before measuring social distance, therefore, a continuum might be constructed of the frequency and extent of women's interaction with men, with the poles conceptualized as ideal types. One extreme would represent a complete "ghetto" status, the woman whose contacts with men were of the most secondary kind. At the other extreme shall we put the woman who has prolonged and repeated associations with men, but only in those situations in which sex-awareness plays a prominent role or the woman who enters into a variety of relationships with men in which her sex identity is to a large extent irrelevant? . . .

Social distance tests as applied to relationships between other dominant and minority groups have for the most part adopted prestige criteria as their basis. The assumption is that the type of situation into which one is willing to enter with average members of another group reflects one's estimate of the status of the group relative to one's own. When the tested group is a sex-group rather than a racial, national, religious, or economic one, several important differences in the use and interpretation of the scale must be noted.

1. Only two groups are involved: men and women. Thus, the test indicates the amount of homogeneity or we-feeling only according to the attribute of sex. If men are a primary group, there are not many groups to be ranked secondary, tertiary, etc., with respect to them, but only one group, women, whose social distance cannot be calculated relative to other groups.

2. Lundberg[3] suggests the possibility of a group of Catholics registering a smaller social distance to Moslems than to Catholics. In such an event the group of Catholics, from any sociological viewpoint, would be classified as Moslems. If women expressed less social distance to men than to women, should they then be classified sociologically as men? Perhaps no more so than the legendary Negro who, when requested to move to the colored section of the train, replied, "Boss, I'se done resigned from the colored race," should be classified as white. It is likely, however, that the group identification of many women in our society is with men. The feminists were charged with wanting to be men, since they associated male physical characteristics with masculine social privileges. A similar statement can be made about men who show greater social distance to other men than to women.

Social distance may be measured from the standpoint of the minority group or the dominant group with different results. In point of fact, tension often arises when one group feels less

3. George A. Lundberg, *Foundations of Sociology* (New York, McKay, 1939), p. 319.

social distance than the other. A type case here is the persistent
suitor who underestimates his desired sweetheart's feeling of
social distance toward him.

  3. In social distance tests the assumption is made of an orderly
progression—although not necessarily by equal intervals—in the
scale. That is, it is not likely that a person would express willingness to have members of a given group as his neighbors, while
simultaneously voicing the desire to have them excluded from
his country. On all scales marriage represents the minimum social
distance, and implies willingness for associations on all levels of
lesser intimacy. May the customary scale be applied to men and
women? If we take the expressed attitude of many men and
women not to marry, we may say that they have feelings of
social distance toward the opposite sex, and in this situation
the usual order of the scale may be preserved.

  In our culture, however, men who wish to marry must per-
force marry women, and even if they accept this relationship,
they may still wish to limit their association with women in
other situations. The male physician may not care for the addition of female physicians to his hospital staff. The male poker
player may be thrown off his game if women participate. A
damper may be put upon the hunting expedition if women come
along. The average man may not wish to consult a woman
lawyer. And so on. In these cases it seems apparent that the
steps in the social distance scale must be reversed. Men will
accept women at the supposed level of greatest intimacy while
rejecting them at lower levels.

  But before concluding that a different scale must be constructed when the dominant group attitude toward a minority
group which is being tested is that of men toward women, the
question may be raised as to whether marriage in fact represents the point of minimum social distance. It may not imply
anything but physical intimacy and work accommodation, as was
frequently true in nonindividuated societies, such as preliterate
groups and the household economy of the Middle Ages, or marriages of convenience in the European upper class. Even in our
own democratic society where marriage is supposedly based on
romantic love there may be little communication between the

partners in marriage. The Lynds[4] report the absence of real companionship between husband and wife in Middletown. Women have been known to say that although they have been married for twenty years, their husband is still a stranger to them. . . . Part of the explanation may be found in the subordination of wives to husbands in our culture which is expressed in the separate spheres of activity for men and women. A recent advertisement in a magazine of national circulation depicts a pensive husband seated by his knitting wife with the caption, "Sometimes a man has moods his wife cannot understand." In this case the husband is worried about a pension plan for his employees. The assumption is that the wife, knowing nothing of the business world, cannot take the role of her husband in this matter.

The presence of love does not in itself argue for either equality of status nor fullness of communication. We may love those who are either inferior or superior to us, and we may love persons whom we do not understand. The supreme literary examples of passion without communication are found in Proust's portrayal of Swann's obsession with Odette, the narrator's infatuation with the elusive Albertine, and, of course, Dante's longing for Beatrice.

In the light of these considerations concerning the relationships between men and women, some doubt may be cast on the propriety of placing marriage on the positive extreme of the social distance scale with respect to ethnic and religious minority groups. Since inequalities of status are preserved in marriage, a dominant group member may be willing to marry a member of a group which, in general, he would not wish admitted to his club. The social distance scale which uses marriage as a sign of an extreme degree of acceptance is inadequate for appreciating the position of women, and perhaps for other minority groups as well. The relationships among similarity of status, communication as a measure of intimacy, and love must be clarified before

4. Robert S. and Helen Merrell Lynd, *Middletown* (Cambridge, Harvard University Press, 1929), p. 120 and *Middletown in Transition* (Cambridge, Harvard University Press, 1937), p. 176.

social distance tests can be applied usefully to attitudes between men and women.

Is the separation between males and females in our society a caste line? Folsom[5] suggests that it is, and Myrdal[6] in his well-known Appendix 5 considers the parallel between the position of and feelings toward women and Negroes in our society. The relation between women and Negroes is historical, as well as analogical. In the seventeenth century the legal status of Negro servants was borrowed from that of women and children, who were under the *patria potestas,* and until the Civil War there was considerable cooperation between the Abolitionist and woman suffrage movements. According to Myrdal, the problems of both groups are resultants of the transition from a preindustrial, paternalistic scheme of life to individualistic, industrial capitalism. Obvious similarities in the status of women and Negroes are indicated in Chart 1.

Chart 1.   Castelike Status of Women and Negroes

NEGROES	WOMEN
1. *High Social Visibility*	
a. Skin color, other "racial" characteristics	a. Secondary sex characteristics
b. (Sometimes) distinctive dress—bandana, flashy clothes	b. Distinctive dress, skirts, etc.
2. *Ascribed Attributes*	
a. Inferior intelligence, smaller brain, less convoluted, scarcity of geniuses	a. ditto
b. More free in instinctual gratifications. More emotional, "primitive" and childlike. Imagined sexual prowess envied.	b. Irresponsible, inconsistent, emotionally unstable. Lack strong super-ego. Women as "temptresses."
c. Common stereotype, "inferior"	c. "Weaker"

5. Joseph Kirk Folsom, *The Family and Democratic Society* (London, Routledge & Kegan Paul, 1948), pp. 623–624.
6. Gunnar Myrdal, *An American Dilemma* (New York, Harper, 1944), pp. 1073–1078.

3. *Rationalizations of Status*

a. Thought all right in his place
b. Myth of contented Negro

a. Woman's place is in the home
b. Myth of contented woman—"feminine" woman is happy in subordinate role

4. *Accommodation Attitudes*

a. Supplicatory whining intonation of voice
b. Deferential manner
c. Concealment of real feelings
d. Outwit "white folks"
e. Careful study of points at which dominant group is susceptible to influence
f. Fake appeals for directives; show of ignorance

a. Rising inflection, smiles, laughs, downward glances
b. Flattering manner
c. "Feminine wiles"
d. Outwit "men-folk"
e. ditto

f. Appearance of helplessness

5. *Discriminations*

a. Limitations on education—should fit "place" in society
b. Confined to traditional jobs—barred from supervisory positions. Their competition feared. No family precedents for new aspirations.
c. Deprived of political importance
d. Social and professional segregation
e. More vulnerable to criticism

a. ditto

b. ditto

c. ditto

d. ditto

e. e.g., conduct in bars [women drivers]

6. *Similar Problems*

a. Roles not clearly defined, but in flux as result of social change. Conflict between achieved status and ascribed status.

While these similarities in the situation of women and Negroes may lead to increased understanding of their social roles, account must also be taken of differences which impose qualifications on the comparison of the two groups. Most importantly, the influence of marriage as a social elevator for women, but not for Negroes, must be considered. Obvious, too, is the greater importance of women to the dominant group, despite the economic, sexual, and prestige gains which Negroes afford the white South. Ambivalence is probably more marked in the attitude of white males toward women than toward Negroes. The "war of the sexes" is only an expression of men's and women's vital need of each other. Again, there is greater polarization in the relationship between men and women. Negroes, although they have borne the brunt of antiminority group feeling in this country, do not constitute the only racial or ethnic minority, but there are only two sexes. And, although we have seen that social distance exists between men and women, it is not to be compared with the social segregation of Negroes.

At the present time, of course, Negroes suffer far greater discrimination than women, but since the latter's problems are rooted in a biological reality less susceptible to cultural manipulation, they prove more lasting. Women's privileges exceed those of Negroes. Protective attitudes toward Negroes have faded into abeyance, even in the South, but most boys are still taught to take care of girls, and many evidences of male chivalry remain. The factor of class introduces variations here. The middle-class Negro endures frustrations largely without the rewards of his white class peer, but the lower-class Negro is still absolved from many responsibilities. The reverse holds true for women. Notwithstanding these and other differences between the position of women and Negroes, the similarities are sufficient to render research on either group applicable in some fashion to the other.

Exemplary of the possible usefulness of applying the caste principle to women is viewing some of the confusion surrounding women's roles as reflecting a conflict between class and caste status. Such a conflict is present in the thinking and feeling of both dominant and minority groups toward upper-class Negroes and educated women. Should a woman judge be treated with the respect due a judge or the gallantry accorded a woman? The extent to which the rights and duties of one role permeate other roles so as to cause a role conflict has been treated elsewhere by the writer. Lower-class Negroes who have acquired dominant group attitudes toward the Negro resent upper-class Negro pretensions to superiority. Similarly, domestic women may feel the career woman is neglecting the duties of her proper station.

Parallels in adjustment of women and Negroes to the class-caste conflict may also be noted. Point 4 "Accommodation Attitudes" of the foregoing chart indicates the kinds of behavior displayed by members of both groups who accept their caste status. Many "sophisticated" women are retreating from emancipation with the support of psycho-analytic derivations.[7] David Riesman has recently provided an interesting discussion of changes "in the denigration by American women of their own sex" in which he explains their new submissiveness as in part a reaction to the weakness of men in the contemporary world.[8] "Parallelism" and "Negroidism" which accept a racially restricted economy reflect allied tendencies in the Negro group.

Role segmentation as a mode of adjustment is illustrated by Negroes who indulge in occasional passing and women who vary their behavior according to their definition of the situation. An example of the latter is the case of the woman lawyer who, after losing a case before a judge who was also her husband, said she would appeal the case, and added, "The judge can lay down the law at home, but I'll argue with him in court."

A third type of reaction is to fight for recognition of class status. Negro race leaders seek greater prerogatives for Negroes. Feminist women, acting either through organizations or as individuals, push for public disavowal of any differential treatment of men and women.

7. As furnished by such books as Helene Deutsch, *The Psychology of Women* (New York, Grune & Stratton, 1944–45); and Ferdinand Lundberg and Marynia F. Farnham, *Modern Woman: The Lost Sex* (New York, Harper, 1947).

8. David Riesman, "The Saving Remnant: An Examination of Character Structure," *Years of the Modern: An American Appraisal,* ed. by John W. Chase (New York, Longmans, Green & Co., 1949), pp. 139–140.

The "race relations cycle," as defined by Robert E. Park,[9] describes the social processes of reduction in tension and increase of communication in the relations between two or more groups who are living in a common territory under a single political or economic system. The sequence of competition, conflict, accommodation, and assimilation may also occur when social change introduces dissociative forces into an assimilated group or causes accommodated groups to seek new definitions of the situation. The ethnic or nationality characteristics of the groups involved are not essential to the cycle. In a complex industrialized society groups are constantly forming and reforming on the basis of new interests and new identities. Women, of course, have always possessed a sex-identification though perhaps not a group awareness. Today they represent a previously accommodated group which is endeavoring to modify the relationships between the sexes in the home, in work, and in the community.

The sex relations cycle bears important similarities to the race relations cycle. In the wake of the Industrial Revolution, as women acquired industrial, business, and professional skills, they increasingly sought employment in competition with men. Men were quick to perceive them as a rival group and made use of economic, legal, and ideological weapons to eliminate or reduce their competition. They excluded women from the trade unions, made contracts with employers to prevent their hiring women, passed laws restricting the employment of married women, caricatured the working woman, and carried on ceaseless propaganda to return women to the home or keep them there. Since the days of the suffragettes there has been no overt conflict between men and women on a group basis. Rather than conflict, the dissociative process between the sexes is that of contravention, a type of opposition intermediate between competition and conflict. . . . It includes rebuffing, repulsing, working against, hindering, protesting, obstructing, restraining, and upsetting another's plans.

9. Robert E. Park, "Our Racial Frontier on the Pacific," *The Survey Graphic*, 56 (May 1, 1926), pp. 192–196.

The present contravention of the sexes, arising from women's competition with men, is manifested in the discriminations against women, as well as in the doubts and uncertainties expressed concerning women's character, abilities, motives. The processes of competition and contravention are continually giving way to accommodation in the relationships between men and women. Like other minority groups, women have sought a protected position, a niche in the economy which they could occupy, and, like other minority groups, they have found these positions in new occupations in which dominant group members had not yet established themselves and in old occupations which they no longer wanted. When women entered fields which represented an extension of services in the home (except medicine!), they encountered least opposition. Evidence is accumulating, however, that women are becoming dissatisfied with the employment conditions of the great women-employing occupations and present accommodations are threatened.

What would assimilation of men and women mean? Park and Burgess in their classic text define assimilation as "a process of interpenetration and fusion in which persons and groups acquire the memories, sentiments, and attitudes of other persons or groups, and, by sharing their experiences and history, are incorporated with them in a cultural life." If accommodation is characterized by secondary contacts, assimilation holds the promise of primary contacts. If men and women were truly assimilated, we would find no cleavages of interest along sex lines. The special provinces of men and women would be abolished. Women's pages would disappear from the newspaper and women's organizations would pass into limbo. The sports page and racing news would be read indifferently by men and women. Interest in cookery and interior decoration would follow individual rather than sex lines. Women's talk would be no different from men's talk, and frank and full communication would obtain between the sexes.

Group relationships are reflected in personal adjustments. Arising out of the present contravention of the sexes is the marginal woman, torn between rejection and acceptance of traditional roles and attributes. Uncertain of the ground on which

she stands, subjected to conflicting cultural expectations, the
marginal woman suffers the psychological ravages of instability,
conflict, self-hate, anxiety, and resentment.

In applying the concept of marginality to women, the term
"role" must be substituted for that of "group." Many of the traditional devices for creating role differentiation among boys and
girls, such as dress, manners, activities, have been de-emphasized
in modern urban middle-class homes. The small girl who wears
a play suit, plays games with boys and girls together, attends a
co-educational school, may have little awareness of sexual differentiation until the approach of adolescence. Parental expectations in the matters of scholarship, conduct toward others, duties
in the home may have differed little for herself and her brother.
But in high school or perhaps not until college, she finds herself
called upon to play a new role. Benedict[10] has called attention
to discontinuities in the life cycle, and the fact that these continuities in cultural conditioning take a greater toll of girls
than of boys is revealed in test scores showing neuroticism and
introversion. In adolescence girls find the frank, spontaneous
behavior toward the neighboring sex no longer rewarding. High
grades are more likely to elicit anxiety than praise from parents,
especially mothers, who seem more pleased if male callers are
frequent. There are subtle indications that to remain home with
a good book on a Saturday night is a fate worse than death. But
even if the die is successfully cast for popularity, all problems
are not solved. Girls are encouraged to heighten their sexual
attractiveness, but to abjure sexual expression.

Assuming new roles in adolescence does not mean the complete relinquishing of old ones. Scholarship, while not so vital
as for the boy, is still important, but must be maintained dis-
creetly and without obvious effort. Komarovsky[11] has supplied
statements of Barnard College girls of the conflicting expectations of their elders. Even more than to the boy is the "all-
round" ideal held up to girls, and it is not always possible to

10. Ruth Benedict, "Continuities and Discontinuities in Cultural Conditioning," *Psychiatry,* 1 (1938), pp. 161–167.
11. Mirra Komarovsky, "Cultural Contradictions and Sex Roles," *The
American Journal of Sociology,* LII (November, 1946), pp. 184–189.

integrate the roles of good date, good daughter, good sorority sister, good student, good friend, and good citizen. The superior achievements of college men over college women bear witness to the crippling division of energies among women. Part of the explanation may lie in women having interiorized cultural notions of feminine inferiority in certain fields, and even the most self-confident or most defensive woman may be filled with doubt as to whether she can do productive work.

It may be expected that as differences in privileges between men and women decrease, the frequency of marginal women will increase. Widening opportunities for women will call forth a growing number of women capable of performing roles formerly reserved for men, but whose acceptance in these new roles may well remain uncertain and problematic. This hypothesis is in accord with Arnold Green's[12] recent critical re-examination of the marginal man concept in which he points out that it is those Negroes and second-generation immigrants whose values and behavior most approximate those of the dominant majority who experience the most severe personal crises. He believes that the classical marginal man symptoms appear only when a person striving to leave the racial or ethnic group into which he was born is deeply identified with the family of orientation and is met with grudging, uncertain, and unpredictable acceptance, rather than with absolute rejection, by the group he is attempting to join, and also that he is committed to success-careerism. Analogically, one would expect to find that women who display marginal symptoms are psychologically bound to the family of orientation in which they experience the imperatives of both the traditional and new feminine roles, and are seeking to expand the occupational (or other) areas open to women rather than those who content themselves with established fields. Concretely, one might suppose women engineers to have greater personality problems than women librarians.

Other avenues of investigation suggested by the minority group approach can only be mentioned. What social types arise

12. Arnold Green, "A Re-Examination of the Marginal Man Concept," *Social Forces,* 26 (December, 1947), pp. 167–171.

as personal adjustments to sex status? What can be done in the
way of experimental modification of the attitudes of men and
women toward each other and themselves? What hypotheses
of inter-group relations may be tested in regard to men and
women? For example, is it true that as women approach the cultural standards of men, they are perceived as a threat and ten-
sions increase? Of what significance are regional and community
variations in the treatment of and degree of participation
permitted women, mindful here that women share responsibility
with men for the perpetuation of attitudes toward women? This
paper is exploratory in suggesting the enhanced possibilities of
fruitful analysis, if women are included in the minority group
corpus, particularly with reference to such concepts and techniques as group belongingness, socialization of the minority group
child, cultural differences, social distance tests, conflict between
class and caste status, race relations cycle, and marginality. I
believe that the concept of the marginal woman should be especially productive, and am now engaged in an empirical study of
role conflicts in professional women.

Simone de Beauvoir / *An Androgynous World*

Simone de Beauvoir's monumental study, *The Second Sex,* is
destined to be a classic critique of the history, sociology, and
psychology of women's oppression. Its thesis is controversial
on many levels, and perhaps in no respect more so than in
De Beauvoir's tendency to substitute a masculine mystique for

From *The Second Sex,* translated and edited by H. M. Parshley (New York,
Knopf, 1953); pp. 682–689. Copyright 1952 by Alfred A. Knopf, Inc. Reprinted by permission of the publisher.

the feminine mystique she so astringently analyzes. For De Beauvoir, the "male principle" represents progress toward "transcendence," an evolutionary and existential necessity for the human race. The truly emancipated woman "accepts masculine values" and seeks to "emerge into the light of transcendence," for only in this way can she take on "the anxiety of liberty." This transition, De Beauvoir argues, would require a socialist economy to support it; but this would be only a minimal condition. Beyond this, she would demand a series of psychological transformations in both men and women which are outlined in the selection presented here.

No single passage from a work of such scope and density as *The Second Sex* could do justice to its richness. The work as a whole is required reading for anyone desiring to achieve an understanding of women's liberation that goes beyond superficialities. The selection offered here—from the conclusion of the work—is among the most subtle and passionately argued passages. Note that while De Beauvoir's hope is for an "androgynous world," she ends by describing that ideal state as one of "brotherhood."

WE HAVE seen why men enslaved women in the first place; the devaluation of femininity has been a necessary step in human evolution, but it might have led to collaboration between the two sexes; oppression is to be explained by the tendency of the existent to flee from himself by means of identification with the other, whom he oppresses to that end. In each individual man that tendency exists today; and the vast majority yield to it. The husband wants to find himself in his wife, the lover in his mistress, in the form of a stone image; he is seeking in her the myth of his virility, of his sovereignty, of his immediate reality. "My husband never goes to the movies," says his wife, and the dubious masculine opinion is graved in the marble of eternity. But he is himself the slave of his double: what an effort to build up an image in which he is always in danger! In spite of everything his success in this depends upon the capricious freedom of women: he must constantly try to keep this propitious to him. Man is concerned with the effort to appear male, important, superior; he pretends so as to get pretense in return; he, too, is aggressive, uneasy; he feels hostility for women because he is afraid of them, he is afraid of them because he is afraid of the personage, the image, with which he identifies himself. What time and strength he squanders in liquidating, sublimating, transferring complexes, in talking about women, in seducing them, in fearing them! He would be liberated himself in their liberation. But this is precisely what he dreads. And so he obstinately persists in the mystifications intended to keep woman in her chains. . . .

A world where men and women would be equal is easy to visualize, for that precisely is what the Soviet Revolution *promised:* women raised and trained exactly like men were to work under the same conditions and for the same wages. Erotic liberty was to be recognized by custom, but the sexual act was not to be considered a "service" to be paid for; woman was to be *obliged* to provide herself with other ways of earning a living; marriage was to be based on a free agreement that the spouses could break at will; maternity was to be voluntary, which meant that contraception and abortion were to be authorized and that, on the other hand, all mothers and their children were to have exactly the same rights, in or out of marriage; pregnancy leaves were to be paid for by the State, which would assume charge of the children, signifying not that they would be *taken away* from their parents, but that they would not be *abandoned* to them.

But is it enough to change laws, institutions, customs, public opinion, and the whole social context, for men and women to become truly equal? "Women will always be women," say the skeptics. Other seers prophesy that in casting off their femininity they will not succeed in changing themselves into men and they will become monsters. This would be to admit that the woman of today is a creation of nature; it must be repeated once more that in human society nothing is natural and that woman, like much else, is a product elaborated by civilization. The intervention of others in her destiny is fundamental: if this action took a different direction, it would produce a quite different result. Woman is determined not by her hormones or by mysterious instincts, but by the manner in which her body and her relation to the world are modified through the action of others than herself. The abyss that separates the adolescent boy and girl has been deliberately opened out between them since earliest childhood; later on, woman could not be other than what she *was made,* and that past was bound to shadow her for life. If we appreciate its influence, we see clearly that her destiny is not predetermined for all eternity.

We must not believe, certainly, that a change in woman's economic condition alone is enough to transform her, though this factor has been and remains the basic factor in her evolution; but until it has brought about the moral, social, cultural, and other consequences that it promises and requires, the new woman cannot appear. At this moment they have been realized nowhere, in Russia no more than in France or the United States; and this explains why the woman of today is torn between the past and the future. She appears most often as a "true woman" disguised as a man, and she feels herself as ill at ease in her flesh as in her masculine garb. She must shed her old skin and cut her own new clothes. This she could do only through a social evolution. No single educator could fashion a *female human being* today who would be the exact homologue of the *male human being;* if she is raised like a boy, the young girl feels she is an oddity and thereby she is given a new kind of sex specification. Stendhal understood this when he said: "The forest must be planted all at once." But if we imagine, on the contrary, a society in which the equality of the sexes would be concretely realized, this equality would find new expression in each individual.

If the little girl were brought up from the first with the same demands and rewards, the same severity and the same freedom, as her brothers, taking part in the same studies, the same games, promised the same future, surrounded with women and men who seemed to her undoubted equals, the meanings of the castration complex and of the Oedipus complex would be profoundly modified. Assuming on the same basis as the father the material and moral responsibility of the couple, the mother would enjoy the same lasting prestige; the child would perceive around her an androgynous world and not a masculine world. Were she emotionally more attracted to her father—which is not even sure —her love for him would be tinged with a will to emulation and not a feeling of powerlessness; she would not be oriented toward passivity. Authorized to test her powers in work and sports, competing actively with the boys, she would not find the absence of the penis—compensated by the promise of a child—enough to give rise to an inferiority complex; correlatively, the boy would not have a superiority complex if it were not instilled into him and if he looked up to women with as much respect as to men. The little girl would not seek sterile compensation in narcissism and dreaming, she would not take her fate for granted; she would be interested in what she was *doing*, she would throw herself without reserve into undertakings.

I have already pointed out how much easier the transformation of puberty would be if she looked beyond it, like the boys, toward a free adult future: menstruation horrifies her only because it is an abrupt descent into femininity. She would also take her young eroticism in much more tranquil fashion if she did not feel a frightened disgust for her destiny as a whole; coherent sexual information would do much to help her over this crisis. And thanks to coeducational schooling, the august mystery of Man would have no occasion to enter her mind: it would be eliminated by everyday familiarity and open rivalry.

Objections raised against this system always imply respect for sexual taboos; but the effort to inhibit all sex curiosity and pleasure in the child is quite useless; one succeeds only in creating repressions, obsessions, neuroses. The excessive sentimentality, homosexual fervors, and platonic crushes of adolescent girls, with all their train of silliness and frivolity, are much more injurious than a little childish sex play and a few definite sex experiences. It would be beneficial above all for the young girl not to be influenced against taking charge herself of her own existence, for then she would not seek a demigod in the male— merely a comrade, a friend, a partner. Eroticism and love would take on the nature of free transcendence and not that of resignation; she could experience them as a relation between equals. There is no intention, of course, to remove by a stroke of the pen all the difficulties that the child has to overcome in changing into an adult; the most intelligent, the most tolerant education could not relieve the child of experiencing things for herself; what could be asked is that obstacles should not be piled gratuitously in her path. Progress is already shown by the fact that "vicious" little girls are no longer cauterized with a red-hot iron. Psychoanalysis has given parents some instruction, but the conditions under which, at the present time, the sexual training and initiation of woman are accomplished are so deplorable that none of the objections advanced against the idea of a radical change could be considered valid. It is not a question of abolishing in woman the contingencies and miseries of the human condition, but of giving her the means for transcending them.

Woman is the victim of no mysterious fatality; the peculiarities that identify her as specifically a woman get their importance from the significance played upon them. They can be surmounted, in the future, when they are regarded in new perspectives. Thus, as we have seen, through her erotic experience woman feels—and often detests—the domination of the male; but this is no reason to conclude that her ovaries condemn her to live forever on her knees. Virile aggressiveness seems like a lordly privilege only within a system that in its entirety conspires to affirm masculine sovereignty; and woman *feels* herself profoundly passive in the sexual act only because she already *thinks* of herself as such. Many modern women who lay claim to their dignity as human beings still envisage their erotic life from the standpoint of a tradition of slavery: since it seems to them humiliating to lie beneath the man, to be penetrated by him, they grow tense in frigidity. But if the reality were different, the meaning expressed symbolically in amorous gestures and postures would be different, too: a woman who pays and dominates her lover can, for example, take pride in her superb idleness and consider that she is enslaving the male who is actively exerting himself. And here and now there are many sexually well-balanced couples whose notions of victory and defeat are giving place to the idea of an exchange.

As a matter of fact, man, like woman, is flesh, therefore passive, the plaything of his hormones and of the species, the restless prey of his desires. And she, like him, in the midst of the carnal fever, is a consenting, a voluntary gift, an activity; they live out in their several fashions the strange ambiguity of existence made body. In those combats where they think they confront one another, it is really against the self that each one struggles, projecting into the partner that part of the self which is repudiated; instead of living out the ambiguities of their situation, each tries to make the other bear the abjection and tries to reserve the honor for the self. If, however, both should assume the ambiguity with a clear-sighted modesty, correlative of an authentic pride, they would see each other as equals and would live out their erotic drama in amity. The fact that we are human beings is infinitely more important than all the peculiarities that distinguish human beings from one another; it is never the given that confers superiorities: "virtue," as the ancients called it, is defined at the level of "that which depends on us." In both sexes is played out the same drama of the flesh and the spirit, of finitude and transcendence; both are gnawed away by time and laid in wait for by death, they have the same essential need for one another; and they can gain from their liberty the same glory. If they were to taste it, they would no longer be tempted to dispute fallacious privileges, and fraternity between them could then come into existence.

I shall be told that all this is utopian fancy, because woman cannot be "made over" unless society has first made her really the equal of man. Conservatives have never failed in such circumstances to refer to that vicious circle; history, however, does not revolve. If a caste is kept in a state of inferiority, no doubt it remains inferior; but liberty can break the circle. Let the Negroes vote and they become worthy of having the vote; let woman be given responsibilities and she is able to assume them. The fact is that oppressors cannot be expected to make a move of gratuitous generosity; but at one time the revolt of the oppressed, at another time even the very evolution of the privileged caste itself, creates new situations; thus men have been led, in their own interest, to give partial emancipation to women: it remains only for women to continue their ascent, and the successes they are obtaining are an encouragement for them to do so. It seems almost certain that sooner or later they will arrive at complete economic and social equality, which will bring about an inner metamorphosis.

However this may be, there will be some to object that if such a world is possible it is not desirable. When woman is "the same" as her male, life will lose its salt and spice. This argument, also, has lost its novelty: those interested in perpetuating present conditions are always in tears about the marvelous past that is about to disappear, without having so much as a smile for the young future. . . .

When the "charming woman" shows herself in all her splendor, she is a much more exalting object than the "idiotic paintings, overdoors, scenery, showman's garish signs, popular chromos," that excited Rimbaud; adorned with the most modern artifices, beautified according to the newest techniques, she comes down from the remoteness of the ages, from Thebes, from Crete, from Chichén-Itzá; and she is also the totem set up deep in the African jungle; she is a helicopter and she is a bird; and there is this, the greatest wonder of all: under her tinted hair the forest murmur becomes a thought, and words issue from her breasts. Men stretch forth avid hands toward the marvel, but when they grasp it it is gone; the wife, the mistress, speak like everybody else through their mouths: their words are worth just what they are worth; their breasts also. Does such a fugitive miracle—and one so rare—justify us in perpetuating a situation that is baneful for both sexes? One can appreciate the beauty of flowers, the charm of women, and appreciate them at their true value; if these treasures cost blood or misery, they must be sacrificed.

But in truth this sacrifice seems to men a peculiarly heavy one; few of them really wish in their hearts for woman to succeed in making it; those among them who hold woman in contempt see in the sacrifice nothing for them to gain, those who cherish her see too much that they would lose. And it is true that the evolution now in progress threatens more than feminine charm alone: in beginning to exist for herself, woman will relinquish the function as double and mediator to which she owes her privileged place in the masculine universe; to man, caught between the silence of nature and the demanding presence of

other free beings, a creature who is at once his like and a passive
thing seems a great treasure. The guise in which he conceives
his companion may be mythical, but the experiences for which
she is the source or the pretext are nonetheless real: there are
hardly any more precious, more intimate, more ardent. There is
no denying that feminine dependence, inferiority, woe, give
women their special character; assuredly woman's autonomy, if
it spares men many troubles, will also deny them many con-
veniences; assuredly there are certain forms of the sexual adventure which will be lost in the world of tomorrow. But this
does not mean that love, happiness, poetry, dream, will be
banished from it.

Let us not forget that our lack of imagination always de-
populates the future; for us it is only an abstraction; each one
of us secretly deplores the absence there of the one who was
himself. But the humanity of tomorrow will be living in its
flesh and in its conscious liberty; that time will be its present and
it will in turn prefer it. New relations of flesh and sentiment of
which we have no conception will arise between the sexes;
already, indeed, there have appeared between men and women
friendships, rivalries, complicities, comradeships—chaste or sen-
sual—which past centuries could not have conceived. To mention
one point, nothing could seem to me more debatable than the
opinion that dooms the new world to uniformity and hence to
boredom. I fail to see that this present world is free from boredom or that liberty ever creates uniformity.

To begin with, there will always be certain differences between man and woman; her eroticism, and therefore her sexual
world, have a special form of their own and therefore cannot fail
to engender a sensuality, a sensitivity, of a special nature. This
means that her relations to her own body, to that of the male,
to the child, will never be identical with those the male bears
to his own body, to that of the female, and to the child; those
who make much of "equality in difference" could not with good
grace refuse to grant me the possible existence of differences in
equality. Then again, it is institutions that create uniformity.
Young and pretty, the slaves of the harem are always the same
in the sultan's embrace; Christianity gave eroticism its savor of

sin and legend when it endowed the human female with a soul; if society restores her sovereign individuality to woman, it will not thereby destroy the power of love's embrace to move the heart.

It is nonsense to assert that revelry, vice, ecstasy, passion, would become impossible if man and woman were equal in concrete matters; the contradictions that put the flesh in opposition to the spirit, the instant to time, the swoon of immanence to the challenge of transcendence, the absolute of pleasure to the nothingness of forgetting, will never be resolved; in sexuality will always be materialized the tension, the anguish, the joy, the frustration, and the triumph of existence. To emancipate woman is to refuse to confine her to the relations she bears to man, not to deny them to her; let her have her independent existence and she will continue nonetheless to exist for him *also:* mutually recognizing each other as subject, each will yet remain for the other an *other.* The reciprocity of their relations will not do away with the miracles—desire, possession, love, dream, adventure—worked by the division of human beings into two separate categories; and the words that move us—giving, conquering, uniting—will not lose their meaning. On the contrary, when we abolish the slavery of half of humanity, together with the whole system of hypocrisy that it implies, then the "division" of humanity will reveal its genuine significance and the human couple will find its true form. "The direct, natural, necessary relation of human creatures is the *relation of man to woman,*" Marx has said. "The nature of this relation determines to what point man himself is to be considered as a *generic being,* as mankind; the relation of man to woman is the most natural relation of human being to human being. By it is shown, therefore, to what point the *natural* behavior of man has become *human* or to what point the *human* being has become his *natural* being, to what point his *human nature* has become his *nature.*"

The case could not be better stated. It is for man to establish the reign of liberty in the midst of the world of the given. To gain the supreme victory, it is necessary, for one thing, that by and through their natural differentiation men and women unequivocally affirm their brotherhood.

Toward Liberation

2. The New Militancy

Juliet Mitchell / *The Longest Revolution*

Juliet Mitchell's essay, *Women: The Longest Revolution* (from which the following is an excerpt), has circulated widely in the women's liberation movement since it first appeared in 1966. It is one of the keenest analyses yet to appear of the way in which socialist theory has failed to make proper ideological sense of women's oppression. Mitchell concludes that woman's condition can only be understood when all four elements of its "complex unity" are included. These elements are production (work and earnings), reproduction, sexuality, and woman's traditional responsibility for socializing children. Most socialist theorists, as well as most feminists, have erred in believing that the liberation of women could be achieved by altering only one or two of these elements. Mitchell argues that *each* must be given special attention in order to see how it functions in any given time or social setting, and that *all* four must be transformed if women are to achieve their full equality.

The problem of the subordination of women and the need for their liberation was recognized by all the great socialist thinkers in the nineteenth century. It is part of the classical heritage of the revolutionary movement. Yet today, in the West, the problem has become a subsidiary, if not an invisible element in

From *The New Left Review* (November-December, 1966), pp. 11–37. Reprinted by permission of *The New Left Review*.

the preoccupations of socialists. Perhaps no other major issue has been so forgotten. . . .

How has this counter-revolution come about? Why has the problem of woman's condition become an area of silence within contemporary socialism? August Bebel, whose book *Woman in the Past, Present and Future* was one of the standard texts of the German Social-Democratic Party in the early years of this century, wrote: "Every socialist recognizes the dependence of the workman on the capitalist, and cannot understand that others, and especially the capitalists themselves, should fail to recognize it also; but the same socialist often does not recognize the dependence of women on men because the question touches his own dear self more or less nearly." But this genre of explanation—psychologistic and moralistic—is clearly inadequate. Much deeper and more structural causes have clearly been at work. To consider these would require a major historical study, impossible here. But it can be said with some certainty that part of the explanation for the decline in socialist debate on the subject lies not only in the real historical processes, but in the original weaknesses in the traditional discussion of the subject in the classics. For while the great studies of the last century all stressed the importance of the problem, they did not *solve* it theoretically. The limitations of their approach have never been subsequently transcended.

Fourier was the most ardent and voluminous advocate of women's liberation and of sexual freedom among the early socialists. In a well-known passage he wrote: "The change in a historical epoch can always be determined by the progress of women towards freedom, because in the relation of woman to man, of the weak to the strong, the victory of human nature over brutality is most evident. The degree of emancipation of women is the natural measure of general emancipation." Marx quoted this formulation with approval in *The Holy Family*.[1] But characteristically in his early writings he gave it a more uni-

1. Charles Fourier, *Théorie des Quatre Mouvements*, in *Oeuvres Complètes* (1841), I, p. 195; cit. Karl Marx, *The Holy Family* (1845), trans. by R. Dixon, (Moscow, Foreign Language Publishing House, 1956), p. 259.

versal and philosophical meaning. The emancipation of women would not only be as Fourier, with his greater preoccupation with sexual liberation saw it, an index of humanization in the civic sense of the victory of humaneness over brutality, but in the more fundamental sense of the progress of the human over the animal, the cultural over the natural: "The relation of man to woman is the *most natural* relation of human being to human being. It indicates, therefore, how far man's *natural* behavior has become human, and how far his *human* essence has become a *natural* essence for him, how far his *human nature* has become *nature* for him."[2] This theme is typical of the early Marx.

Fourier's ideas remained at the level of utopian moral injunction. Marx used and transformed them, integrating them into a philosophical critique of human history. But he retained the abstraction of Fourier's conception of the position of women as an index of general social advance. This in effect makes it merely a symbol—it accords the problem a universal importance at the cost of depriving it of its specific substance. Symbols are allusions to or derivations of something else. In Marx's early writings woman becomes an anthropological entity, an ontological category, of a highly abstract kind. Contrarily, in his later work, where he is concerned with describing the family, Marx differentiates it as a phenomenon according to time and place:

. . . marriage, property, the family remain unattacked, in theory, because they are the practical basis on which the bourgeoisie has erected its domination, and because in their bourgeois form they are the conditions which make the bourgeois a bourgeois. . . . This attitude of the bourgeois to the conditions of his existence acquires one of its universal forms in bourgeois morality. One cannot, in general, speak of the family *as such*. Historically, the bourgeois gives the family the character of the bourgeois family, in which boredom and money are the binding link, and which also includes the bourgeois dissolution of the family, which does not prevent the family itself from always continuing to exist. Its dirty existence has its counterpart in the holy concept of it in official phraseology and uni-

2. Karl Marx, *Private Property and Communism* (1844) in *Early Writings*, translated by T. B. Bottomore (London, C. Watts & Co., 1963), p. 154.

versal hypocrisy. . . . (Among the proletariat) the concept of the family does not exist at all. . . . In the eighteenth century the concept of the family was abolished by the philosophers, because the actual family was already in process of dissolution at the highest pinnacles of civilization. The internal family bond was dissolved, the separate components constituting the concept of the family were dissolved, for example, obedience, piety, fidelity in marriage, etc.; but the real body of the family, the property relation, the exclusive attitude in relation to other families, forced cohabitation—relations produced by the existence of children, the structure of modern towns, the formation of capital, etc.—all these were preserved, although with numerous violations because the existence of the family has been made necessary by its connection with the mode of production that exists independently of the will of bourgeois society.[3]

. . . What is striking is that here the problem of women has been submerged in an analysis of the family. The difficulties of this approach can be seen in the somewhat apocalyptic note of Marx's comments on the fate of the bourgeois family here and elsewhere (for example, in the *Communist Manifesto*). There was little historical warrant for the idea that it was in effective dissolution, and indeed could no longer be seen in the working-class. Marx thus moves from general philosophical formulations about women in the early writings to specific historical comments on the family in the later texts. There is a serious disjunction between the two. The common framework of both, of course, was his analysis of the economy, and of the evolution of property.

It was left to Engels to systematize these theses in *The Origin of the Family, Private Property and the State,* after Marx's death. Engels declared that the inequality of the sexes was one of the first antagonisms within the human species. The first class antagonism "coincides with the development of the antagonism between man and woman in the monogamous marriage, and the first class oppression with that of the female sex by the male." Basing much of his theory on Lewis H. Morgan's inaccurate anthropological investigations, Engels nevertheless had some val-

3. Karl Marx, *The German Ideology* (1845–46), trans. by Clemens Dutt, (Moscow, Progress Publishers, 1965), pp. 192–193.

uable insights. Inheritance, which is the key to his economist account, was first matrilineal, but with the increase of wealth became patrilineal. This was woman's greatest single setback. The wife's fidelity becomes essential and monogamy is irrevocably established. The wife in the communistic, patriarchal family is a public servant, with monogamy she becomes a private one. Engels effectively reduces the problem of woman to her capacity to work. He therefore gave her physiological weakness as a primary cause of her oppression. He locates the moment of her exploitation at the point of the transition from communal to private property. If inability to work is the cause of her inferior status, ability to work will bring her liberation: ". . . the emancipation of women and their equality with men are impossible and must remain so as long as women are excluded from socially productive work and restricted to housework, which is private. The emancipation of women becomes possible only when women are enabled to take part in production on a large, social scale, and when domestic duties require their attention only to a minor degree." . . . Engels thus finds a solution schematically appropriate to his analysis of the origin of feminine oppression. The position of women, then, in the work of Marx and Engels remains dissociated from, or subsidiary to, a discussion of the family, which is in its turn subordinated as merely a precondition of private property. Their solutions retain this overly economist stress, or enter the realm of dislocated speculation.

Bebel, Engels' disciple, attempted to provide a programmatic account of woman's oppression as such, not simply as a by-product of the evolution of the family and of private property: "From the beginning of time oppression was the common lot of woman and the labourer. . . . *Woman was the first human being that tasted bondage,* woman was a slave *before the slave existed.*" He acknowledged, with Marx and Engels, the importance of physical inferiority in accounting for woman's subordination, but while stressing inheritance, added that a biological element—her maternal function—was one of the fundamental conditions that made her economically dependent on the man. But Bebel, too, was unable to do more than state that sexual equality was impossible without socialism. His vision of the future was a vague reverie, quite disconnected from his description of the past. The absence of a strategic concern forced him into voluntarist optimism divorced from reality. Lenin himself, although he made a number of specific suggestions, inherited a tradition of thought which simply pointed to the *a priori* equation of socialism with feminine liberation without showing concretely how it would transform woman's condition: "Unless women are brought to take an independent part not only in political life generally, but also in daily and universal public service, it is no use talking about full and stable democracy, let alone socialism."[4]

The liberation of women remains a normative ideal, an adjunct to socialist theory, not structurally integrated into it.

The contrary is true of De Beauvoir's massive work *The Second Sex*—to this day the greatest single contribution on the subject. Here the focus is the status of women through the ages. But socialism as such emerges as a curiously contingent solution at the end of the work, in a muffled epilogue. De Beauvoir's main theoretical innovation was to fuse the "economic" and "reproductive" explanations of women's subordination by a psychological interpretation of both. Man asserts himself as subject and free being by opposing other consciousnesses. He is distinct from animals precisely in that he creates and invents (not in that he reproduces himself), but he tries to escape the burden of his freedom by giving himself a spurious "immortality" in his children. He dominates woman both to imprison another consciousness which reflects his own and to provide him with children that are securely his (his fear of illegitimacy). The notions obviously have a considerable force. But they are very atemporal: it is not easy to see why socialism should modify the basic "ontological" desire for a thinglike freedom which De Beauvoir sees as the motor behind the fixation with inheritance in the property system, or the enslavement of women which derived from it. . . .

Thus, the classical literature on the problem of woman's condition is predominantly economist in emphasis, stressing her simple subordination to the institutions of private property. Her

4. V. I. Lenin, *The Tasks of the Proletariat in Our Revolution* (1917), in *Collected Works*, XXIV, p. 70.

biological status underpins both her weakness as a producer, in work relations, and her importance as a possession, in reproductive relations. The fullest and most recent interpretation gives both factors a psychological cast. The framework of discussion is an evolutionist one which nevertheless fails noticeably to project a convincing image of the future, beyond asserting that socialism will involve the liberation of women as one of its constituent "moments."

What is the solution to this impasse? It must lie in differentiating woman's condition, much more radically than in the past, into its separate structures, which together form a complex—not a simple—unity. This will mean rejecting the idea that woman's condition can be deduced derivatively from the economy or equated symbolically with society. Rather, it must be seen as a *specific* structure, which is a unity of different elements. . . . The [four] key structures can be listed as follows: *Production, Reproduction, Sex,* and *Socialization of children.* The concrete combination of these produces the "complex unity" of her position; but each separate structure may have reached a different "moment" at any given historical time. Each then must be examined separately in order to see what the present unity is and how it might be changed. . . .

The liberation of women can only be achieved if *all four* structures in which they are integrated are transformed. A modification of any one of them can be offset by a reinforcement of another, so that mere permutation of the form of exploitation is achieved. The history of the last sixty years provides ample evidence of this. In the early twentieth century, militant feminism in England or the United States surpassed the labour movement in the violence of its assault on bourgeois society, in pursuit of suffrage. This political right was eventually won. Nonetheless, though a simple completion of the formal legal equality of bourgeois society, it left the socio-economic situation of women virtually unchanged. The wider legacy of the suffrage was nil: the suffragettes proved quite unable to move beyond their own initial demands, and many of their leading figures later became extreme reactionaries. The Russian Revolution produced a quite different experience. In the Soviet Union in the 1920's, advanced social legislation aimed at liberating women above all in the field of sexuality: divorce was made free and automatic for either partner, thus effectively liquidating marriage; illegitimacy was abolished, abortion was free, etc. The social and demographic effects of these laws in a backward, semi-literate society bent on rapid industrialization (needing, therefore, a high birth-rate) were—predictably—catastrophic. Stalinism soon produced a restoration of iron traditional norms. Inheritance was reinstated, divorce inaccessible, abortion illegal, etc. "The State cannot exist without the family. Marriage is a positive value for the Socialist Soviet State only if the partners see in it a lifelong union. So-called free-love is a bourgeois invention and has nothing in common with the principles of conduct of a Soviet citizen. Moreover, marriage receives its full value for the State only if there is progeny, and the consorts experience the highest happiness of parenthood," wrote the official journal of the Commissariat of Justice in 1939.[5] Women still retained the right and obligation to work, but because these gains were not integrated into the earlier attempts to abolish the family and free sexuality no general liberation has occurred. In China, still another experience is being played out today. At a comparable stage of the revolution, all the emphasis is being placed on liberating women in *production*. This has produced an impressive social promotion of women. But it has been accompanied by a tremendous repression of sexuality and a rigorous puritanism (currently rampant in civic life). This corresponds not only to the need to mobilize women massively in economic life, but to a deep cultural reaction against the corruption and prostitution prevalent in Imperial and Kuo Ming Tang China (a phenomenon unlike anything in Czarist Russia). Because the exploitation of women was so great in the *ancien régime,* women's participation at village level in the Chinese Revolution was uniquely high. As for reproduction, the Russian cult of maternity in the 1930's and 1940's has not been repeated for demographic reasons: indeed, China may be one of the first

5. *Sotsialisticheskaya Żakonnost* No. 2 (1939), cit. N. Timasheff, "The Attempt to Abolish the Family in Russia," in *The Family,* ed. N. W. Bell and E. F. Vogel (New York, Free Press, 1960), p. 59.

countries in the world to provide free State authorized contraception on a universal scale to the population. Again, however, given the low level of industrialization and fear produced by imperialist encirclement, no all-round advance could be expected.

It is only in the highly developed societies of the West that an authentic liberation of women can be envisaged today. But for this to occur, there must be a transformation of all the structures into which they are integrated. . . . A revolutionary movement must base its analysis on the uneven development of each, and attack the weakest link in the combination. This may then become the point of departure for a general transformation. What is the situation of the different structures today?

1. *Production:* The long-term development of the forces of production must command any socialist perspective. . . . Today, automation promises the *technical* possibility of abolishing completely the physical differential between man and woman in production, but under capitalist relations of production, the *social* possibility of this abolition is permanently threatened, and can easily be turned into its opposite, the actual diminution of woman's role in production as the labour force contracts.

This concerns the future; for the present the main fact to register is that woman's role in production is virtually stationary, and has been so for a long time now. In England in 1911, 30 percent of the work-force were women; in the 1960's 34 percent. The composition of these jobs has not changed decisively either. The jobs are very rarely "careers." When they are not in the lowest positions on the factory-floor, they are normally white-collar auxiliary positions (such as secretaries)—supportive to masculine roles. . . .

Thus, in all essentials, work as such—of the amount and type effectively available today—has not proved a salvation for women.

2. *Reproduction:* Scientific advance in contraception could . . . make involuntary reproduction—which accounts for the vast majority of births in the world today, and for a major proportion even in the West—a phenomenon of the past. But oral contraception—which has so far been developed in a form which exactly repeats the sexual inequality of Western society—is only at its

beginnings. It is inadequately distributed across classes and countries and awaits further technical improvements. Its main initial impact is, in the advanced countries, likely to be psychological—it will certainly free women's sexual experience from many of the anxieties and inhibitions which have always afflicted it. It will definitely divorce sexuality from procreation, as necessary complements.

The demographic pattern of reproduction in the West may or may not be widely affected by oral contraception. One of the most striking phenomena of very recent years in the United States has been the sudden increase in the birth-rate. In the last decade it has been higher than that of under-developed countries such as India, Pakistan, and Burma. In fact, this reflects simply the lesser economic burden of a large family in conditions of economic boom in the richest country in the world. But it also reflects the magnification of familial ideology as a social force. This leads to the next structure.

3. *Socialization:* The changes in the composition of the work force, the size of the family, the structure of education, etc.—however limited from an ideal standpoint—have undoubtedly diminished the societal function and importance of the family. As an organization it is not a significant unit in the political power system, it plays little part in economic production and it is rarely the sole agency of integration into the larger society; thus at the macroscopic level it serves very little purpose.

The result has been a major displacement of emphasis on to the family's psycho-social function, for the infant and for the couple. Parsons writes: "The trend of the evidence points to the beginning of the relative stabilization of a *new* type of family structure in a new relation to a general social structure, one in which the family is more specialized than before, but not in any general sense less important, because the society is dependent *more* exclusively on it for the performance of *certain* of its vital functions."[6] The vital nucleus of truth in the emphasis on socialization of the child has been discussed. It is essential that social-

6. Talcott Parsons and Robert F. Bales, *Family, Socialization, and Interaction Process* (Glencoe, Mich., Free Press, 1956), pp. 9–10.

ists should acknowledge it and integrate it entirely into any pro-
gramme for the liberation of women. . . . The attempt to focus
women's existence exclusively on bringing up children is mani-
festly harmful to children. Socialization as an exceptionally delicate process requires a serene and mature socializer—a type which
the frustrations of a *purely* familial role are not liable to produce.
Exclusive maternity is often in this sense "counter-productive."
The mother discharges her own frustrations and anxieties in a
fixation on the child. An increased awareness of the critical importance of socialization, far from leading to a restitution of
classical maternal roles, should lead to a reconsideration of them
—of what makes a good socializing agent, who can genuinely
provide security and stability for the child. . . .

4. *Sexuality:* It is difficult not to conclude that the major structure which at present is in rapid evolution is sexuality. Production, reproduction, and socialization are all more or less stationary in the West today, in the sense that they have not changed
for three or more decades. There is, moreover, no widespread
demand for changes in them on the part of women themselves—
the governing ideology has effectively prevented critical consciousness. By contrast, the dominant sexual ideology is proving
less and less successful in regulating spontaneous behaviour. Marriage in its classical form is increasingly threatened by the lib-
eralization of relationships before and after it which affects all
classes today. In this sense, it is evidently the weak link in the
chain—the particular structure that is the site of the most contradictions. . . . The liberation of sexual experience from relations which are extraneous to it—whether procreation or property—could lead to true inter-sexual freedom. But it could also
lead simply to new forms of neocapitalist ideology and practice.
For one of the forces behind the current acceleration of sexual
freedom has undoubtedly been the conversion of contemporary
capitalism from a production-and-work ethos to a consumption-
and-fun ethos. Riesman commented on this development early
in the 1950's: ". . . there is not only a growth of leisure, but work
itself becomes both less interesting and less demanding for many
. . . more than before, as job-mindedness declines, sex permeates
the daytime as well as the playtime consciousness. It is viewed

as a consumption good not only by the old leisure classes, but by the modern leisure masses."[7] The gist of Riesman's argument is that in a society bored by work, sex is the only activity, the only reminder of one's energies, the only competitive act; the last defence against *vis inertiae*. . . . These considerations make it clear that sexuality, while it presently may contain the greatest potential for liberation—can equally well be organized against any increase of its human possibilities. New forms of reification are emerging which may void sexual freedom of any meaning. This is a reminder that while one structure may be the *weak link* in a unity like that of woman's condition, there can never be a solution through it alone. . . .

What, then, is the responsible revolutionary attitude? It must include both immediate and fundamental demands, in a single critique of the *whole* of women's situation, that does not fetishize any dimension of it. . . .

In practical terms this means a coherent system of demands. The four elements of women's condition cannot merely be considered each in isolation; they form a structure of specific interrelations. The contemporary bourgeois family can be seen as a triptych of sexual, reproductive, and socializatory functions (the woman's world) embraced by production (the man's world)— precisely a structure which in the final instance is determined by the economy. The exclusion of women from production—social human activity—and their confinement to a monolithic condensation of functions in a unity—the family—which is precisely unified in the *natural part* of each function, is the root cause of the contemporary *social* definition of women as *natural* beings. Hence the main thrust of any emancipation movement must still concentrate on the economic element—the entry of women fully into public industry. The error of the old socialists was to see the other elements as reducible to the economic; hence the call for the entry of women into production was accompanied by the purely abstract slogan of the abolition of the family. Economic demands are still primary, but must be accompanied by coherent

7. David Riesman, *The Lonely Crowd* (New Haven, Conn., Yale University Press, 1950), p. 154.

policies for the other three elements, policies which at particular junctures may take over the primary role in immediate action. . . .

Traditionally, the socialist movement has called for the "abolition of the bourgeois family." This slogan must be rejected as incorrect today. It is maximalist in the bad sense, posing a demand which is merely a negation without any coherent construction subsequent to it. . . . The reasons for the historic weakness of the notion is that the family was never analysed structurally—in terms of its different functions. It was a hypostasized entity; the abstraction of its abolition corresponds to the abstraction of its conception. The strategic concern for socialists should be for the equality of the sexes, not the abolition of the family. The consequences of this demand are no less radical, but they are concrete and positive, and can be integrated into the real course of history. The family as it exists at present is, in fact, incompatible with the equality of the sexes. But this equality will not come from its administrative abolition, but from the historical differentiation of its functions. The revolutionary demand should be for the liberation of these functions from a monolithic fusion which oppresses each. Thus dissociation of reproduction from sexuality frees sexuality from alienation in unwanted reproduction (and fear of it), and reproduction from subjugation to chance and uncontrollable causality. It is thus an elementary demand to press for free State provision of oral contraception. The legalization of homosexuality—which is one of the forms of non-reproductive sexuality—should be supported for just the same reason, and regressive campaigns against it in Cuba or elsewhere should be unhesitatingly criticized. The straightforward abolition of illegitimacy as a legal notion as in Sweden and Russia has a similar implication; it would separate marriage civically from parenthood.

The problem of socialization poses more difficult questions, as has been seen. But the need for intensive maternal care in the early years of a child's life does not mean that the present single sanctioned form of socialization—marriage and family—is inevitable. Far from it. The fundamental characteristic of the present system of marriage and family is in our society its *monolithism*: there is only one institutionalized form of intersexual or intergenerational relationship possible. It is that or nothing. This is why it is essentially a denial of life. For all human experience shows that intersexual and intergenerational relationships are infinitely various—indeed, much of our creative literature is a celebration of the fact—while the institutionalized expression of them in our capitalist society is utterly simple and rigid. It is the poverty and simplicity of the institutions in this area of life which are such an oppression. Any society will require some institutionalized and social recognition of personal relationships. But there is absolutely no reason why there should be only one legitimized form—and a multitude of unlegitimized experience. Socialism should properly mean not the abolition of the family, but the diversification of the socially acknowledged relationships which are today forcibly and rigidly compressed into it. This would mean a plural range of institutions—where the family is only one, and its abolition implies none. Couples living together or not living together, long-term unions with children, single parents bringing up children, children socialized by conventional rather than biological parents, extended kin groups, etc.—all these could be encompassed in a range of institutions which matched the free invention and variety of men and women.

Alice Rossi / *Sex Equality: The Beginning of Ideology*

Alice Rossi, who is a professor of sociology at Goucher College, has been speaking and writing for years in the cause of women's rights. In this recent essay she employs the current sociological concepts of the pluralist and assimilation models of

From *The Humanist*, xxix, 5 (September-October, 1969), pp. 3–6, 16. Reprinted by permission of *The Humanist*.

equality in order to examine the possibilities for women in such societies. For Rossi, it is only a hybrid model in which the dominating group changes in order to accept women as equals, that can offer women a chance for true equality. Pluralism and assimilation are dead ends for women. She sees in the current agitation of the New Left and in women's liberation groups a hopeful sign of a movement toward such a hybrid model.

It is 2400 years since Lysistrata organized a sex strike among Athenian women in a play that masked a serious antiwar opposition beneath a thin veneer of bawdy hilarity. The play is unique in drama as a theme of women power and sex solidarity, and takes on a fresh relevance when read in the tumultuous 1960's. Women in our day are active as students, as blacks, as workers, as war protesters, but far less often as women *qua* women pressing for equality with men, or actively engaging in a dialogue of what such equality should mean. . . .

The major objective of this article is to examine three possible goals of equality between the sexes, while a secondary objective is to pinpoint the ways in which inequality on sex grounds differs from racial, ethnic, or religious inequality.

A group may be said to suffer from inequality if its members are restricted in access to legitimate valued positions or rewards in a society for which their ascribed status is not a relevant consideration. In our day, this is perhaps least ambiguous where the status of citizen is concerned: We do not consider race, sex, religion, or national background relevant criteria for the right to vote or to run for public office. Here we are dealing with a particular *form* of inequality—codified law—and a particular *type* of inequality—civil and political rights of an individual as a citizen. There are several other forms of inequality in addition to legal statute: corporate or organizational policies and regulations, and most importantly, those covert social pressures which restrict the aspirations or depress the motivation of individuals on the ascribed grounds of their membership in certain categories. Thus, a teacher who scoffs at a black boy or white girl who aspires to become an engineer, or a society which uniformly applies pressure on girls to avoid occupational choices in medicine and law are examples of covert pressures which bolster racial and sexual inequality. *Forms* of inequality therefore range from explicit legal statute to informal social pressure.

Type of inequality adds a second dimension: the area of life in which the inequality is evidenced. There are inequalities in the *public* sector, as citizens, employees, consumers, or students; and there are inequalities in the *private* sector as family, organization, or club members. Throughout American history, the gains made for greater racial and sexual equality have been based on constitutional protection of individual rights in the public area of inequality, as citizens, students, and workers. But precisely because of constitutional protection of privacy of home, family, and person, it is more difficult to remove inequalities rooted in the private sphere of life. . . . We have yet to devise a means to compensate [for example] for the influences of parents who depress a daughter's aspiration to become a physician, while urging a son to aspire beyond his capacity or preference. . . .

There is, thus, a continuum of increasing difficulty in effecting social and political change along both dimensions of inequality: by *form,* from legal statute to corporate regulation to covert and deeply embedded social mores; by *type,* from citizenship to schooling and employment, to the private sector of family. Hence, the easiest target in removing inequality involves legal statute change or judicial interpretation of rights in the public sector, and the most difficult area involves changes in the covert social mores in family and social life. It is far easier to change laws which presently penalize women as workers, students, or citizens than it will be to effect social changes in family life and higher education which depress the aspirations and motivations of women.

An example of this last point can be seen in higher education. Few graduate schools discriminate against women applicants, but there are widespread subtle pressures once women are registered as students in graduate departments—from both faculty and male peers. In one graduate department of sociology, women represent a full third of the students, and, hence, the faculty cannot be charged with discriminatory practices toward the ad-

mission of women students. On the other hand, it was not un-
common in that department to hear faculty members charac-
terize a woman graduate student who showed strong commitment and independence as an "unfeminine bitch," and others
who were quiet and unassertive as "lacking ambition"—women
who will "never amount to much." Since it is difficult to be simultaneously independent and ambitious, but conventionally feminine and dependent, it would appear that the informal rules
prevent many women from winning the game, although they
are accepted as players.

Discrimination against women in hiring or promotion may be
barred by statute and corporate policy, but this does not magically stimulate any great movement of women up the occupational status ladder. Progress on the legal front must be accompanied by compensatory tactics to free girls and women from
the covert depression of their motivations and aspirations through
ridicule and double-bind pressures to be contradictory things.

Many women find an easy empathy with the plight of the poor,
the black, and minority religious groups—not from any innate
feminine intuition, but simply because a subordinate group is
sensitive to both unintended and intentional debasement or discrimination where another subordinate group is concerned. Wom-
en know from personal experience what it is like to be "put down"
by men, and can therefore understand what it is to be "put
down" as a black by whites. But there are also fundamental
differences between sex as a category of social inequality and
the categories of race, religion, or ethnicity. I shall discuss three
of the most important differences.

1. *Category Size and Residence:* In the case of race, religion,
and ethnicity, we are literally dealing with minority groups in
the American population, whether Mexican, Indian, Jewish, Catholic, or black. This is not the case for sex, since women are actually a numerical majority in the population.

While the potential is present for numerical strength to press
for the removal of inequalities, this is counterbalanced by other
ways in which women are prevented from effectively utilizing
their numerical strength. The Irish, the Italians, and the Jews
in an earlier period, and blacks in more recent history, have

been able to exert political pressure for representation and legislative change because residential concentration gave them voter strength in large urban centers. By contrast, women are for the most part *evenly distributed throughout the population.* Women can exert political pressure in segmental roles as consumers, workers, New Yorkers, or the aged; but not as a cohesive political group based on sex solidarity. It is inconceivable that a political organization of blacks would avoid the "race" issue, yet the League of Women Voters does precisely this when it takes pride in avoiding "women's" issues.

2. *Early Sex Role Socialization:* Age and sex are the earliest social categories an individual learns. The differentiation between mother and father, or parent and child, is learned at a tender, formative stage of life; and consequently, we carry into adulthood a set of age and sex role expectations that are extremely resistant to change. Not only do girls learn to accept authority from the older generation and from men, but they learn this lesson in intense, intimate relationships. By the time they reach adulthood, women are well socialized to seek and to find gratification in an intimate dependence on men, and in responsible authority over children. They may be dominant and affirmative mothers with their own children, or as teachers in classrooms, but pliant and submissive as wives.

Sex role expectations tend to remain a stubborn part of our impulse lives. This is often not visible among young men and women until they become parents. Many young people are egalitarian peers in school, courtship, and early marriage. With the birth of a child, deeper layers of their personalities come into play. Since there is little or no formal education for parenthood in our society, only a thin veneer of Spock-reading hides the acting out of old parental models that have been observed and internalized in childhood, triggering a regression to traditional sex roles that gradually spreads from the parental role to the marriage and self-definition of both sexes.

As a result of early sex-role socialization, there is bound to be a lag between political and economic emancipation of women and the inner adjustment to equality of both men and women. Even in radical political movements, women have often had to

caucus and fight for their acceptance as equal peers to men.
Without such efforts on their own behalf, women are as likely
to be "girl-Friday" assistants in a radical movement espousing
class and racial equality as they are in a business corporation,
a labor union, or a conservative political party.

3. *Pressures Against Sex Solidarity:* Racial, ethnic, and religious conflict can reach an acute stage of political strife in the
movement for equality, without affecting the solidarity of the
families of blacks, whites, Jews, or Gentiles. Such strife may, in
fact, increase the solidarity of these family units. A "we versus
them" dichotomy does not cut into family units in the case of
race, religion, or ethnicity as it does in the case of sex. Since
women typically live in greater intimacy with men than they do
with other women, there is potential conflict within family units
when women press hard for sex equality. Their demands are on
predominantly male legislators and employers in the public do-
main—husbands and fathers in the private sector. A married black
woman can affiliate with an activist civil rights group with no
implicit threat to her marriage. For a married woman to affiliate
with an activist women's rights group might very well trigger
tension in her marriage. . . . A large proportion of married
women [who] have not combated sex discrimination . . . fear
conflict with men, or benefit in terms of a comfortable high
status in exchange for economic dependence upon their husbands. There are many more women in the middle class who
benefit from sex inequality than there are blacks in the middle
class who benefit from racial inequality.

The size of a women's rights movement has, therefore, been
responsive to the proportion of "unattached" women in a population. An excess of females over males, a late age at marriage,
postponement of childbearing, a high divorce rate, a low remar-
riage rate, and greater longevity for women, all increase the
number of unattached women in a society, and therefore, increase the potential for sex equality activism. The hard core of
activists in past suffrage and feminist movements were women
without marital and family ties: ex-wives, nonwives, or childless
wives, whose need to support themselves triggered their concern
for equal rights to vote, to work, and to advance in their work.

The lull in the women's rights movement in the 1950's was related to the fact that this same decade saw the lowest age at marriage and the highest proportion of the population married in all of our history.

Since 1960, the age at marriage has moved up; the birth rate is down to what it was in the late 1930's; the divorce rate is up among couples married a long time, and more married women are in the labor force than ever before. These are all relevant contributors to the renascence of women's rights activism in the mid-1960's. The presence of older and married women in women's rights organizations (like the National Organization for Women) is also responsible for a broadening of the range of issues that concern women activists—from the civil, political, and economic concerns they share with feminists of an earlier day, to a host of changes affecting family roles; repeal of abortion laws, revision of divorce laws, community provision of child-care facilities, equal treatment under Social Security in old age, and a de-bunking of the clinging-vine or tempting-Eve image of married women that pervades the American mass media.

The point remains, however, that movement toward sex equality is restricted by the fact that our most intimate human relation is the heterosexual one of marriage. This places a major brake on the development of sex solidarity among women, a brake that is not present in other social inequalities. . . .

Courses in social stratification, minority groups, prejudice, and discrimination have been traditional fare in sociological curriculum for a long time. Many sociologists studied immigrants and their children and puzzled about the eventual shape of a society that underwent so massive an injection of diverse cultures. From these writings, we can extract three potential models that will be useful in sketching the alternate goals not only for the relations between ethnic groups, but for those of race and sex as well.

Three such models may be briefly defined, and then each in turn explored in somewhat greater detail:

1. *Pluralist Model:* This model anticipates a society in which marked racial, religious, and ethnic differences are retained and valued for their diversity, yielding a heterogeneous society in

which it is hoped cultural strength is increased by the diverse strands making up the whole society.

2. *Assimilation Model:* This model anticipates a society in which the minority groups are gradually absorbed into the mainstream by losing their distinguishing characteristics and acquiring the language, occupational skills, and life style of the majority of the host culture.

3. *Hybrid Model:* This model anticipates a society in which there is change in both the ascendant group and the minority groups—a "melting-pot" hybrid requiring changes not only in blacks and Jews and women, but white male Protestants as well.

It is dubious whether any society has ever been truly pluralist in the sense that all groups which comprise it are on an equal footing of status, power, or rewards. Pluralism often disguises a social system in which one group dominates the upper classes (white Anglo-Saxon Protestants) and minority ethnic, religious, or racial groups are confined to the lower classes. The upper classes may ceremonially invoke the country's cultural heterogeneity, and delight in ethnic food, art, and music, but exclude the ethnic members themselves from their professions, country clubs, and neighborhoods. Bagels and lox for breakfast, soul food for lunch, and lasagne for dinner; but no Jews, blacks, or Italians on the professional and neighborhood turf! Pluralism has been a congenial model for the race segregationist as well, rationalizing the confinement of blacks to unskilled labor, segregated schools and neighborhoods.

In the case of sex, the pluralist model posits the necessity of traditional sex role differentiation between the sexes on the grounds of fundamental physiological and hence social differences between the sexes. This is the perspective subscribed to by most behavioral scientists, clinical psychologists, and psychoanalysts, despite the fact that the women they have studied and analyzed are the products of a society that systematically *produces* such sex differences through child rearing and schooling practices. . . .

Freudian theory has contributed to the assumption of innate sex differences on which recent scholars in psychology and sociology have built their case for the necessity of social role and status differentiation between the sexes. Freud codified the belief that men get more pleasure than women from sex in his theory of the sexual development of the female: the transition from an early stage in which girls experience the clitoris as the leading erogenous zone of their bodies to a mature stage in which vaginal orgasm provides the woman with her major sexual pleasure. Women who did not make this transition were then viewed as sexually "anaesthetic" and "psychosexually immature." Psychological theory often seems sterner and more resistant to change than the people to whom it is applied. It is incredible that the Freudian theory of female sexuality was retained for decades despite thousands of hours of intimate therapeutic data from women, only recently showing signs of weakening under the impact of research conducted by Masters and Johnson and reported in their *Human Sexual Response,* that there is no anatomical difference between clitoral and vaginal orgasm.

Implicit in both psychological theory of sex differences and the Freudian, vaginal orgasm theory was a basic assumption that women should be exclusively dependent on men for their sexual pleasure, hiding from view the realization that masturbation may be different from, but not necessarily less gratifying sexually than sexual intercourse. Much the same function has been served by the strong pressures to dissociate sex from maternity. Physicians have long known that nursing is associated with uterine contractions and have noted that male babies often have erections while nursing, but no one has suggested that the starry-eyed contentment of a nursing mother is a blend of genital as well as maternal pleasure. The cultural insistence upon separating sex from maternity, as the insistence that vaginal orgasm is the only "normal satisfaction" of a mature woman, serves the function of preventing women from seeing that they can find pleasure and fulfillment from themselves, other women, and their children and do not have to depend exclusively upon men for such gratification.

Coupled with this is the further assumption, peculiar to American society, that childbearing is the exclusive responsibility of the parents themselves, and not a community responsibility to assure every child a healthy physical and social development (as it is, for example, in East European countries, Israel, and Sweden).

This belief keeps women tied closely to the home for the most vigorous years of their adulthood. The "new" look to a woman's life span, now institutionalized by over one hundred centers for continuing education for women in the United States, does nothing to alter this basic assumption, but merely adapts to our lengthened life span. Women are urged to withdraw from outside obligations during the childbearing and rearing years and to return for further training and participation in the labor force when children reach an appropriate mature age. The consequences of such late return to active work away from the home are lower incomes, work at levels below the ability of the women, and withdrawal for the very years all studies show to be the peaks of creativity in work, their twenties and thirties.

Why does American society persist in maintaining erroneous myths concerning female sexuality, contrary to research evidence, as it does in urging women to believe their children's development requires their daily attendance upon them, again contrary to research evidence? I believe the answer lies in the economic demand that men work at persistent levels of high efficiency and creativity. To free men to do this requires a social arrangement in which the family system serves as the shock-absorbing handmaiden of the occupational system. The stimulation of women's desires for an affluent style of life and a bountiful maternity—to be eager and persistent consumers of goods and producers of babies—serves the function of adding continual pressure on men to be high earners. . . . As a result, the broad sweep of many an American woman's life span is caught by the transitions from Bill's daughter to John's wife to Johnny's mother and Billy's grandmother.

Behind the veneer of modern emancipation is a woman isolated in an apartment or suburban home, exclusively responsible for the care of young children, dependent on her husband for income, misled to believe that sex gratification is only possible via a vaginal orgasm simultaneous with male ejaculation, and urged to buy more and more clothes and household possessions, which she then takes more time but little pleasure in maintaining. Complementing the life of the woman in the pluralist model of sex roles, the American male is prodded to seek success and achievement in a competitive job world at the emotional cost of limited time or psychic energy for his marriage or his children, tempted by the same consumption-stimulating media and promises of easy credit, expected to uproot his family if a move is "good for his career," and ridiculed if he seeks to participate more extensively in home and child care as "unmanly."

The odds are heavily stacked against the pluralist model of society as a goal in terms of which racial, ethnic, or sex equality can be achieved.

The [assimilation] model anticipates that with time, the minority groups will be gradually absorbed into the mainstream of society by losing their distinguishing characteristics, acquiring the language, educational attainment, and occupational skills of the majority host culture. Concern for inequality along ethnic or racial lines is concentrated on the political, educational, and economic institutions of society. Little sociological interest or political concern is shown once men in the minority group are distributed throughout the occupational system in roughly the same proportion as mainstream males.

Feminist ideology is but one variant of the assimilation model, calling upon women to seek their place with men in the political and occupational world in sufficient numbers to eventually show a fifty-fifty distribution by sex in the prestigious occupations and political organizations of the society. The federal government has served as a pacesetter for the economy in urging the appointment and promotion of competent women to the highest civil service posts and encouraging private employers to follow the federal example by facilitating the movement of women into executive posts.

The feminist-assimilation model has an implicit fallacy, however. No amount of entreaty will yield an equitable distribution of women and men in the top strata of business and professional occupations, for the simple reason that the life men have led in these strata has been possible only because their own wives were leading traditional lives as homemakers, doing double parent and household duty, and carrying the major burden of civic responsibilities. If it were not for their wives in the background, successful men in American society would have to be single or childless. This is why so many professional women complain privately that what they most need in life is a "wife"!

The assimilation model also makes an assumption that the institutional structure of American society developed over decades by predominantly white Protestant males, constitutes the best of all possible worlds. Whether the call is to blacks or to women to join white men in the mainstream of American society, both racial integration and a feminist ideology accept the structure of American society as it now exists. The assimilation model rejects the psychological theses of innate racial or sex differences implicit in most versions of the pluralist model, but it accepts the social institutions formed by the ascendant group. This is precisely the assumption numerous blacks, women, and members of the younger generation have recently been questioning and rejecting.

The hybrid model of equality rejects both traditional psychological assumptions and the institutional structure we have inherited. It anticipates a society in which the lives of men and of whites will be different, not only women and blacks. In fact, it might be that this hybrid model would involve greater change in the role of men than of women, because institutional changes it would require involve a restructuring to bring the world of jobs and politics closer to the fulfillment of individual human needs for both creativity and fellowship. From this point of view, the values many young men and women subscribe to today are congenial to the hybrid model of equality: the desire for a more meaningful sense of community and a greater depth to personal relations across class, sex, and racial lines; a stress on human fellowship and individual scope for creativity rather than merely rationality and efficiency in our bureaucracies; heightened interest in the humanities and the social sciences from an activated value base; and a social responsibility commitment to medicine and law rather than a thirst for status by the younger generation in our time that are closer to the values and interests women have held than they are to the values and interests of men. They represent an ardent "no" to the image of society projected by the new crop of male technitronic futurists—a machine and consumption-oriented society that rewards technological prowess in a "plasticWasp-9-5america."

Because women have tended to play the passive, adaptive role in the past, they have not been prominent as social and political critics of American institutions. In fact, the traditional roles of women confined them to the most conservative institutions of the society: the family, the public schools, and the church. Women deviant enough to seek greater equality with men in professional, business, and academic life have tended to share the values of their masculine colleagues, while professional women who did not share these values have been quiet, either because they distrusted their own critical bent as a vestige of unwanted "womanliness," or because they feared exclusion from the masculine turf they have precariously established themselves on.

But there is a new ground swell in American society, which is a hopeful sign of a movement toward the hybrid model briefly sketched here. One finds it in women's liberation groups across the country, particularly on the university campus. I would predict, for example, that these young women, unlike their professional older sisters, will not bemoan the fact that academic women have been less "productive" than men, but will be critical of the criteria used to assess academic productivity. . . . The new breed of women will ask, as many young students are now demanding, that the quality of teaching, the degree of colleagueship with students, the extent of service to both an academic institution and its surrounding community, become part of the criteria on which the productivity of an academic man or woman is evaluated. No one has conducted research on academic productivity with this enlarged net of criteria, and it is a moot point whether men would show greater productivity than women if such criteria were applied. . . .

CONCLUSION

A *pluralist* model of social equality is implicitly a conservative goal, a descriptive model that accepts what exists at a given point in time as desirable and good. The *assimilation* model is implicitly a liberal goal, a Horatio Alger model that accepts the present structure of society as stable and desirable, and urges minority groups to accept the values and goals of the dominant group within that system as their own. The *hybrid* model is a radical goal which rejects the present structure of society and seeks instead a new breed of men and women and a new vision of the future. . . .

An analysis of sex equality goals may start with the reality of contemporary life, but soon requires an imaginative leap to a new conception of what a future good society should be. With the hybrid model of equality one envisages a future in which family, community, and play are valued on a par with politics and work for both sexes, for all the races, and for all social classes and nations which comprise the human family. We are on the brink not of the "end" of ideology, but its "beginning."

Marlene Dixon / *The Rise of Women's Liberation*

Marlene Dixon is a New Left sociologist whose dismissal from the University of Chicago in 1968 became a *cause célèbre*. She now teaches sociology at McGill University in Canada and is one of the most active spokeswomen of the burgeoning women's liberation movement. In this essay, she reviews the beginnings of the new feminism, analyzes its constituents, and examines marriage, labor, and male attitudes from the standpoint of women's oppression. Hers is an impassioned plea for radical change from the present society's false and damaging stereotypes to a new, authentic conception of humanity, both male and female.

From *Ramparts*, 8, 6 (December, 1969), pp. 57–64. Copyright Ramparts Magazine, Inc., 1969. By permission of the editors.

THE 1960's has been a decade of liberation; women have been swept up by that ferment along with blacks, Latins, American Indians, and poor whites—the whole soft underbelly of this society. As each oppressed group in turn discovered the nature of its oppression in American society, so women have discovered that they too thirst for free and fully human lives. The result has been the growth of a new women's movement, whose base encompasses poor black and poor white women on relief, working women exploited in the labor force, middle-class women incarcerated in the split-level dream house, college girls awakening to the fact that sexiness is not the crowning achievement in life, and movement women who have discovered that in a freedom movement they themselves are not free. In less than four years women have created a variety of organizations, from the nationally based middle-class National Organization of Women (NOW) to local radical and radical feminist groups in every major city in North America. The new movement includes caucuses within nearly every New Left group and within most professional associations in the social sciences. Ranging in politics from reform to revolution, it has produced critiques of almost every segment of American society and constructed an ideology that rejects every hallowed cultural assumption about the nature and role of women.

As is typical of a young movement, much of its growth has been underground. The papers and manifestoes written and circulated would surely comprise two very large volumes if published, but this literature is almost unknown outside of women's liberation. Nevertheless, where even a year ago organizing was slow and painful, with small cells of six or ten women, high turnover, and an uphill struggle against fear and resistance, in 1969 all that changed. Groups are growing up everywhere with women eager to hear a hard line, to articulate and express their own rage and bitterness. Moving about the country, I have found an electric atmosphere of excitement and responsiveness. Everywhere there are doubts, stirrings, a desire to listen, to find out what it's all about. The extent to which groups have become politically radical is astounding. A year ago the movement stressed male chauvinism and psychological op-

pression; now the emphasis is on understanding the economic
and social roots of women's oppression, and the analyses range
from social democracy to Marxism. But the most striking change
of all in the last year has been the loss of fear. Women are no
longer afraid that their rebellion will threaten their very identity
as women. They are not frightened by their own militancy, but
liberated by it. Women's liberation is an idea whose time has
come.

The old women's movement burned itself out in the frantic
decade of the 1920's. After a hundred years of struggle, women
won a battle, only to lose the campaign: the vote was obtained,
but the new millennium did not arrive. Women got the vote and
achieved a measure of legal emancipation, but the real social
and cultural barriers to full equality for women remained
untouched.

For over thirty years the movement remained buried in its own
ashes. Women were born and grew to maturity virtually ignorant
of their own history of rebellion, aware only of a caricature of
blue-stockings and suffragettes. Even as increasing numbers of
women were being driven into the labor force by the brutal
conditions of the 1930's and by the massive drain of men into the
military in the 1940's, the old ideal remained: a woman's place
was in the home and behind her man. As the war ended and men
returned to resume their jobs in factories and offices, women were
forced back to the kitchen and nursery with a vengeance. This
story has been repeated after each war and the reason is clear:
women form a flexible, cheap labor pool which is essential to a
capitalist system. When labor is scarce, they are forced onto the
labor market. When labor is plentiful, they are forced out.
Women and blacks have provided a reserve army of unemployed
workers, benefiting capitalists and the stable male white working
class alike. Yet the system imposes untold suffering on the victims, blacks and women, through low wages and chronic un-
employment.

With the end of the war the average age at marriage declined,
the average size of families went up, and the suburban migration
began in earnest. The political conservatism of the 1950's was
echoed in a social conservatism which stressed a Victorian ideal

of the woman's life: a full womb and selfless devotion to husband and children.

As the bleak decade played itself out, however, three important social developments emerged which were to make a rebirth of the women's struggle inevitable. First, women came to make up more than a third of the labor force, the number of working women being twice the prewar figure. Yet the market increase in female employment did nothing to better the position of women, who were more occupationally disadvantaged in the 1960's than they had been twenty-five years earlier. Rather than moving equally into all sectors of the occupational structure, they were being forced into the low-paying service, clerical and semi-skilled categories. In 1940, women had held 45 per cent of all professional and technical positions; in 1967, they held only 37 per cent. The proportion of women in service jobs meanwhile rose from 50 to 55 per cent.

Second, the intoxicating wine of marriage and suburban life was turning sour; a generation of women woke up to find their children grown and a life (roughly thirty more productive years) of housework and bridge parties stretching out before them like a wasteland. For many younger women, the empty drudgery they saw in the suburban life was a sobering contradiction to adolescent dreams of romantic love and the fulfilling role of woman as wife and mother.

Third, a growing civil rights movement was sweeping thousands of young men and women into a moral crusade—a crusade which harsh political experience was to transmute into the New Left. The American Dream was riven and tattered in Mississippi and finally napalmed in Viet-Nam. Young Americans were drawn not to Levittown, but to Berkeley, the Haight-Ashbury, and the East Village. Traditional political ideologies and cultural myths, sexual mores and sex roles with them, began to disintegrate in an explosion of rebellion and protest.

The three major groups which make up the new women's movement—working women, middle-class married women and students—bring very different kinds of interests and objectives to women's liberation. Working women are most concerned with the economic issues of guaranteed employment, fair wages, job discrimination, and child care. Their most immediate oppression is rooted in industrial capitalism and felt directly through the vicissitudes of an exploitative labor market.

Middle-class women, oppressed by the psychological mutilation and injustice of institutionalized segregation, discrimination, and imposed inferiority, are most sensitive to the dehumanizing consequences of severely limited lives. Usually well educated and capable, these women are rebelling against being forced to trivialize their lives, to live vicariously through husbands and children.

Students, as unmarried middle-class girls, have been most sensitized to the sexual exploitation of women. They have experienced the frustration of one-way relationships in which the girl is forced into a "wife" and companion role with none of the supposed benefits of marriage. Young women have increasingly rebelled not only against passivity and dependency in their relationships but also against the notion that they must function as sexual objects, being defined in purely sexual rather than human terms, and being forced to package and sell themselves as commodities on the sex market.

Each group represents an independent aspect of the total institutionalized oppression of women. Their differences are those of emphasis and immediate interest rather than of fundamental goals. All women suffer from economic exploitation, from psychological deprivation, and from exploitative sexuality. Within women's liberation there is a growing understanding that the common oppression of women provides the basis for uniting across class and race lines to form a powerful and radical movement.

Clearly, for the liberation of women to become a reality it is necessary to destroy the ideology of male supremacy which asserts the biological and social inferiority of women in order to justify massive institutionalized oppression. Yet we all know that many women are as loud in their disavowal of this oppression as are the men who chant the litany of "a woman's place is in the home and behind her man." In fact, women are as trapped in their false consciousness as were the mass of blacks twenty years ago, and for much the same reason.

As blacks were defined and limited socially by their color, so women are defined and limited by their sex. While blacks, it was argued, were preordained by God or nature, or both, to be hewers of wood and drawers of water, so women are destined to bear and rear children, and to sustain their husbands with obedience and compassion. The Sky-God tramples through the heavens and the Earth/Mother-Goddess is always flat on her back with her legs spread, putting out for one and all.

Indeed, the phenomenon of male chauvinism can only be understood when it is perceived as a form of racism, based on stereotypes drawn from a deep belief in the biological inferiority of women. The so-called "black analogy" is no analogy at all; it is the same social process that is at work, a process which both justifies and helps perpetuate the exploitation of one group of human beings by another.

The very stereotypes that express the society's belief in the biological inferiority of women recall the images used to justify the oppression of blacks. The nature of women, like that of slaves, is depicted as dependent, incapable of reasoned thought, childlike in its simplicity and warmth, martyred in the role of mother, and mystical in the role of sexual partner. In its benevolent form, the inferior position of women results in paternalism; in its malevolent form, a domestic tyranny which can be unbelievably brutal.

It has taken over fifty years to discredit the scientific and social "proof" which once gave legitimacy to the myths of black racial inferiority. Today most people can see that the theory of the genetic inferiority of blacks is absurd. Yet few are shocked by the fact that scientists are still busy "proving" the biological inferiority of women.

In recent years, in which blacks have led the struggle for liberation, the emphasis on racism has focused only upon racism against blacks. The fact that "racism" has been practiced against many groups other than blacks has been pushed into the background. Indeed, a less forceful but more accurate term for the phenomenon would be "Social Darwinism." It was the opinion of the Social Darwinists that in the natural course of things the "fit" succeed (i.e., oppress) and the "unfit" (i.e., the biologically inferior) sink to the bottom. According to this view, the very fact of a group's oppression proves its inferiority and the inevitable correctness of its low position. In this way each successive immigrant group coming to America was decked out in the garments of "racial" or biological inferiority until the group was sufficiently assimilated, whereupon Anglo-Saxon venom would turn on a new group filling up the space at the bottom. Now two groups remain, neither of which has been assimilated according to the classic American pattern: the "visibles"—blacks and women. It is equally true for both: "It won't wear off."

Yet the greatest obstacle facing those who would organize women remains women's belief in their own inferiority. Just as all subject populations are controlled by their acceptance of the rightness of their own status, so women remain subject because they believe in the rightness of their own oppression. This dilemma is not a fortuitous one, for the entire society is geared to socialize women to believe in and adopt as immutable necessity their traditional and inferior role. From earliest training to the grave, women are constrained and propagandized. Spend an evening at the movies or watching television, and you will see a grotesque figure called woman presented in a hundred variations upon the themes of "children, church, kitchen" or "the chick sex-pot."

For those who believe in the "rights of mankind," the "dignity of man," consider that to make a woman a person, a human being in her own right, you would have to change her sex: imagine Stokely Carmichael "prone and silent"; imagine Mark Rudd as a Laugh-In girl; picture Rennie Davis as Miss America. Such contradictions as these show how pervasive and deep-rooted is the cultural contempt for women, how difficult it is to imagine a woman as a serious human being, or conversely, how empty and degrading is the image of woman that floods the culture.

Countless studies have shown that black acceptance of white stereotypes leads to mutilated identity, to alienation, to rage and self-hatred. Human beings cannot bear in their own hearts the contradictions of those who hold them in contempt. The ideology of male supremacy and its effect upon women merits as serious study as has been given to the effects of prejudice upon Jews, blacks, and immigrant groups.

It is customary to shame those who would draw the parallel between women and blacks by a great show of concern and chest beating over the suffering of black people. Yet this response itself reveals a refined combination of white middle-class guilt and male chauvinism, for it overlooks several essential facts. For example, the most oppressed group within the feminine population is made up of black women, many of whom take a dim view of the black male intellectual's adoption of white male attitudes of sexual superiority (an irony too cruel to require comment). . . .

Among whites, women remain the most oppressed—and the most unorganized—group. Although they constitute a potential mass base for the radical movement, in terms of movement priorities they are ignored; indeed they might as well be invisible. Far from being an accident, this omission is a direct outgrowth of the solid male supremist beliefs of white radical and left-liberal men. Even now, faced with both fact and agitation, leftist men find the idea of placing any serious priority upon women so outrageous, such a degrading notion, that they respond with a virulence far out of proportion to the modest requests of movement women. This only shows that women must stop wasting their time worrying about the chauvinism of men in the movement and focus instead on their real priority: organizing women.

The institution of marriage is the chief vehicle for the perpetuation of the oppression of women; it is through the role of wife that the subjugation of women is maintained. . . .

Looking at marriage from a detached point of view one may well ask why anyone gets married, much less women. One answer lies in the economics of women's position, for women are so occupationally limited that drudgery in the home is considered to be infinitely superior to drudgery in the factory. Secondly, women themselves have no independent social status. Indeed, there is no clearer index of the social worth of a woman in this society than the fact that she has none in her own right. A woman is first defined by the man to whom she is attached, but more particularly by the man she marries, and secondly by the children she bears and rears—hence the anxiety over sexual attractiveness, the frantic scramble for boy friends and husbands. Having obtained and married a man the race is then on to have children, in order that their attractiveness and accomplishments may add more social worth. In a woman, not having children is seen as an incapacity somewhat akin to impotence in a man.

Beneath all of the pressures of the sexual market place and the marital status game, however, there is a far more sinister organization of economic exploitation and psychological mutilation. The housewife role, usually defined in terms of the biological duty of a woman to reproduce and her "innate" suitability for a nurturant and companionship role, is actually crucial to industrial capitalism in an advanced state of technological development. In fact, the housewife . . . provides, unpaid, absolutely essential services and labor. In turn, her assumption of all household duties makes it possible for the man to spend the majority of his time at the work place. . . . Margaret Benston, a radical women's liberation leader, points out: "In sheer quantity, household labor, including child care, constitutes a huge amount of socially necessary production. Nevertheless, in a society based on commodity production, it is not usually considered even as 'real work' since it is outside of trade and the market place. This assignment of household work as the function of a special category 'women' means that this group *does* stand in a different relationship to production. . . . The material basis for the inferior status of women is to be found in just this definition of women. In a society in which money determines value, women are a group who work outside the money economy. Their work is not worth money, is therefore valueless, is therefore not even real work. And women themselves, who do this valueless work, can hardly be expected to be worth as much as men, who work for money."

Women are essential to the economy not only as free labor, but also as consumers. The American system of capitalism depends for its survival on the consumption of vast amounts of socially wasteful goods, and a prime target for the unloading of this waste is the housewife. She is the purchasing agent for the family, but beyond that she is eager to buy because her own identity depends on her accomplishments as a consumer and her ability to satisfy the wants of her husband and children. This is not, of course, to say that she has any power in the economy. Although she spends the wealth, she does not own or control it—it simply passes through her hands.

In addition to their role as housewives and consumers, increasing numbers of women are taking outside employment. These women leave the home to join an exploited labor force, only to return at night to assume the double burden of housework on top of wage work—that is, they are forced to work at two full-time jobs. No man is required or expected to take on such a burden. The result: two workers from one household in the labor force with no cutback in essential female functions—three for the price of two, quite a bargain.

Frederick Engels, now widely read in women's liberation, argues that, regardless of her status in the larger society, within the context of the family the woman's relationship to the man is one of proletariat to bourgeoisie. One consequence of this class division in the family is to weaken the capacity of men and women oppressed by the society to struggle together against it.

In all classes and groups, the institution of marriage functions to a greater or lesser degree to oppress women; the unity of women of different classes hinges upon our understanding of that common oppression. The nineteenth-century women's movement refused to deal with marriage and sexuality, and chose instead to fight for the vote and elevate the feminine mystique to a political ideology. That decision retarded the movement for decades. But . . . there now exist alternatives to marriage. The most original and creative politics of the women's movement has come from a direct confrontation with the issue of marriage and sexuality. The cultural revolution—experimentation with life-styles, communal living, collective child-rearing—have all come from the rebellion against dehumanized sexual relationships, against the notion of women as sexual commodities, against the constriction and spiritual strangulation inherent in the role of wife.

Lessons have been learned from the failures of the earlier movement as well. The feminine mystique is no longer mistaken for politics, nor gaining the vote for winning human rights. Women are now all together at the bottom of the work world, and the basis exists for a common focus of struggle for all women in American society. It remains for the movement to understand this, to avoid the mistakes of the past, to respond creatively to the possibilities of the present.

Women's oppression, although rooted in the institution of marriage, does not stop at the kitchen or the bedroom door. . . .

Women have always represented the most exploited sector of the industrial labor force. Child and female labor were introduced during the early stages of industrial capitalism, at a time when most men were gainfully employed in crafts. As industrialization developed and craft jobs were eliminated, men entered the industrial labor force, driving women and children into the lowest categories of work and pay. Indeed, the position of women and children industrial workers was so pitiful, and their wages so small, that the craft unions refused to organize them. Even when women organized themselves and engaged in militant strikes and labor agitation—from the shoemakers of Lynn, Massachusetts, to the International Ladies' Garment Workers and their great strike of 1909—male unionists continued to ignore their needs. As a result of this male supremacy in the unions, women remain essentially unorganized, despite the fact that they are becoming an ever larger part of the labor force.

The trend is clearly toward increasing numbers of women entering the work force: women represented 55 per cent of the growth of the total labor force in 1962, and the number of working women rose from 16.9 million in 1957 to 24 million in 1962. There is every indication that the number of women in the labor force will continue to grow as rapidly in the future.

Job discrimination against women exists in all sectors of work, even in occupations which are predominantly made up of women. This discrimination is reinforced in the field of education, where women are being short-changed at a time when the job market demands higher educational levels. In 1962, for example, while women constituted 53 per cent of the graduating high school class, only 42 per cent of the entering college class were women. Only one in three people who received a B.A. or M.A. in that year was a woman, and only one in ten who received a Ph.D. was a woman. These figures represent a decline in educational achievement for women since the 1930's, when women received two out of five of the B.A. and M.A. degrees given, and one out of seven of the Ph.D.'s. While there has been a dramatic increase in the number of people, including women, who go to college, women have not kept pace with men in terms of educational achievement. Furthermore, women have lost ground in professional employment. In 1960 only 22 per cent of the faculty and other professional staff at colleges and universities were women—down from 28 per cent in 1949, 27 per cent in 1930, 26 per cent in 1920. 1960 does beat 1919 with only 20 per cent—"you've come a long way, baby"—right back to where you started! In other professional categories: 10 per cent of all scientists are women, 7 per cent of all physicians, 3 per cent of all lawyers, and 1 per cent of all engineers.

Even when women do obtain an education, in many cases it does them little good. . . . Most women are forced to work at clerical jobs, for which they are paid, on the average, $1600 less per year than men doing the same work. Working-class women in the service and operative (semi-skilled) categories, making up 30 per cent of working women, are paid $1900 less per year on the average than are men. Of all working women, only 13 per cent are professionals (including low-pay and low-status work such as teaching, nursing and social work), and they earn $2600 less per year than do professional men. Household workers, the lowest category of all, are predominantly women (over 2 million) and predominantly black and third world, earning for their labor barely over $1000 per year.

. . . While women might passively accept low status jobs, limited opportunities for advancement, and discrimination in the factory, office and university, they choke finally on the daily fact that the male worker next to them earns more, and usually does less. In 1965 the median wage or salary income of year-round full-time women workers was only 60 per cent that of men, a 4 per cent loss since 1955. Twenty-nine per cent of working women earned less than $3000 a year as compared with 11 per cent of the men; 43 per cent of the women earned from $3000 to $5000 a year as compared with 19 per cent of the men; and 9 per cent of the women earned $7000 or more as compared with 43 per cent of the men.

What most people do not know is that in certain respects, women suffer more than do non-white men, and that black and third world women suffer most of all. . . .

Women, regardless of race, are more disadvantaged than are men, including non-white men. White women earn $2600 less than white men and $1500 less than non-white men. The brunt of the inequality is carried by 2.5 million non-white women, 94 per cent of whom are black. They earn $3800 less than white men, $1900 less than non-white men, and $1200 less than white women.

There is no more bitter paradox in the racism of this country than that the white man, articulating the male supremacy of the white male middle class, should provide the rationale for the oppression of black women by black men. Black women constitute the largest minority in the United States, and they are the most disadvantaged group in the labor force. The further oppression of black women will not liberate black men, for black women were never the oppressors of their men—that is a myth of the liberal white man. The oppression of black men comes from institutionalized racism and economic exploitation: from the world of the white man. . . .

The percentage of black working women has always been proportionately greater than that of white women. In 1900, 41 per cent of black women were employed, as compared to 17 per cent for white women. In 1963, the proportion of black women employed was still a fourth greater than that of whites. In 1960, 44 per cent of black married women with children under six years were in the labor force, in contrast to 29 per cent for white women. While job competition requires ever higher levels of education, the bulk of illiterate women are black. On the whole, black women—who often have the greatest need for employment—are the most discriminated against in terms of opportunity. Forced by an oppressive and racist society to carry unbelievably heavy economic and social burdens, black women stand at the bottom of that society, doubly marked by the caste signs of color and sex.

The rise of new agitation for the occupational equality of women also coincided with the re-entry of the "lost generation"—

the housewives of the 1950's—into the job market. Women from middle class backgrounds, faced with an "empty nest" (children grown or in school) and a widowed or divorced rate of one-fourth to one-third of all marriages, returned to the work place in large numbers. But once there they discovered that women, middle class or otherwise, are the last hired, the lowest paid, the least often promoted, and the first fired. Furthermore, women are more likely to suffer job discrimination on the basis of age, so the widowed and divorced suffer particularly, even though their economic need to work is often urgent. Age discrimination also means that the option of work after child-rearing is limited. Even highly qualified older women find themselves forced into low-paid, unskilled or semi-skilled work—if they are lucky enough to find a job in the first place.

The realities of the work world for most middle class women— that they become members of the working class, like it or not— are understandably distant to many young men and women in college who have never had to work, and who tend to think of the industrial "proletariat" as a revolutionary force, to the exclusion of "bourgeois" working women. Their image of the "pampered middle class woman" is factually incorrect and politically naïve. It is middle class women forced into working class life who are often the first to become conscious of the contradiction between the "American Dream" and their daily experience.

Faced with discrimination on the job—after being forced into the lower levels of the occupational structure—millions of women are inescapably presented with the fundamental contradictions in their unequal treatment and their massive exploitation. The rapid growth of women's liberation as a movement is related in part to the exploitation of working women in all occupational categories.

Male supremacy, marriage, and the structure of wage labor— each of these aspects of women's oppression has been crucial to the resurgence of the women's struggle. It must be abundantly clear that radical social change must occur before there can be significant improvement in the social position of women. Some form of socialism is a minimum requirement, considering the changes that must come in the institutions of marriage and the family alone. The intrinsic radicalism of the struggle for women's liberation necessarily links women with all other oppressed groups.

The heart of the movement, as in all freedom movements, rests in women's knowledge, whether articulated or still only an illness without a name, that they are not inferior—not chicks, nor bunnies, nor quail, nor cows, nor bitches, nor ass, nor meat. . . . Women know that male supremacy is a lie. They know they are not animals or sexual objects or commodities. They know their lives are mutilated, because they see within themselves a promise of creativity and personal integration. Feeling the contradiction between the essentially creative and self-actualizing human being within her, and the cruel and degrading less-than-human role she is compelled to play, a woman begins to perceive the falseness of what her society has forced her to be. And once she perceives this, she knows that she must fight.

Women must learn the meaning of rage, the violence that liberates the human spirit. The rhetoric of invective is an equally essential stage, for in discovering and venting their rage against the enemy—and the enemy in everyday life is men—women also experience the justice of their own violence. They learn the first lessons in their own latent strength. Women must learn to know themselves as revolutionaries. They must become hard and strong in their determination, while retaining their humanity and tenderness.

There is a rage that impels women into a total commitment to women's liberation. That ferocity stems from a denial of mutilation; it is a cry for life, a cry for the liberation of the spirit. Roxanne Dunbar, surely one of the most impressive women in the movement, conveys the feelings of many: "We are damaged— we women, we oppressed, we disinherited. There are very few who are not damaged, and they rule. . . . The oppressed trust those who rule more than they trust themselves, because self-contempt emerges from powerlessness. Anyway, few oppressed people believe that life could be much different. . . . We are damaged and we have the right to hate and have contempt and to kill and to scream. But for what? . . . Do we want the oppressor to admit he is wrong, to withdraw his misuse of us? He is only too happy to admit guilt—then do nothing but try to absorb and exorcize the new thought. . . . That does not make up for what I have lost, what I never had, and what all those others who are worse off than I never had. . . . Nothing will compensate for the irreparable harm it has done to my sisters. . . . How could we possibly settle for anything remotely less, even take a crumb in the meantime less, than total annihilation of a system which systematically destroys half its people."

Susan Lydon / *Understanding Orgasm*

Aristotle is said to have concluded—on the basis of pure theory —that women have fewer teeth than men. Apparently he never checked to see. In this essay, Susan Lydon shows that Freud's pontifical speculations regarding female sexuality were scarcely sounder than Aristotle's about female denture—but they have been far more fateful. They have, in fact, been among the cruelest and most effective means of obfuscating women's efforts to break free of their man-made identity. Along with Ann Koedt's pamphlet, "The Myth of the Vaginal Orgasm," Lydon's essay has been one of the most influential writings on the sexual aspect of women's liberation.

From *Ramparts* (December, 1968), pp. 59–63. Copyright Ramparts Magazine, Inc., 1968. By permission of the editors.

TIRESIAS, WHO had been both man and woman, was asked, as Ovid's legend goes, to mediate in a dispute between Jove and Juno as to which sex got more pleasure from lovemaking. Tiresias unhesitatingly answered that women did. Yet in the intervening 2000 years between Ovid's time and our own, a mythology has been built up which not only holds the opposite to be true, but has made this belief an unswerving ideology dictating the quality of relations between the sexes. Women's sexuality, defined by men to benefit men, has been downgraded and perverted, repressed and channeled, denied and abused until women themselves, thoroughly convinced of their sexual inferiority to men, would probably be dumbfounded to learn that there is scientific proof that Tiresias was indeed right.

The myth was codified by Freud as much as anyone else. In *Three Essays on the Theory of Sexuality,* Freud formulated his basic ideas concerning feminine sexuality: for little girls, the leading erogenous zone in their bodies is the clitoris; in order for the transition to womanhood to be successful, the clitoris must abandon its sexual primacy to the vagina; women in whom this transition has not been complete remain clitorally oriented, or "sexually anaesthetic," and "psychosexually immature." In the context of Freud's total psychoanalytic view of women—that they are not whole human beings but mutilated males who long all their lives for a penis and must struggle to reconcile themselves to its lack—the requirement of a transfer of erotic sensation from clitoris to vagina became a *prima facie* case for their inevitable sexual inferiority. In Freud's logic, those who struggle to become what they are not must be inferior to that to which they aspire.

Freud himself admitted near the end of his life that his knowledge of women was inadequate. "If you want to know more about femininity, you must interrogate your own experience, or turn to the poets, or wait until science can give you more profound and more coherent information," he said; he also hoped the female psychoanalysts who followed him would be able to find out more. But the post-Freudians adhered rigidly to the doctrine of the master, and, as with most of his work, what Freud hoped would be taken as a thesis for future study became instead a kind of canon law.

While the neo-Freudians haggled over the correct reading of the Freudian bible, watered-down Freudianism was wending its way into the cultural mythology via Broadway plays, novels, popular magazines, social scientists, marriage counselors and experts of various kinds who found it useful in projecting desired images of woman. The superiority of the vaginal over the clitoral orgasm was particularly useful as a theory since it provided a convenient basis for categorization: clitoral women were deemed immature, neurotic, bitchy and masculine; women who had vaginal orgasms were maternal, feminine, mature, and normal. Though frigidity should technically be defined as total inability to achieve orgasm, the orthodox Freudians (and pseudo-Freudians) preferred to define it as inability to achieve vaginal orgasm, by which definition, in 1944, Edmond Bergler adjudged between 70 and 80 per cent of all women frigid. The clitoral versus vaginal debate raged hot and heavy among the sexologists—Kinsey's writings stressed the importance of the clitoris to female orgasm and contradicted Bergler's statistics—but it became clear that there was something indispensable to society in the Freudian view which allowed it to remain unchallenged in the public consciousness.

In 1966, Dr. William H. Masters and Mrs. Virginia E. Johnson published *Human Sexual Response*, a massive clinical study of the physiology of sex. Briefly and simply, the Masters and Johnson conclusions about the female orgasm, based on observation of and interviews with 487 women, were these:

1) That the dichotomy of vaginal and clitoral orgasms is entirely false. Anatomically, all orgasms are centered in the clitoris, whether they result from direct manual pressure applied to the clitoris, indirect pressure resulting from the thrusting of penis during intercourse, or generalized sexual stimulation of other erogenous zones like the breasts.

2) That women are naturally multiorgasmic; that is, if a woman is immediately stimulated following orgasm, she is likely to experience several orgasms in rapid succession. This is not an exceptional occurrence, but one of which most women are capable.

3) That while women's orgasms do not vary in kind, they vary

in intensity. The most intense orgasms experienced by the research subjects were by masturbatory manual stimulation, followed in intensity by manual stimulation by the partner; the least intense orgasms were experienced during intercourse.

4) That there is an "infinite variety in female sexual response" as regards intensity and duration of orgasms.

To anyone acquainted with the body of existing knowledge of feminine sexuality, the Masters and Johnson findings were truly revolutionary and liberating in the extent to which they demolished the established myths. Yet two years after the study was published, it seems hardly to have made any impact at all. Certainly it is not for lack of information that the myths persist; *Human Sexual Response,* despite its weighty scientific language, was an immediate best seller, and popular paperbacks explicated it to millions of people in simpler language and at a cheaper price. The myths remain because a male-dominated American culture has a vested interest in their continuance.

Before Masters and Johnson, men defined feminine sexuality in a way as favorable to themselves as possible. If woman's pleasure was obtained through the vagina, then she was totally dependent on the man's erect penis to achieve orgasm; she would receive her satisfaction only as a concomitant of man's seeking his. With the clitoral orgasm, woman's sexual pleasure was independent of the male's, and she could seek her satisfaction as aggressively as the man sought his, a prospect which didn't appeal to too many men. The definition of feminine sexuality as normally vaginal, in other words, was a part of keeping women down, of making them sexually as well as economically, socially and politically subservient.

In retrospect, particularly with the additional perspective of our own times, Freud's theory of feminine sexuality appears an historical rationalization for the realities of Victorian society. A prisoner of the Victorian ethos, Freud had to play the paterfamilias. Freud's analysis implied that woman's low status had not been conferred upon her by men, but by God, who created her without a penis.

The superiority of the vaginal orgasm seems almost a demoniac determination on Freud's part to complete the Victorians' repression of feminine eroticism, to stigmatize the remaining vestiges of pleasure felt by women and thus make them unacceptable to the women themselves. For there were still women whose sexuality hadn't been completely destroyed, as evidenced by one Dr. Isaac Brown Baker, a surgeon who performed numerous clitoridectomies on women to prevent the sexual excitement which, he was convinced, caused "insanities," "catalepsy," "hysteria," "epilepsy" and other diseases. The Victorians needed to repress sexuality for the success of Western industrialized society; in particular, the total repression of woman's sexuality was crucial to ensure her subjugation. So the Victorians honored only that aspect of sexuality which was necessary to the survival of the species—the male ejaculation; made women submissive to sex by creating a mystique of the sanctity of motherhood; and, supported by Freud, passed on to us the heritage of the double standard.

When Kinsey laid to rest the part of the double standard that maintained women got no pleasure at all from sex, everyone cried out that there was a sexual revolution afoot. But such talk, as usual, was deceptive. Morality, outside the marriage bed, remained the same, and children were socialized as though Kinsey had never described what they would be like when they grew up. Boys were taught that they should get their sex where they could find it, "go as far" as they could. On the old assumption that women were asexual creatures, girls were taught that since they needed sex less than boys did, it was up to them to impose sexual restraints. In whatever sex education adolescents did manage to receive, they were told that men had penises and women vaginas; the existence of the clitoris was not mentioned, and *pleasure* in sex was never discussed at all.

Adolescent boys growing up begging for sexual crumbs from girls frightened for their "reputations"—a situation that remains unchanged to this day—hardly constitutes the vanguard of a sexual revolution. However, the marriage manual craze that followed Kinsey assumed that a lifetime of psychological destruction could, with the aid of a little booklet, be abandoned after marriage, and that husband and wife should be able to make sure that the wife was not robbed of her sexual birthright to orgasm, just so long

as it was *vaginal* (though the marriage manuals did rather reluctantly admit that since the clitoris was the most sexually sensitive organ in the female body, a little clitoral stimulation was in
order), and so long as their orgasms were *simultaneous*.

The effect of the marriage manuals of course ran counter to
their ostensible purpose. Under the guise of frankness and sexual
liberation, they dictated prudery and restraint. Sex was made so
mechanized, detached and intellectual that it was robbed of its
sensuality. Man became a spectator of his own sexual experience. And the marriage manuals put new pressure on women.
The swing was from repression to preoccupation with the orgasm.
Men took the marriage manuals to mean that their sexuality
would be enhanced by bringing women to orgasm and, again co-
opting feminine sexuality for their own ends, they put pressure
on women to perform. The marriage manuals' endorsement of the
desirability of vaginal orgasm insured that women would be
asked not only, "Did you come?" but also, "Did you conform to
Freud's conception of a psychosexually mature woman, and thereby validate my masculinity?"

Appearances notwithstanding, the age-old taboos against conversation about personal sexual experience haven't yet been
broken down. This reticence has allowed the mind-manipulators
of the media to create myths of sexual supermen and super-
women. So the bed becomes a competitive arena, where men
and women measure themselves against these mythical rivals,
while simultaneously trying to live up to the ecstasies promised
them by the marriage manuals and the fantasies of the media
("If the earth doesn't move for me, I must be missing something"). Our society has made sex a sport, with its record-break-
ers, its judges, its rules and its spectators.

As anthropologists have shown, woman's sexual response is
culturally conditioned; historically, women defer to whatever
model of their sexuality is offered them by men. So the sad
thing for women is that they have participated in the destruction of their own eroticism. Women have helped make the
vaginal orgasm into a status symbol in a male-dictated system
of values. A woman would now perceive her preference for
clitoral orgasm as a "secret shame," ignominious in the eyes of

other women as well as those of men. This internalization can be seen in literature: Mary McCarthy and Doris Lessing's writings on orgasm do not differ substantially from Ernest Hemingway's, and Simone de Beauvoir, in *The Second Sex,* refers to vaginal orgasm as the only "normal satisfaction."

One factor that has made this possible is that female sexuality is subtle and delicate, conditioned as much by the emotions as by physiology and sociology. Masters and Johnson proved that the orgasm experienced during intercourse, the misnamed vaginal orgasm, did not differ *anatomically* from the clitoral orgasm. But this should not be seen as their most significant contribution to the sexual emancipation of women. A difference remains in the *subjective* experience of orgasm during intercourse and orgasm apart from intercourse. In the complex of emotional factors affecting feminine sexuality, there is a whole panoply of pleasures: the pleasure of being penetrated and filled by a man, the pleasure of sexual communication, the pleasure of affording a man his orgasm, the erotic pleasure that exists even when sex is not terminated by orgasmic release. Masters and Johnson's real contribution was to show this "infinite variety in female sexual response"; that one experience is not better than another, but merely different.

There is no doubt that Masters and Johnson were fully aware of the implications of their study to the sexual liberation of women. As they wrote, "With orgasmic physiology established, the human female now has an undeniable opportunity to develop realistically her own sexual response levels." Two years later this statement seems naïve and entirely too optimistic. Certainly the sexual problems of our society will never be solved until there is real and unfeigned equality between men and women. This idea is usually misconstrued: sexual liberation for women is wrongly understood to mean that women will adopt all the forms of masculine sexuality. As in the whole issue of women's liberation, that's really not the point. Women don't aspire to imitate the mistakes of men in sexual matters, to view sexual experiences as conquest and ego-enhancement, to use other people to serve their own ends. But if the Masters and Johnson material is allowed to filter into the public consciousness, hopefully to replace the enshrined Freudian myths, then woman at long last will be allowed to take the first step toward her emancipation: to define and enjoy the forms of her own sexuality.

Patricia Robinson / *Poor Black Women,* and A Collective Statement, *Black Sisters*

Patricia Robinson has been a psychiatric social worker in the Boston area and now has a private practice in psychotherapy in New York. She has also spent several years doing voluntary therapy for poor black families and has been a correspondent for the *Afro-American.* The following essay and collective statement were circulated among women in 1968 as a reply to black men's argument that the promulgation of birth control in black communities is a form of genocide. These were among the first widely read and discussed analyses by poor black women of their own domination, not only by white capitalist society, but by their own black men.

POOR BLACK WOMEN

IT IS time to speak to the whole question of the position of poor black women in this society and in this historical period of

From *Poor Black Women* (Boston, New England Free Press, 1968). Reprinted by permission of the author.

revolution and counterrevolution. We have . . . some very concrete points.

First, that the class hierarchy as seen from the poor black woman's position is one of white male in power, followed by the white female, then the black male and lastly the black female.

Historically, the myth in the black world is that there are only two free people in the United States, the white man and the black woman. The myth was established by the black man in the long period of his frustration when he longed to be free to have the material and social advantages of his oppressor, the white man. On examination of the myth, this so-called freedom was based on the sexual prerogatives taken by the white man on the black female. It was fantasied by the black man that she enjoyed it.

The black woman was needed and valued by the white female as a domestic. The black female diluted much of the actual oppression of the white female by the white male. With the help of the black woman, the white woman had free time from mother and housewife responsibilities and could escape her domestic prison overseered by the white male.

The poor black woman still occupies the position of a domestic in this society, rising no higher than public welfare, when the frustrated male deserts her and the children. (Public welfare was instituted primarily for poor whites during the depression of the thirties to stave off their rising revolutionary violence. It was considered as a temporary stop-gap only.)

The poor black male deserted the poor black female and fled to the cities where he made his living by his wits—hustling. The black male did not question the kind of society he lived in other than on the basis of racism: "The white man won't let me up 'cause I'm black!" Other rationalizations included blaming the black woman, which has been a much described phenomenon. The black man wanted to take the master's place and all that went with it.

Simultaneously, the poor black woman did not question the social and economic system. She saw her main problem as described in the accompanying article—social, economic and psychological oppression by the black man. But awareness in this case has moved to a second phase and exposes an important fact in the whole process of oppression. It takes two to oppress, a proper dialectical perspective to examine at this point in our movement.

An examination of the process of oppression in any or all of its forms shows simply that at least two parties are involved. The need for the white man, particularly, to oppress others reveals his own anxiety and inadequacy about his own maleness and humanity. Many black male writers have eloquently analyzed this social and psychological fact. Generally a feeling of inadequacy can be traced to all those who desperately need power and authority over others throughout history.

In other words, one's concept of oneself becomes based on one's class or power position in a hierarchy. Any endangering of this power position brings on a state of madness and irrationality within the individual which exposes the basic fear and insecurity beneath—politically speaking, the imperialists are paper tigers.

But the oppressor must have the cooperation of the oppressed, of those he must feel better than. The oppressed and the damned are placed in an inferior position by force of arms, physical strength, and later, by threats of such force. But the long-time maintenance of power over others is secured by psychological manipulation and seduction. The oppressed must begin to believe in the divine right and position of kings, the inherent right of an elite to rule, the supremacy of a class or an ethnic group, the power of such condensed wealth as money and private property to give to its owners high social status. So a gigantic and complex myth has been woven by those who have power in this society of the inevitability of classes and the superiority and inferiority of certain groups. The oppressed begin to believe in their own inferiority and are left in their lifetime with two general choices: to identify with the oppressor (imitate him) or to rebel against him. Rebellion does not take place as long as the oppressed are certain of their inferiority and the innate superiority of the powerful, in essence a neurotic illusion. The oppressed appear to be in love with their chains.

In a capitalist society, all power to rule is imagined in male symbols and, in fact, all power in a capitalist society is in male hands. Capitalism is a male supremacist society. Western religious gods are all male. The city, basis of "civilization," is male as opposed to the country which is female. The city is a revolt against earlier female principles of nature and man's dependence on them. All domestic and international political and economic decisions are made by men and enforced by males and their symbolic extension—guns. Women have become the largest oppressed group in a dominant, male, aggressive, capitalistic culture. The next largest oppressed group is the product of their wombs, the children, who are *ever* pressed into service and labor for the maintenance of a male-dominated class society.

If it is granted that it takes two to oppress, those who neurotically need to oppress and those who neurotically need to be oppressed, then what happens when the female in a capitalist society awakens to the reality? She can either identify with the male and opportunistically imitate him, appearing to share his power and giving him the surplus product of her body, the child, to use and exploit. Or she can rebel and remove the children from exploitative and oppressive male authority.

Rebellion by poor black women, the bottom of a class hierarchy heretofore not discussed, places the question of what kind of society will the poor black woman demand and struggle for. Already she demands the right to have birth control, like middle-class black and white women. She is aware that it takes two to oppress and that she and other poor people no longer are submitting to oppression, in this case genocide. She allies herself with the have-nots in the wider world and their revolutionary struggles. She has been forced by historical conditions to withdraw the children from male dominance and to educate and support them herself. In this very process, male authority and exploitation are seriously weakened. Further, she realizes that the children will be used as all poor children have been used through history—as poorly paid mercenaries fighting to keep or put an elite group in power. Through these steps in the accompanying analytic article, she has begun to question aggressive male domination and the class society which enforces it, capitalism. This question, in time, will be posed to the entire black movement in this country.

Black Sisters

POOR BLACK sisters decide for themselves whether to have a baby or not to have a baby. If we take the pills or practice birth control in other ways, it's because of poor black men.

Now here's how it is. Poor black men won't support their families, won't stick by their women—all they think about is the street, dope and liquor, women, a piece of ass, and their cars. That's all that counts. Poor black women would be fools to sit up in the house with a whole lot of children and eventually go crazy, sick, heartbroken, no place to go, no sign of affection—nothing. Middle class white men have always done this to their women—only more sophisticated like.

So when whitey put out the pill and poor black sisters spread the word, we saw how simple it was not to be a fool for men any more (politically we would say men could no longer exploit us sexually or for money and leave the babies with us to bring up). That was the first step in our waking up!

Black women have always been told by black men that we were black, ugly, evil, bitches and whores—in other words, we were the real niggers in this society—oppressed by whites, male and female, and the black man, too.

Now a lot of the black brothers are into a new bag. Black women are being asked by militant black brothers not to practice birth control because it is a form of whitey committing genocide on black people. Well, true enough, but it takes two to practice genocide and black women are able to decide for themselves, just like poor people all over the world, whether they will submit to genocide. For us, birth control is freedom to fight genocide of black women and children.

Like the Vietnamese have decided to fight genocide, the South American poor are beginning to fight back, and the African poor will fight back, too. Poor black women in the U.S. have to fight back out of our own experience of oppression.

Having too many babies stops us from supporting our children, teaching them the truth or stopping the brainwashing as you say, and fighting black men who still want to use and exploit us.

But we don't think you are going to understand us because you are a bunch of little middle class people and we are poor black women. The middle class never understands the poor because they always need to use them as you want to use poor black women's children to gain power for yourself. You'll run the black community with your kind of black power— you on top!

> PATRICIA HADEN—welfare recipient
> SUE RUDOLPH—housewife
> JOYCE HOYT—domestic
> RITA VAN LEW—welfare recipient
> CATHERINE HOYT—grandmother
> PATRICIA ROBINSON—housewife and psychotherapist

Beverly Jones / *Radical Women as Students,* and Judith Benninger Brown / *Female Liberation First, and Now*

Judith Brown and Beverly Jones were members of the Gainesville, Florida, chapter of S.D.S. when they wrote the pamphlet from which the following two excerpts are taken. It was written first as a response to an S.D.S. woman's manifesto which appeared in 1967 and was meant to challenge radical women

From *Toward a Female Liberation Movement,* pamphlet (Boston, New England Free Press, 1968), pp. 5–11, 27–33. Reprinted by permission of the authors.

in the movement to define a new position (not prone, not submissive) within the male-dominated New Left. Their suggestions for action and their fervent analyses are an example of many similar mimeographed papers circulated among hundreds of women in the movement all over the country from the late sixties to the present. However, the following excerpts are important not only as examples but also for what they say about women in the New Left. Note the authors' concern with what male radicals say about them, with the continuing sense of inferiority and self-rejection of women, and with the desire to experiment with new life styles in order to gain an independent identity.

Radical Women as Students

Radical women do not really understand the desperate condition of women in general. . . . As students, they occupy some sexy, sexless, limbo territory where they are treated by the administration and by males in general with less discrimination than they will ever again face. It may seem strange but one of the main advantages of a female student, married or unmarried, with or without children, is that she is still public. She has in her classes, in her contacts on campus, the opportunity to express her ideas publicly to males and females of all rank. Indeed, she is expected to do so . . . on an equal basis with men.

Moreover, her competition with men, at least scholastically, is condoned—built into the system. This creates in the girl the illusion of equality and harmony between the sexes very much as a good integrated school (where students visit each others' homes even for weekends and are always polite) creates in the black the illusion of change and the faith in continued good relations upon graduation.

These female illusions are further nurtured by the social life of students. Since many live in dorms or other places where they cannot entertain members of the opposite sex, most social intercourse of necessity takes place in public. . . . People congregate in coffee houses, pubs, movies, or at parties of the privileged few with off-campus apartments or houses. And since most students are unmarried, unsure of themselves, and lonely, they are constantly on the make. Thus they dance with each other, and talk with each other. The conversation between the sexes is not necessarily serious or profound but it takes place, and . . . takes place in the great main, publicly. Each tries to find out more about the other, attempts to discover what future relations might be possible between them, tries to impress the other in some way.

So the female student feels like a citizen, like an individual among others in the body politic, in the civil society, in the world of the intellect. What she doesn't understand is that upon graduation she is stripped of her public life and relegated to the level of private property. Enslavement is her farewell present. As things stand now, she is doomed to become someone's secretary, or someone's nurse, or someone's wife, or someone's mistress. From now on if she has some contribution to make to society she is expected to make it privately through the man who owns some part of her. . . .

What is feared most [by men] is that women, looking out at their natural surroundings, will suffer a reversal of perspective like that one experiences looking at optically balanced drawings where background suddenly becomes the subject. That one day, looking at men and women in full-blown stereotype, a woman will suddenly perceive individuals of varying ability, honesty, warmth, and understanding. When that day comes her master stands before her stripped of his historical prerogative, just another individual with individual attributes. That has ponderous implications for their relationship, for all of society.

In the world of the graduated and married this situation is forestalled in perhaps the most expeditious way. Men simply refuse to talk to women publicly about anything but the most trivial affairs: home, cooking, the weather, her job, perhaps a local school-board election, etc. In these areas they are bound to be able to compete and if they fail—well, men aren't supposed to know anything about those things anyway. They're really just trying to give the girls a little play.

But even that routine has its dangers. Women are liable to change the topic, to get to something of substance. So generally to be absolutely safe men just don't talk to women at all. At parties they congregate on one side of the room, standing up as befits their condition and position (desk workers in the main), and exhausted women (servants and mothers) are left propped up by girdles, pancake make-up, and hair spray, on the couch and surrounding chairs. If the place is big and informal enough the men may actually go into another room, generally under the pretext of being closer to the liquor.

Of course, most women don't understand this game for what it is. The newcomer to it often thinks it is the women who withdraw and may seek out what she imagines to be the most stimulating company of the men. When she does, she is quickly disillusioned. As she approaches each group of men the conversation they were so engrossed in usually dies. The individual members begin to drift off—to get a refill, to talk with someone they have just noticed across the room, etc. If she manages to ensnare a residual member of the group in conversation, he very soon develops a nervous and distressed look on his face as though he had to go to the bathroom; and he leaves as soon as possible, perhaps to make that trip.

There is another phenomenon not to be confused here. Namely, men being stimulated to show off in the presence of an attractive female, to display in verbal exchange what they imagine to be their monstrous cleverness. But the rules of this game require the woman to stand by semi-mute, just gasping and giggling, awed, and somewhat sexually aroused. The verbal exchange is strictly between the men. Any attempt on the woman's part to become a participant instead of a prize breaks up the game and the group.

This kind of desperate attempt by men to defend their power by refusing to participate in open public discussion with women would be amusing if it were not so effective. And one sees the beginnings of it even now while still students, in S.D.S. meetings. You are allowed to participate and to speak, only the men stop listening when you do. How many times have you seen a woman enter the discussion only to have it resume at the exact point from which she made her departure, as though she had never said anything at all? How many times have you seen men get up and actually walk out of a room while a woman speaks, or begin to whisper to each other as she starts?

In that kind of a hostile, unresponsive atmosphere, it is difficult for anyone to speak in an organized, stringent manner. Being insulted [the woman] becomes angry, in order to say what she wanted to say and not launch an attack upon the manners of her "audience" she musters the energy to control her temper, and finally she wonders why she is bothering at all since no one is listening. Under the pressure of all this extraneous stimulation she speaks haltingly, and if she gets to the point at all hits it obliquely.

And thus the male purpose is accomplished. Someone may comment, "Well, that is kind of interesting but it is sort of beside the main point here." Or, whoever is in charge may just look at her blankly as if, "What was that all about?" The conversation resumes and perhaps the woman feels angry but she also feels stupid. In this manner the slave relationship is learned and reinforced.

Even [in] the exceptional case—the woman who does sometimes get up front—the argument holds. . . . [I am] thinking about the girl who has thirty I.Q. points over almost anyone in the group and therefore can't be altogether put down. She is much too intelligent, much too valuable. So she is sometimes asked by the male leadership to explain a plan or chair a meeting, and since it is obvious that she is exercising a *male*-delegated authority and because she is so bright, people will sometimes listen to her. But have you ever known the top dog in an S.D.S. group to be a woman, or have you ever known a woman to be second in command? Have you ever seen one argue substance or tactics with one of the top males *in front* of the full group? She may forget her place and do so, but if she does she receives the same treatment as all other females. The rules may and sometimes have to be stretched for the exceptional but never at the price of male authority and male control.

Of course, being a student, having not as yet come under the full heel of male domination, and not identifying with women in general, you may view S.D.S. group dynamics somewhat differently. You may grant the male domination but think it is a function of the particular males in command or you may grant its existence but blame the women for not asserting themselves.

With regard to the first assumption let me point out that almost all men are involved in the male mystique. No matter how unnecessary it may be, particularly for the most bright and most able among them, each rests his ego in some measure on the basic common denominator, being a man. In the same way white people, consciously or unconsciously, derive ego support from being white, and Americans from being American.

Allowing females to participate in some group on the basis of full equality presents a direct threat to each man in that group. And though an individual male leader may be able to rise above this personal threat he cannot deviate from the rules of the game without jeopardizing his own leadership and the group itself. If he permits the public disclosure in an irrefutable manner, of the basic superiority of half the women to half the men, of some of the women to some of the men, he breaks the covenant and the men will not follow him. Since they are not obliged to, they will not suffer this emasculation and the group will fall apart.

To think that women, by asserting themselves individually in S.D.S., can democratize it, can remove the factor of sex, is equally silly. In the first place the men will not permit it and in the second place, as things stand now, the women are simply incapable of that kind of aggressive individual assertion. The socialization process has gone too far, they are already scrambled. Meeting after meeting their silence bears witness to their feelings of inferiority. Who knows what they get out of it? Are they listening, do they understand what is being said, do they accept it? . . . Would urging them to speak out have any effect other than to cut down their numbers at the next meeting?

Though female students objectively have more freedom than most older married women their life is already a nightmare. Totally unaware, they long ago accepted the miserable role male society assigned to them: help-mate and maintenance worker. Upon coming to college they eagerly and "voluntarily" flood the great service schools: the college of education, the college of nursing, the departments of social work, physical therapy, counseling, and clinical psychology. In some places they even major in home economics.

Denied most of them forever is the great discovery, the power and beauty of logic and mathematics, the sweeping syntheses, the perspective of history. The academic education in these service schools varies from thin to sick—two semester courses in history of Western civilization, watered down one-quarter courses on statistics for nurses, and the mumbo-jumbo courses on psychoanalysis.

It is no wonder that women who may have come to college with perfect confidence in themselves begin to feel stupid. They are being systematically stupefied. Trying to think without knowledge is just a cut above trying to think without language. The wheels go around but nothing much happens.

The position of these women in college is very much like the position of black kids in the black public schools. They start out with the same I.Q. and achievement scores as their white counterparts but after the third year they begin to lag further and further behind in both measurements. Those blacks still around to graduate from high school usually measure at least two years below graduating whites. Of course, black kids blame the discrepancy on the schools, on the environment, on all kinds of legitimate things. But always there is the gnawing doubt. It is hard to believe the schools could be so different; white women, being at the same school and from the same families understand that they are simply, though individually, inferior.

But that is not the only reason female students are scrambled. They are also in a panic, an absolute frenzy, to fulfill their destiny: to find a man and get married. It is not that they have all been brainwashed by the media to want a husband, split-level house, three children, a dog, a cat, and a station wagon. Many just want out from under their parents. They just can't take the slow slaughter any more but they don't have the courage to break away. They fear the wrath of the explosion but even more they fear the ensuing loneliness and isolation.

Generally a single girl's best friend is still her family. They are the only people she can rely upon for conversation, for attention, for concern with her welfare, no matter how misdirected. And everyone needs some personal attention or they begin to experience a lack of identity. Thus the big push to find the prince charming who will replace the chains with a golden ring.

But that is not as simple as it may seem. It is not proper for women to ask men out. They are never permitted the direct approach to anything. So women must set traps and, depending upon their looks and brains, that can be terribly time-consuming, nerve-racking, and disappointing. Thus the great rash of nose jobs, the desperate dieting, the hours consumed in pursuit of the proper attire. There is skin care, putting up one's hair each night, visits to the hairdressers, keeping up with, buying, applying, and taking off make-up, etc. The average American woman spends two hours a day in personal grooming, not including shopping or sewing. That is one-twelfth of her whole life and one-eighth of the time she spends awake. If she lives to be eighty, a woman will have spent ten whole years of her time awake in this one facet of the complex business of making herself attractive to men. It is staggering to think what that figure would be if one were to include the endless hours spent looking through fashion magazines, shopping and window shopping, discussing and worrying about clothes, hair style, diet, and make-up. Surely one-fourth of a woman's waking time would be a conservative estimate here. Twenty years of wakeful life!

So, one-fourth of a female student's day goes down the drain in this manner, another one-fourth to one-half is spent getting brainwashed in school and studying. . . . What does she do with the rest of the time? Often she must work to support herself and she must eat, clean, wash clothes, date, etc. That leaves her just enough time to worry about her behavior on her last date and her behavior on her next one. Did she say and do the right thing, should she change her approach? Does he love her or does he not? . . . It is taken for granted amongst the more sophisticated that it helps to nail a man if one sleeps with him. Still, it is no guarantee and there are only so many men with whom a woman can cohabit in the same circle and still expect a proposal. Movement men seem prone to marry the "purer" non-movement types.

And at that age and stage, when girls are worried about being used, about pregnancy and privacy, still ignorant of the potentials of their bodies, and hung-up by the old male sexual code which classifies so much as perversion and then demands it, sex usually offers only minimal gratification anyway. Given the girls' hang-ups and the insecurity and ineptness of young men, even that gratification is more often psychological than sexual.

Sex becomes the vehicle for momentary exchanges of human warmth and affection. It provides periods in which anxiety is temporarily allayed and girls feel wanted and appreciated, periods in which they develop some identity as individuals. It is ironic indeed that a woman attains this sense of identity and individuality through performing an act common to all mankind and all mammals. It bespeaks her understanding that society as it is presently organized will not permit her to function at all except through some male. . . .

In this terrible delirium between adolescence and marriage the friendship of female to female all but disappears. Girls, because they are growing duller, become less interesting to each other. As they slip into the role of submissiveness, of respondent to male initiative, male intelligence, they also become increasingly uneasy with one another. To be the benefactor of female intelligence and to respond with warmth and affection brings with it anxieties of "homosexual tendencies." To initiate, direct, or dominate brings with it the same apprehensions. To ensure a female for every male (if he wants one), to ensure his freedom and his power through the enslavement of our sex, males have made of homosexuality *the* abomination. Everyone knows what happens to them: they go crazy and get buried at some intersection. It is too horrible to think about; it can only be feared.

And that fear, initiated by men, is reinforced by both men and women. Perform a simple spontaneous act like lighting another woman's cigarette with the same match you've just lit your own with, and there is panic on all sides. Women have to learn to inhibit these natural, asexual gestures. And any close and prolonged friendship between women is always suspect.

So women use each other as best they can under the circumstances, to keep out the cold. . . . No woman trusts another because she understands the desperation. The older a woman becomes the more oppressive the syndrome. As one by one her contemporaries marry she begins to feel the way old people must when one by one their friends and relatives die. Though an individual in the latter condition is not necessarily burdened with a sense of failure and shame.

So there you have the typical coed, ignorant, suffering from a sense of inferiority, barely perceiving other women except as mindless, lonely, and terrified. Hardly in any condition to aggressively and individually fight for her rights in S.D.S. It seems, in a way, the least of her problems. To solve them all she is fixated on marriage.

FEMALE LIBERATION FIRST, AND NOW

A RESPECTABLE canon of New Left philosophy . . . is that central theme that human beings, by combining in organizations, by seeking to participate in decision-making which affects their lives, can achieve a democratic society, and hence, a life experience perhaps approximating their potentiality. . . .

We want to make a few tentative comments about the form of the marriage institution, for we hope that radical women will begin to turn from psychiatry to each other for insight about their oppressive sexual relationships. Family arrangements, as we all know, vary from culture to culture. While the female has a biological requirement for some support immediately after childbirth, anthropology suggests that the form of this support is not always that which we find institutionalized in the West—namely, one man providing economic aid so that one female can be a full-time mother, with this relationship extended then, perhaps for a lifetime.

The institution of marriage given us in the United States is the pawn of other, more powerful, institutions. It is a potent instrument for maintaining the status quo in American society. It is in the family that children learn so well the dominance-submission game by observation and participation. Each family, reflecting the perversities of the larger order and split off from the others, is powerless to force change on other institutions, let alone attack or transform its own. And this serves the Savage Society well.

The family owes its characteristic features to the economic necessities of frontier America (nation-building) and its monogamous form to a statistical and cultural happenstance (monogamy seems to prevail where the sex ratio is about 50–50 and there is a pretense to democracy). The particular division of labor was designed to contribute to the Industrial Revolution, a requirement of the most powerful national institution. Claude Lévi-Strauss suggests that "like the form of the family, the division of labor stems more from social and cultural considerations than from natural ones." He recalls the "Nambikwara father nursing his baby and cleaning it when it soils itself" as a contrast to the European nobleman who rarely sees his children. And he notes that the "young concubines of the Nambikwara chieftain disdain domestic activities and prefer to share in their husband's adventurous expeditions." In the absence of household servants, the American emigré man first subdued one woman and with her aid produced a family of servants sufficient at least to manage the homestead and offer him the leisure to participate in town politics and even revolutions.

Now, with birth control, higher education for women, and the movement itself, it is becoming clear to some women that the marriage institution, like so many others, is an anachronism. For unmarried women it offers only a sanctional security and the promise of love. The married woman knows that love is, at its best, an inadequate reward for her unnecessary and bizarre heritage of oppression. The marriage institution does not free women; it does not provide for emotional and intellectual growth; and it offers no political resources. Were it not for male-legislated discrimination in employment, it would show little economic advantage.

[The married woman] is locked into a relationship which is oppressive politically, exhausting physically, stereotyped emotionally and sexually, and atrophying intellectually. She teams up with an individual groomed from birth to rule, and she is equipped for revolt only with the foot-shuffling, head-scratching

gestures of "feminine guile." We conceptualize the significance
of the marriage institution this way:

$$\frac{\text{Marriage}}{\text{Integration}} \sim \frac{\text{Women}}{\text{Blacks}}$$

Marriage as we know it is for women as integration is for blacks.
It is the atomization of a sex so as to render it politically powerless. The anachronism remains because men derive valuable
benefits from it and will not give them up and because, even
given a willingness among men and women to transform the
institution, it is at the mercy of the more powerful institutions
which use it and give it its form.

We would return to our relational model and suggest that
some women will have to remove themselves totally from the
marriage arrangement which insists that they love, in a predetermined style, their own personal masters. And married women
will have to do this periodically to revitalize their commitment
to their sex and the liberation movement.

Many younger, unmarried women live in all-female groups
now. The problem . . . is that these domiciles are not self-
consciously arranged to serve political as well as personal needs.
They are not a temporary stopping-off place for women who need
to re-evaluate their lives. They are no sanctuary from destructive
male-female encounters. They are no base for female liberation
work.

Some radical women, in deciding to live together, ought to
fashion homes which have definite political goals. A woman, married or unmarried, could move into such a center for a period
of time and be relieved of the terrible compulsion to one-up her
sisters in dating, grooming, and so on. The commune should
decide on house rules, experiment with sexual relationships on an
equal basis with men (that is, remove the bordello element from
the place). The commune should be a center for women to live
in during decision periods in their lives. We all know about these
crisis periods; most of the time we manage to suffer through
them while at the same time carrying all the burdens of "keeping face," maintaining some sexual life, etc. The commune would
define itself as a female place. Innumerable experiments in liv-

ing, political forays, and serious and uninterrupted thinking could center in the commune.

While sexual and emotional alliances with men may continue to be of some benefit, the peculiar domestic institution is not. Only women can define what "womanhood" might best be. Theoretically, such women and men might, in the future, liberated from this master-slave hang-up, meet and work out a new domestic institution, but we are certain that it will be designed most rapidly and most reasonably by liberated souls. . . .

Let us review briefly why this program at least parallels in importance the antidraft, anti-imperialistic movements we all know. People get radicalized fighting their own battles. For woman, these are her chains, and she will ultimately invest more energy, and in the process become radicalized, breaking them, than attacking the other forms of colonialism men urge her to fight. Men have accelerated their rate of history-making beyond humane proportions. With their slaves secure at home, they have the time to play abstractly and inhumanly with their technology and to make history more rapidly than they can effectively comprehend or control. Robbed of a faithful custodial class (women, blacks, etc.) they will be less effective, and time may finally overtake them so that where they're at is also where it's at. Women who organize other women to slow down male history-making are functioning, in this country, at their political best.

The goal of the New Left is to dismantle outworn institutions and replace them with better arrangements. Presently, the energies of radical women are not wholeheartedly with this effort, because it has no program which speaks to their needs. Women mobilized where they stand against the nearest oppressor will make their most effective contribution to this process. . . .

I would like to cover briefly some topics which may serve in the over-all strategy of female liberation. Most women are integrated with men in an ongoing institutionalized setup. One or two all-female meetings, or even one a month, will not begin to solve our problems or guide our programming intelligently. The particular need to get together is shared by the youngest and the older, married women who have children. We are all separated from each other. This does not mean that the constituency should meet together—there is no little hostility among older women toward what they imagine to be their more liberated younger sisters, and the problems differ. The tactics will differ. But both groups need to plan programs in which women can meet for extended periods to talk about the political issues of female liberation. And this meeting, this talking, in itself, is more difficult than we had imagined.

But women are beginning to meet, and they are beginning to talk to each other. That some of these discussions produce ideas or actions at which male radicals giggle is a measure of what we are up against.

The big push to have children, whether we are married or not, should be viewed as one of the strong links in the chain which enslaves us. Biological arguments are romantically blown-up out of proportion by men. We have plenty of so-called biological needs which we have learned to control or rechannel for political purposes. Let us remember that many of us have been willing to exchange, for principle, what are bound to be even more basic needs: food during hunger strikes and our lives in police battles and the more extended confrontations on dirt roads in the civil rights South. We were willing to face being shotgunned to death for black voter registration; I think we can defer dropping children on cultural command for our own thing, if we think that necessary. I am not making a call for eternal celibacy, but for intelligent birth control and a rethinking of the compulsion to have children. . . . The same radical woman who thinks draft resistance is more important than female liberation ends up having a baby, and then she is immobilized for both battles. . . .

Control over our own sexuality is another short-term goal. We all believe in birth control and legalized abortion. However, there is little talk of periodic, self-imposed celibacy. We are besieged by the media with sexy commercials and talk in the movement about screwing as often as possible; many of us have already been on the pill for longer than we can medically afford. And a good many of us, I would suspect, are desperately screwing some guy because we think we should and wonder what our friends would think if we didn't at all for a while. . . . It requires, from an unmarried woman, a lot more time to maintain a sexual relationship than it does for her male partner. Radical women could gain a lot in time, energy, and getting themselves together if they would avail themselves of the tactic [of celibacy] occasionally. We must stop being pawns in the media's sexuality game and reconsider the whole scene.

Those radical females already married, but without children, should be prepared to make a decision about how they will live their lives in order to have time for their political activities. Regardless of who is working, going to school, and so on, you should demand equal time for your own things. This requires your husband to assume half of the burden of maintaining a home: . . . cooking, cleaning, laundering, entertaining. . . . If you plan to live with your husband, you will have to begin making changes in the marital pattern. And the chances are that unless he has a radical analysis which is pretty thorough, your marriage will end in divorce if you take this route.

If you have children already, the most devastating pattern of the male-female relationship has set in long ago. If you are serious about political activities and female liberation, you may have to make important adjustments in your life. Presently you work from daybreak until the time when your husband falls asleep. He will have to assume enough of the child caring and housekeeping . . . so that you each have equal time off during each day. His posture of dominance will be threatened, his time consumed . . . by such a plan. Stopgap measures such as communal evening-care centers and communal eating are short-term tactics which serve the long-term goal of freeing women for . . . personal and political activity. What is central to our problem is our complete alienation from other women. We will have to get out of our houses and meet them on serious issues. . . . We will need each other's support and advice to achieve liberation. We will need time to read, to study, to write, to debate, among ourselves. . . . No woman can go this alone. The territory is new, frightening, and appears lonely. We must begin by forming organizations which will provide emotional support and an intellectual base for framing action. . . .

Underlying much of the evasiveness and the apparent lack of

self-confidence among women when confronted with the possibility of a female liberation movement is the big male gun—the
charge of homosexuality. . . .

The radical woman, for very specific reasons, is probably more
uptight about homosexuality than other women. This is one of
the curious paradoxes in the movement; in many ways movement
people tend to maintain some Puritan mores to excess. Most of
us entered the movement on the basis of simple, middle-class
idealistic hang-ups. Our parents taught us all the tenets of "clean
living," including equality for the races and humanity among
men, and when we got to college we recognized that this was
science fiction. Our minds were momentarily blown, we went to
a meeting somewhere, got involved, and a few of us got radicalized along the way. While younger radicals tend to be more
cynical, perhaps have freer life styles, all of us have a heritage
which is essentially puritanical. Homosexuality is "wrong." . . .

Women who turn from men for a time, to look to each other
for political relationships, movement thinking, and an organizational milieu are bound to see here and there someone they love.
The slightest measure of female liberation will bring with it an
ability to perceive again the precise qualities and degree of
responsiveness which inhere in other women. For those in serious
communes or political trenches, a continued fear of homosexuality may be the one last strand by which the male order can pull
us back into tow. It has been our past error to repress the
political attraction we have for our own kind. It would be
equally wrong to turn female communes into anything less than
a tentative experiment with a new domestic arrangement. . . .
It will be in these communes, or their less rigorous counterparts
in female rediscovery, that we may learn to design new living
arrangements which will make our coexistence with men in the
future all the more equal and all the more humane. And, exploring the possibilities of nonelitist, noncolonial love may teach us
forms of political strength far more valuable than guerrilla
theater.

We have got to stop throwing around terms like "fag," "pimp,"
"queer," and "dyke," to reassure men of our absolute loyalty to
them. This is the language which helps to ensure that each man

has his female slave, and that each woman eventually becomes one.

Indirect male sniping insinuating homosexuality is a horror which is bound to attend female liberation activity and has some interesting analogies in our movement experience. It's like the signal Southern whites put out: "If you leave a white and a black alone for five minutes, there's no telling what might happen." And it's a lot like Red-baiting. Our answers to Red-baiting will serve us well here. The charge of homosexuality—which will be more openly voiced by nonmovement males—stands for a fear of something greater, as did the charge of Communism against Southern blacks and whites getting together: that they might get together. An indigenous movement of any people determined to gain their liberation is a more serious threat than "Communism" or "homosexuality," and the charge is merely a delaying tactic to obstruct organization. . . .

As we begin talking to women about female liberation, most of them accept our description of our lot with little argument. But they do come on with honest fears about engaging in the movement, and they tell us how incompetent they feel, how they lack self-confidence, and how they don't have much time (a lot of custodial tasks on the home front), and most important, how they're scared.

Being afraid has been a genuine response of oppressed people to their initial encounter with a vision of liberation. As is always the case, discipline and organization are the antidote, the means by which the exploited are drawn out of the routine of their ghettos. We cannot meet fear with rhetoric or statistics. We must become ready to organize, support, and act. . . .

Gayle Rubin / *Woman as Nigger*

Gayle Rubin is a student at the University of Michigan, where she is active in the women's liberation movement. She wrote the following essay for a campus newspaper as an introduction to the subject. She says of this effort, "it was written with the enthusiasm of the first flush of excitement about the growing feeling that an old private concern of mine was becoming a political issue." It seemed to the editors remarkable for Rubin's sophisticated grasp of the psychological ramifications of women's oppression, for the depth and breadth of her reading, and for the sense of personal discovery and passion with which her argument is imbued.

In 1903 Daniel De Leon, a nineteenth-century American Marxist, attacked the wrongs done to women, observing that this oppression "touches a nerve that aches from end to end of the capitalist world. . . . Accordingly, the innovation of the 'Rights of Woman' . . . arouses the spirit of the heaviest sufferers under capitalist society." Jesse Lemisch, in a paper describing his course on radicalism at Northwestern, notes that the last 20 per cent of it is devoted to women's liberation. He says,

One reason for concluding a history of radicalism with the subject of women's liberation is this: the idea of women's liberation is ludicrous, not only to Americans in general, but, more importantly, to most of

From *The Argus*, Ann Arbor, Michigan (March 28–April 11; April 14–28, 1969), pp. 7–15; 14. Reprinted by permission of the author and *The Argus*.

the movement. Thus women's liberation defines the limits of contemporary radicalism—and suggests directions for the future—by indicating the point at which the movement ceases to be literal and thoroughgoing in its belief in human rights. . . . It is a measure of how far we have to go that such a course should have to begin by convincing students that a problem does in fact exist, that women are *not* inferior, and that there is injustice and brutality in this area. People are more sophisticated about blacks than about women. Black history courses do not have to begin by convincing people that blacks are not in fact genetically better suited to dancing than to thinking. . . .

The basic premise of women's liberation is that women are an exploited class, like black people, but that unlike blacks, they are not marginal to our technocratic society. So that one might expect that social control of women is less slipshod and more subtle than that of black people. In other words, women suffer from some form of racism, as that word is currently used. Racism has come to refer . . . to something enormously more complex than what it meant in the days of the first sit-ins. It refers to any dynamic system of social, political, economic, and psychological pressures that tend to suppress a group, whose members may be influenced by some form of biologically determined distinction, and whose suppression may be contrary to what would be expected by normal divisions of class. That is, blacks are oppressed as workers, but their blackness makes them more vulnerable than white workers.

They are a class within a class. Women form a class within every class. Sometimes they are oppressed despite their class. I started thinking seriously about the "woman as nigger" . . . at a training session on racism held by People Against Racism. As the speaker explained the dynamics of black-white interaction, I kept substituting female for black, and was astonished by the similarities. . . . There is a paper by Helen Hacker which contains a chart on the parallels between blacks and women in regard to such matters as discrimination, rationalization of status, ascribed attributes, and means of accommodation, such as "Supplicatory whining intonations of the voice" for blacks, "rising inflections, smiles, laughter, downward glances" for women; "con-

cealment of real feelings" for blacks, and "feminine wiles" for
women; "outwit white folks," and "outwit men." [See Helen
Mayer Hacker, "Women as a Minority Group," in this anthology.]

Girls, don't you remember? Never let on to your real feelings,
boost their egos, and don't beat them in games, use your head
and you can always get around them, never trust a boy. We are
raised to think of all male-female relationships as huge games
of win or lose—win and marry, lose and get pregnant. It's so sick,
it's so neurotic.

The socially defined role of a woman is a modified form of
hysteria. A hysterical person has shallow relationships, based on
security needs instead of the personality of the people involved.
A hysteric relationship with one's body is one of distance, in
which the body is an alienated object. Hysterical women are
characterized in psychology books by descriptions indistinguish-
able from the All American Ideal Woman, i.e., a tease who is
enormously attractive, yet withholds herself after leading people
on. Hysterical perception is defined as vague, global, unanalytic,
simplistic, emotive, non-intellectual. A hysteric is very dependent
on others for his identity—he is only what others think of him, so
his enterprise is to fulfill what roles are expected of him, to
always be what anyone wants him to be. All of these descriptions are held up as ideals of feminine behavior, particularly this
last. A girl is trained to worry most about how she appears to
men, what impression she gives, how to play the role he wants
her to play (ego-booster, sweet, demure, non-assertive, etc.).
The important point about the woman's role isn't even that it is
necessarily inferior; it is rather that a woman's unique identity
is made irrelevant. . . .

The heroine of the *Story of O* is named, simply "O." Susan
Sontag refers to this as a cartoon of her sex—an empty zero to
be filled. In fact, some critics have referred to the book as being
the logical, extreme conclusion of the cultural stereotype of
women—a following-through of the consequences of an ideology.

Think about the cultural myths in Aldous Huxley's parody of
Christianity, *Ape and Essence*. Women are referred to as "ves-
sels of unholiness." This is no more than is implied by the entire
Christian ideology of sex that has been adopted since Saint Paul.

Women are always held responsible for the supposed evilness of sex—it's not just Eve and Pandora. The prostitution laws are a contemporary example. Soliciting is an offense in thirty-four states, whereas customers are subject to legal action in only fourteen states. Moreover, prostitutes are jailed in virtually every state, and customers—men—not at all.

In general, the legal status of women in America has improved. It is no longer true that, as Gunnar Myrdal pointed out, the nearest analogy to the legal status of Negro slaves in the seventeenth century was the status of women. However, although women now are independent legal entities, there are still tremendous inequities. The law does not permit a woman control over her own body. Most states restrict the dispersal of birth-control information and devices (except for poor people, where its use is faintly reminiscent of genocide). Hospital abortions are illegal in most states except for rare cases. More women die each year from medically unsafe abortions than American soldiers die in Vietnam! And the word "sex" was included in the 1964 Civil Rights Act as a joke. It was opposed by all the liberals on the ground that it would make the whole Civil Rights Act more difficult to pass.

Despite the Civil Rights Act, blacks and women still suffer tremendous job discrimination. The percentage of women faculty members at the University of Michigan is appallingly low. Those departments which do hire women are usually "service" professions—nursing, social work, some psychology. The History department has one female professor. Philosophy and English have none. In Classics, Math, and the hard sciences, they are sparse.

For women outside the university, there are jobs—mostly low-paid, part-time, or shit-work ones. Look at any office—not a single male secretary, which is more telling than the occasional female exceptions. Women working at the same job as men frequently receive lower salaries, whether or not they are self-supporting.

Every racism needs an ideology. A primary ideological support of racism is psychology. The black man is contented with his lot because he is suited for it. "His intelligence is not the logic of a white man, but a shifting intuitiveness that makes him more

sensitive to, for instance, religion. . . . But he lacks the pur-
posive, disciplined intelligence of his betters. . . ." As Heather
Dean says, "Read woman for black man. Read woman for good
nigra. Read male chauvinist for Southerner. For the Southerner's
ideology, read Freud."

I am going to quote most of a section of her paper entitled
"Penis-Envy—the Ideology of the Master Sex."

Freud's dualism is most marked in his understanding of masculinity
and femininity . . . his essence a protuberance, woman as orifice, man
is active, woman is passive, man logical, woman intuitive, man aggressive, woman submissive. When a woman wants to undertake
"male" activities such as voting (pushing a vote through a slot) she
is flying in the face of what God and nature had created for her.
Why? Well, at the age of three or four, a little girl discovers the
difference. She deduces that she has been castrated. In the normal
course of her development, per Freud, she resolves the resulting
turmoil by accepting her punishment, her mutilation, with total resignation, and adopts the passive feminine role.

But some little girls do not. They strive for physical and intellectual
competence, but not because these are good in themselves. They
resent discrimination in education, the arts, and employment, and are
frustrated rather than fulfilled by male domination and not for the
reasons the black man in America reacts this way, not because of an
essential human drive to activity and self-realization; rather because
she perceives these male activities as a symbolic substitution for the
penis of which she was robbed in infancy.

It might seem more plausible to explain a neurotic desire for the
freedom entailed in the male role than to explain a desire for "male"
freedom as a symbolic repossession of a hypothetical lost penis. But
it is observable in the sociology of knowledge that the "free and
unbiased" pursuit of scientific truth seems to lead inexorably in every
era to a rationalization of the power relations of that era. (Heather
Dean, "The Sexual Caste System," in *Random*, University of Toronto,
Oct. 1966.)

Women entering psychoanalysis are encouraged to adjust to
their traditional role. Indeed, it is usually thought that the source
of their problem, whatever brought them into analysis, is precisely a failure to adapt to that role. A paper by Sandra and
Daryl Bem ("Case Study of a Nonconscious Ideology: Training

the Woman to Know Her Place," in D. J. Bem, *Beliefs, Attitudes and Human Affairs,* Belmont, California, 1970) documents early socialization of women, showing that girl children, like black children, are very early taught low self-esteem and how not to be self-initiating and highly motivated.

One thing that should be made clear about women's liberation is that it doesn't mean turning women into men. To use the black power analogy, no one wants to obliterate the differences between male and female. Rather the point is to destroy some of the myths about the nature of male and female and find more satisfying role definitions for male and female alike. Moreover, radical women, at least, don't want to become like men in the additional sense that we find so much wrong with the role the American male has to fulfill, both in terms of his relationships with women and his relationships with society as a whole. It may be true that a man is so . . . battered and belittled by his days in the office or plant or whatever, that he needs an ego-boosting fragile woman at home in order to keep him going. But if the solution to that man's problems is not to provide him with a diligent wife at the expense of her own independence, then neither would it help to send women into the same office, plant, or factory for forty-hour weeks. Rather, atrocious dehumanizing working conditions should be changed, and working patterns must be changed. As working patterns are now set up, one of the family must work a forty-hour week. Part-time labor in this country has no security, no benefits, and is always cheap. An essential step towards liberating men and women would be to set up twenty-hour work weeks with job security and fringe benefits.

Heather Dean points out in yet another sense why women's liberation is "not a struggle against men." The phrase "the battle of the sexes" was not coined to describe the female liberation movement. It applies to the underhanded, sometimes terrible revenge women exact from men for their frustrations. Jiggs and Dagwood are not victims of free women, but of women who are playing the game. Listen to the jokes at pre-nuptial stags; play ritual murder (contract bridge) with suburbanites; read statistics on divorce, frigidity, impotence, child-bearing, psycho-

somatic illness and nervous breakdown; watch your parents'
friends. And be assured that men will not suffer from an initiative by women to change their relationships to men and society.

Doris Lessing, in her novel *The Golden Notebook*, is more explicit about this reason for women's liberation, which is precisely
to avoid taking out an impersonal resentment on the people
who are close to you . . . your lover or husband. She points out
that it takes conscious effort not to personalize that resentment
and blame it on your specific man. It takes conscious effort
not to use those weapons with which anyone is familiar from
his family—emotional blackmail, unspoken and unacknowledged.
I had always thought that sort of thing happened in families,
with parents, but never among my friends and peers, until I
found myself using it with men out of frustration and resentment. It is the most concrete, most horrible manifestation of the
oppression of women that they use such emotional tactics. I want
to give you Lessing's description. The narrator is waking up in
bed with Michael, her lover. She associates:

It must be six o'clock. . . . I realize the "housewife disease" has taken
hold of me. . . . I must dress Janet, get her breakfast, don't forget to
buy tea, etc., etc. With all this useless tension a resentment is also
switched on against unfairness . . . that I should have to spend so
much of my time worrying over details. . . . The resentment focuses
on Michael, though I know with my intelligence it has nothing to do
with Michael. And yet I do resent him, because he will spend his day
served by secretaries, nurses, women in all kinds of capacities, who
will take this weight off him. . . . But the anger is not related to
him . . . the anger is the disease of women in our time. The woman's
emotional resentment against injustice, an impersonal poison. The
unlucky ones who do not know it is impersonal turn it against their
men. The lucky ones, like me—fight it.

The misplaced blame for the hardships of housewifery is only
one of the emotional strategy mistakes for which we need
women's liberation, so that we can destroy the neurosis. Another
is the problem of negative identity. [Recently] people started
talking about white racism. Part of that discussion centered on
the way that blacks couldn't form black identities in a white
culture, except in self-hatred. But the discussion also included

the white man, and how so much of his self picture consists in not being black. What happens to the white man in this case is that he too is not independent, because a certain number of his actions must prove that he is not black. He is trapped and oppressed by his own system.

This is even more true of men who define themselves as not feminine. The all-American Not-Woman is dour, unemotional, dresses drably in an invariable uniform, doesn't cry, can't take care of himself (can't cook, do laundry, take care of his living quarters), works like a dog at a boring job, etc. Wouldn't he be better off if he were free to be himself, instead of not-feminine?

Yet another aspect of the many-sided neurosis which woman's liberation should attempt to cure is the kind of interaction resulting from a woman's being defined by whom she sleeps with. While this has been true for centuries, it takes on a new twist in an age of sexual freedom. There are, scattered all over the country, girls recently labelled as "groupies." . . . The groupies hang around backstage in the big auditoriums when rock bands play, and compete to fuck members of the band. The objects of their choice are pretty much interchangeable; they aren't fucking people at all, just an interchangeable male body and a symbol of status (for example, it's better to screw Jimi Hendrix than, say, the guitarist for the Strawberry Alarm Clock). I can't help but think of the similar syndrome of black men wanting to sleep with white women. One of the most important steps in black liberation was for black men to appreciate their own women. One of the priorities of women's liberation would be for girls to start sleeping with real, human men instead of sexual objects, father figures, or images of authority.

I think that Sartre's analysis of racism leads towards the best understanding of feminine sexuality in our culture. In *Anti-Semite and Jew*, Sartre discusses the core psychological hardships endured by someone who is treated in a racist way. First I should explain that for Sartre, there is for each of us a fundamental relationship with other people. All the difficulties in interpersonal contact arise from this relationship which is that we see ourselves as subject, whereas others see us as object, and as something different from our own self-perception. Describing the Jew, he says,

Within himself, the Jew considers himself the same as others. He speaks the same language, he has the same class interests, the same national interests, he reads the newspapers others read, he votes as they do, he understands and shares their opinions. Yet they give him to understand that he does not belong, that he has a "Jewish" way of speaking, of reading, of voting, and if he asks for an explanation, they sketch a portrait which he does not recognize as himself. There can be no doubt of its being his portrait, since millions of people maintain that it is. What can he do? We shall see that the root of Jewish disquietude is the necessity imposed upon the Jew of subjecting himself to endless self-examination and finally of assuming a phantom personality, at once strange and familiar, that haunts him and which is nothing but himself—himself as others see him. You may say that this is the lot of all, that each of us has a character familiar to those close to us which we ourselves don't see. No doubt this is the expression of our fundamental relationship to the Other. But the Jew has a personality like the rest of us, and on top of that is Jewish. It amounts in a sense to a doubling of the fundamental relationship with the Other.

This, in a nutshell, is the root of my disquietude as a woman.

But Sartre goes on, in *Saint Genet,* to describe Genet's situation as the object which he is to others over the subject he is to himself. Sartre says,

this type of alienation is widespread. Most of the time however, it is a matter of partial or temporary alienation. But when children are subjected, from their earliest days, to great social pressure, when their Being-For-Others is the subject of a collective image accompanied by value judgments and social prohibitions, the alienation is sometimes total and definitive.

Genet is subject to this alienation as is every woman. . . . The fact that Genet is first an object indicates the origin of his particular brand of sexuality.

Simone de Beauvoir has pointed out that feminine sexuality derives its chief characteristics from the fact that a woman is an object to the other and to herself before being a subject. One can expect that Genet, who is the object *par excellence,* will make himself an object in sexual relations and that his eroticism will bear a resemblance to feminine eroticism.

Sartre points out directions for a detailed analysis of this eroticism in his characterization of Evil as "totally other" as well. . . . [His analysis of Evil] is too complicated to bring in here, but to summarize, one could expect that eroticism to resemble, in its extreme form, the *Story of O*. Thus, if women are passive sexually, if they do perceive the man as an overbearing, invading force, and yet derive pleasure from him, it may be because of their oppressed historical situation rather than any biological reason at all.

The importance of sex relationships to political relationships should never be underestimated. To fully appreciate the implications of woman's liberation for radical politics one should read the analyses of sex and politics by such men as Eldridge Cleaver and Herbert Marcuse. Radical men who think of woman's liberation as a secondary, unimportant issue are blinded by their own chauvinism. They fail to see real, concrete oppression and even more, they fail to see the explosive political potential of the issue. On the other hand, there are women who refuse to link a woman's movement with radical politics. They are naïve enough to think that any of their demands can be met without radical change in the system, although the system can accommodate individuals. . . .

As Julius Lester has written,

it has always been men who have said that a woman's function in life was to serve a man. Now, the women within the movement are talking to each other and seeking to define who they are, first in relationship to themselves. Any man who cannot see the beauty of this should question any claims he may make of being more than liberal. . . . As long as men accept this society's definition of women and male-female relationships, then men remain oppressed by this society; to the degree that a man views a woman as an object, he is himself an object. No man who is fully human can be threatened by woman's liberation. Rather, he is overjoyed by it. (From his column, "From the Other Side of the Tracks," *The Guardian,* July 20, 1968)

There are some women who recognize the importance of woman's liberation, and who integrate it into a radical perspec-

tive, but who see it as something which should not be pressed
to the exclusion of their other political activity. I disagree—I
think that for radical women it is necessary to devote most of
their time towards organizing women. Otherwise, I think their
time is being wasted, because women are now politically ineffec-
tive. . . . Before we talk to people, we should make sure that
women are listened to, and responded to. But even more than
that, women, no matter how free compared to other women, are
paralyzed in their use of themselves. I find this in myself—I
suspect that a thoroughgoing examination will find it in others.
I mean by this that when I fight some political battle, I first
have to fight my own training and the paralysis that training was
designed to produce. So for me, political agitation must start
with myself. . . . I think this is the key to understanding the
phrase, "We cannot free others until we free ourselves." In other
words, giving primacy to woman's liberation is not, as student
power demands may be, an attempt to get more power for an
already privileged group. Rather it is a means to free energy
and competence that are badly needed in all areas of activity.
We are all "castrated" by the society, men and women alike, and
each of us must overcome our alienation from ourselves. . . . We
must recover our minds and our hands, which have been
severed from us since socialization began. Then we can use them
to alter the power relationships that oppress Vietnamese, blacks,
poor people, and ourselves. That is my vision of what woman's
liberation is about.

Robin Morgan / *Goodbye to All That*

Robin Morgan, one of the leading voices of the women's liberation movement, is a poet and a frequent contributor to the underground press. She is also the editor of an anthology of women's liberation writings. In this essay, she bids goodbye to the male vanities and hypocrisies of sham-left radicalism. Like all good prophecy, her statement is both denunciation and celebration: a denunciation of all that has disguised the oppression of women . . . a celebration of the new feminism as at last an independent radical movement.

So. *Rat* has been liberated, for this week, at least. Next week? If the men return to reinstate the porny photos, the sexist comic strips, the "nude-chickie" covers (along with their patronizing rhetoric about being in favor of Women's Liberation)—if this happens, our alternatives are clear. *Rat* must be taken over permanently by women—or *Rat* must be destroyed.

Why *Rat*? Why not EVO or even the obvious new pornzines (Mafia-distributed alongside the human pornography of prostitution)? First, they'll get theirs—but it won't be a takeover, which is reserved for something at least *worth* taking over. Nor should they be censored. They should just be helped not to exist—by any means necessary. But *Rat*, which has always tried to be a really radical *cum* life-style paper—that's another matter. It's the liberal co-optative masks on the face of sexist hate and fear, worn by real nice guys we all know and like, right? We have met the enemy and he's our friend. And dangerous. "What the hell, let the chicks do an issue; maybe it'll satisfy 'em for a while, it's a good controversy,

From *Rat: Subterranean News,* New York, 2, 27 (February 6, 1970), pp. 6–7. Reprinted by permission of the author.

and it'll maybe sell papers"—runs an unheard conversation that I'm sure took place at some point last week.

And that's what I wanted to write about—the friends, brothers, lovers in the counterfeit male-dominated Left. The good guys who think they know what "Women's Lib," as they so chummily call it, is all about—and who then proceed to degrade and destroy women by almost everything they say and do: The cover on the last issue of *Rat* (front *and* back). The token "pussy power" or "clit militancy" articles. The snide descriptions of women staffers on the masthead. The little jokes, the personal ads, the smile, the snarl. No more, brothers. No more well-meaning ignorance, no more co-optation, no more assuming that this thing we're all fighting for is the same: one revolution under *man,* with liberty and justice for all. No more.

Let's run it on down. White males are most responsible for the destruction of human life and environment on the planet today. Yet who is controlling the supposed revolution to change all that? White males (yes, yes, even with their pasty fingers back in black and brown pies again). It just could make one a bit uneasy. It seems obvious that a legitimate revolution must be led by, *made* by those who have been most oppressed: black, brown, and white *women*—with men relating to that the best they can. A genuine Left doesn't consider anyone's suffering irrelevant or titillating; nor does it function as a microcosm of capitalist economy, with men competing for power and status at the top, and women doing all the work at the bottom (and functioning as objectified prizes or "coin" as well). Goodbye to all that.

Run it all the way down.

Goodbye to the male-dominated peace movement, where sweet old Uncle Dave [Dellinger] can say with impunity to a woman on the staff of *Liberation,* "The trouble with you is you're an aggressive woman."

Goodbye to the "straight" male-dominated Left: to Progressive Labor who will allow that some workers are women, but won't see all women (say, housewives) as workers (just like the System itself); to all the old Leftover parties who offer their "Women's Liberation caucuses" to us as if that were not a contradiction in terms; to the individual anti-leadership leaders who hand-pick certain women to be leaders and then relate only to them, either in the male Left or in Women's Liberation—bringing their hang-ups about power-dominance and manipulation to everything they touch.

Goodbye to the WeatherVain, with the Stanley Kowalski image and theory of free sexuality—but practice of sex on demand for males. "Left Out!"—not Right On—to the Weather Sisters who, and they know better, reject their own radical feminism for that last desperate grab at male approval that we all know so well, for claiming that the *machismo* style and the gratuitous violence is their own style by "free choice" and for believing that this is the way for a woman to make her revolution . . . all the while, oh my sister, not meeting my eyes because WeatherMen chose Manson as their—and your—Hero. (Honest, at least . . . since Manson is only the logical extreme of the normal American male's fantasy [whether he is Dick Nixon or Mark Rudd]: master of a harem, women to do all the shitwork, from raising babies and cooking and hustling to killing people on order.) Goodbye to all that shit that sets women apart from women; shit that covers the face of any Weatherwoman which is the face of any Manson Slave which is the face of Sharon Tate which is the face of Mary Jo Kopechne which is the face of Beulah Saunders which is the face of me which is the face of Pat Nixon which is the face of Pat Swinton.

In the dark we are all the same—and you better believe it: we're in the dark, baby. (Remember the old joke: Know what they call a black man with a Ph.D.? A nigger. Variation: Know what they call a Weatherwoman? A heavy cunt. Know what they call a Hip Revolutionary Woman? A groovy cunt. Know what they call a radical militant feminist? A crazy cunt.) Amerika is a land of free choice—take your pick of titles. Left Out, my Sister —don't you see? Goodbye to the illusion of strength when you run hand in hand with your oppressors; goodbye to the dream that being in the leadership collective will get you anything but gonorrhea.

Goodbye to Revolutionary Youth Movement II, as well, and all the other Revolutionary Youth Movements—not that the Sisters there didn't pull a cool number by seizing control, but because they let the men back in after only *a day or so* of self-criticism on male

chauvinism. (And goodbye to the inaccurate blanket use of that
phrase, for that matter: male chauvinism is an *attitude*—male
supremacy is the *objective reality, the fact.*) Goodbye to the Conspiracy who, when lunching with fellow sexist bastards Norman
Mailer and Terry Southern in a bunny-type club in Chicago, found
Judge Hoffman at the neighboring table—no surprise: *in the light
they are all the same.*

Goodbye to Hip Culture and the so-called Sexual Revolution,
which has functioned toward women's freedom as did the Reconstruction toward former slaves—reinstituted oppression by another
name. Goodbye to the assumption that Hugh Romney is safe in his
"cultural revolution," safe enough to refer to "our women, who
make all our clothes" without somebody not forgiving that. Goodbye to the arrogance of power indeed that lets Czar Stan Freeman
of the Electric Circus sleep without fear at night, or permits Tomi
Ungerer to walk unafraid in the street after executing the drawings
for the Circus advertising campaign against women. Goodbye to
the idea that Hugh Hefner is groovy 'cause he lets Conspirators
come to parties at the Mansion—goodbye to Hefner's dream of a
ripe old age. Goodbye to Tuli and the Fugs and all the boys in the
front room—who always knew they hated the women they loved.
Goodbye to the notion that good ol' Abbie is any different from any
other up and coming movie star (like, say Cliff Robertson) who
ditches the first wife and kids, good enough for the old days but
awkward once you're Making It. Goodbye to his hypocritical
double standard that reeks through all the tattered charm. Goodbye to lovely pro-Women's-Liberation Paul Krassner, with all his
astonished anger that women have lost their sense of humor "on
this issue" and don't laugh any more at little funnies that degrade
and hurt them; farewell to the memory of his "Instant Pussy"
aerosol-can poster, to his column for *Cavalier,* to his dream of a
Rape-In against legislators' wives, to his Scapegoats and Realist
Nuns and cute anecdotes about the little daughter he sees as often
as any proper divorced Scarsdale middle-aged (38) father; goodbye forever to the notion that he is my brother who, like Paul, buys
a prostitute for the night as a birthday gift for a male friend, or
who, like Paul, reels off the names in alphabetical order of people
in the Women's Movement he has fucked, reels off names in the

best locker-room tradition—as proof that *he's* no sexist oppressor.

Let it all hang out. Let it seem bitchy, catty, dykey, frustrated, crazy, Solanasesque, nutty, frigid, ridiculous, bitter, embarrassing, man-hating, libelous, pure, unfair, envious, intuitive, low-down, stupid, petty, liberating. We are the women that men have warned us about.

And let's put one lie to rest for all time: the lie that men are oppressed, too, by sexism—the lie that there can be such a thing as "men's liberation groups." Oppression is something that one group of people commits against another group specifically be-cause of a "threatening" characteristic shared by the latter group —skin color or sex or age, etc. The oppressors are indeed *fucked up* by being masters (racism hurts whites, sexual stereotypes are harmful to men) but those masters are not *oppressed*. Any master has the alternative of divesting himself of sexism or racism—the oppressed have no alternative—for they have no power—but to fight. In the long run, Women's Liberation will of course free men—but in the short run it's going to *cost* men a lot of privilege, which no one gives up willingly or easily. Sexism is *not* the fault of women—kill your fathers, not your mothers.

Run it on down. Goodbye to a beautiful new ecology move-ment that could fight to save us all if it would stop tripping off women as earth-mother types or frontier chicks, if it would *right now* cede leadership to those who have *not* polluted the planet because that action implies power and women haven't had any power in about 5,000 years, cede leadership to those whose brains are as tough and clear as any man's but whose bodies are also unavoidably aware of the locked-in relationship between humans and their biosphere—the earth, the tides, the atmosphere, the moon. Ecology is no big schtick if you're a woman—it's always been there.

Goodbye to the complicity inherent in the Berkeley Tribes-men being part publishers of Trashman Comics; goodbye, for that matter, to the reasoning that finds whoremaster Trashman a fitting model, however comic-strip far out, for a revolutionary man—somehow related to the same Supermale reasoning that permits the first statement on Women's Liberation and male chauvinism that came out of the Black Panther Party to be made *by a man,* talkin' a whole lot 'bout how the Sisters should speak up for themselves. Such ignorance and arrogance ill befits a revolutionary.

We know how racism is worked deep into the unconscious by our System—the same way sexism is, as it appears in the very name of the Young Lords. What are you if you're a "macho woman"—a female Lord? Or, god forbid, a Young Lady? Change it, change it to the Young Gentry if you must, or never assume that the name itself is innocent of pain, of oppression.

Theory and practice and the light years between them. "Do it!" says Jerry Rubin in *Rat*'s last issue—but he doesn't, or every *Rat* reader would have known the pictured face next to his article as well as they know his own much-photographed face: it was Nancy Kurshan, the power behind the clown.

Goodbye to the New Nation and Earth People's Park, for that matter, conceived by men, announced by men, led by men—doomed before its birth by the rotting seeds of male supremacy which are to be transplanted in fresh soil.

Was it my brother who listed human beings among the *objects* which would be easily available after the Revolution: "Free grass, free food, free women, free acid, free clothes, etc.?" Was it my brother who wrote "Fuck your women till they can't stand up" and said that groupies were liberated chicks 'cause they dug a tit-shake instead of a hand-shake? The epitome of female exclusionism—"men will make the Revolution—and their chicks." Not my brother, no. Not my revolution. Not one breath of my support for the new counterleft Christ—John Sinclair. Just one less to worry about for ten years. I do not choose my enemy for my brother.

Goodbye, goodbye. The hell with the simplistic notion that automatic freedom for women—or non-white peoples—will come about ZAP! with the advent of a socialist revolution. Bullshit. Two evils pre-date capitalism and have been clearly able to survive and post-date socialism: sexism and racism. Women were the first property when the Primary Contradiction occurred: when one half of the human species decided to subjugate the other half, because it was "different," alien, the Other. From there it was an easy enough step to extend the Other to some-

one of different skin shade, different height or weight or language—or strength to resist. Goodbye to those simple-minded
optimistic dreams of socialist equality all our good socialist
brothers want us to believe. How liberal a politics that is! How
much further we will have to go to create those profound
changes that would give birth to a genderless society. *Profound*,
Sister. Beyond what is male or female. Beyond standards we all
adhere to now without daring to examine them as male-created,
male-dominated, male-fucked-up, and in male self-interest. *Beyond all known standards*, especially those easily articulated
revolutionary ones we all rhetorically invoke. Beyond, to a
species with a new name, that would not dare define itself
as Man.

I once said, "I'm a revolutionary, not just a woman," and knew
my own lie even as I said the words. The pity of that statement's
eagerness to be acceptable to those whose revolutionary zeal no
one would question, i.e., any male supremacist in the counterleft.
But to become a true revolutionary one must first become one
of the oppressed (not organize or educate or manipulate them,
but become one of them)—or realize that you *are* one of them
already. No woman wants that. Because that realization is humiliating, it hurts. It hurts to understand that at Woodstock or
Altamont a woman could be declared uptight or a poor sport if
she didn't want to be raped. It hurts to learn that the Sisters still
in male-Left captivity are putting down the crazy feminists to
make themselves look okay and unthreatening to our mutual
oppressors. It hurts to be pawns in those games. It hurts to try
and change each day *of your life right now*—not in talk, not
"in your head," and not only conveniently "out there" in the
Third World (half of which is women) or the black and brown
communities (half of which are women) but in your own home,
kitchen, bed. No getting away, no matter how else you are
oppressed, from the primary oppression of being female in a
patriarchal world. It hurts to hear that the Sisters in the Gay
Liberation Front, too, have to struggle continually against the
male chauvinism of their gay brothers. It hurts that Jane Alpert
was cheered when rapping about imperialism, racism, the Third

World, and All Those Safe Topics but hissed and booed by a
Movement crowd of men who wanted none of it when she began to
talk about Women's Liberation. The backlash is upon us.

They tell us the alternative is to hang in there and "struggle,"
to confront male domination in the counterleft, to fight beside
or behind or beneath our brothers—to show 'em we're just as
tough, just as revolushunerry, just as whatever-image-they-now-
want-of-us-as-once-they-wanted-us-to-be-feminine-and-keep-the-
home-fire-burning. They will bestow titular leadership on our
grateful shoulders, whether it's being a token woman on the
Movement Speakers Bureau Advisory Board, or being a Conspiracy groupie or one of the "respectable" chain-swinging
Motor City Nine. Sisters all, with only one real alternative: to
seize our own power into our own hands, all women, separate
and together, and make the Revolution the way it must be made
—no priorities this time, no suffering group told to wait until after.

It is the job of revolutionary feminists to build an ever
stronger independent Women's Liberation Movement, so that
the Sisters in counterleft captivity will have somewhere to turn,
to use their power and rage and beauty and coolness in their
own behalf for once, on their own terms, on their own issues,
in their own style—whatever that may be. Not for us in Women's
Liberation to hassle them and confront them the way their
men do, nor to blame them—or ourselves—for what any of us
are: an oppressed people, but a people raising our consciousness
toward something that is the other side of anger, something
bright and smooth and cool, like action unlike anything yet con-
templated or carried out. It is for us to survive (something the
white male radical has the luxury of never really worrying about,
what with all his options), to talk, to plan, to be patient, to welcome new fugitives from the counterfeit Left with no arrogance
but only humility and delight, to plan, to push—to strike.

There is something every woman wears around her neck on a
thin chain of fear—an amulet of madness. For each of us, there
exists somewhere a moment of insult so intense that she will
reach up and rip the amulet off, even if the chain tears at the
flesh of her neck. And the last protection from seeing the truth
will be gone. Do you think, tugging furtively every day at the

chain and going nicely insane as I am, that I can be concerned with the puerile squabbles of a counterfeit Left that laughs at my pain? Do you think such a concern is noticeable when set alongside the suffering of more than half the human species for the past 5,000 years—due to a whim of the other half? No, no, no, goodbye to all that.

Women are Something Else. This time, we're going to kick out all the jams, and the boys will just have to hustle to keep up, or else drop out and openly join the power structure of which they are already the illegitimate sons. Any man who claims he is serious about wanting to divest himself of cock privilege should trip on this: all male leadership out of the Left is the only way; and it's going to happen, whether through men stepping down or through women seizing the helm. It's up to the "brothers"— after all, sexism is their concern, not ours; we're too busy getting ourselves together to have to deal with their bigotry. So they'll have to make up their own minds as to whether they will be divested of just cock privilege or—what the hell, why not say it, say it?—divested of cocks. How deep the fear of that loss must be, that it can be suppressed only by the building of empires and the waging of genocidal wars!

Goodbye, goodbye forever, counterfeit Left, counterleft, male-dominated cracked-glass-mirror reflection of the Amerikan Nightmare. Women are the real Left. We are rising, powerful in our unclean bodies; bright glowing mad in our inferior brains; wild voices keening; undaunted by blood we who hemorrhage every twenty-eight days; laughing at our own beauty we who have lost our sense of humor; mourning for all each precious one of us might have been in this one living time-place had she not been born a woman; stuffing fingers into our mouths to stop the screams of fear and hate and pity for men we have loved and love still; tears in our eyes and bitterness in our mouths for children we couldn't have, or couldn't *not* have, or didn't want, or didn't want *yet*, or wanted and had in this place and this time of horror. We are rising with a fury older and potentially greater than any force in history, and this time we will be free or no one will survive. Power to all the people or to none.

All the way down, this time.

Free Kathleen Cleaver!
Free Anita Hoffman!
Free Bernardine Dohrn!
Free Donna Malone!
Free Ruth Ann Miller!
Free Leni Sinclair!
Free Jane Alpert!
Free Gumbo!
Free Bonnie Cohen!
Free Judy Lampe!

Free Kim Agnew!
Free Holly Krassner!
Free Lois Hart!
Free Alice Embree!
Free Nancy Kurshan!
Free Lynn Phillips!
Free Dinky Forman!
Free Sharon Krebs!
Free Iris Luciano!
Free Robin Morgan!

Free Valerie Solanas!

FREE OUR SISTERS!   **FREE OURSELVES!**

Rattling the Invisible Chains

A Collection of Women's
Liberation Manifestoes

Judi Bernstein, Peggy Morton, Linda Seese, Myrna Wood / *Sisters, Brothers, Lovers . . . Listen . . .*

The writers of this manifesto are women who were active in SUPA (Student Union for Peace Action), the Canadian equivalent of S.D.S. It was written for a membership conference and was instrumental in organizing the first women's liberation group in Canada.

WE ASSERT that SUPA people have the same hang-ups, frustrations, and neuroses as the rest of society. One attempted solution to our lack of real ego identity was finding it within SUPA. . . . We tried to make such a group our family, peer group, and society. We created or allowed to be created father figures. . . . As a result of this kind of psychological seeking we never gained the principles of participatory democracy. A few people were allowed to lead. Many people were excluded from leadership. The largest excluded group was women. SUPA in respect to women totally accepted the mores of the dominant society.

Stokely once said, "The only position for women in S.N.C.C. is prone." We cannot imagine any of the fine SUPA men uttering such a statement, but we can imagine many of them thinking it.

Pamphlet (Boston, New England Free Press, 1967), pp. 6–7.

In fact they put women in SUPA in two categories or roles—
the workers and the "wives."

One role for women is that of servicing the organization's men.
These women maintain the stable, homey atmosphere which the
radical man needs to survive. They raise the future radicals of
Canada. They earn the money in the mundane jobs that our
society pays people to do, so the radical men can be at home
and be political, creative, and so forth. Of course, these relationships are ones of "freedom." But it is, in fact, a one-sided freedom and we all know which side is "free." This, we feel, is a
situation not unsimilar to that of the dominant society—behind
every successful man is a successful woman. While these "real"
women are being women (earning money, cooking, and house-
cleaning), their radical partners can run around being political,
creative—writing, thinking, and oozing charisma.

But in order to do this, these men need followers and main-
tainers. Therefore the workers of the Movement—the second role
of women in SUPA—are the typists, fund raisers, and community
organizers. The vast majority of community organizers were
women and we must ask why. Community organizing was considered tedious. It required patience, sensitivity, understanding,
and more patience. It is a sad commentary that so few men felt
they could do this kind of work.

Every so often one of these workers would try, through her
efforts and work, to attain a position of leadership. They, as we
all know too well, were labeled "castrating females" and not
"real women." (They were no longer good niggers.) These women
were forced out of the organization by various unconscious means,
or accepted their subservient roles. . . .

The myth of participatory democracy is just that, if one looks
at the participation of women in SUPA. Old Leftists, who agree
totally with the aims and goals of SUPA, are astounded that we
permit the degree of male chauvinism that abounds in it to exist.
One sometimes gets the feeling that we are like a civil rights
organization with a leadership of Southern racists. . . . An organization that permits half its membership to be kept from using
their talents and energies is in sad shape. Because of the attitude
within the Movement (in the minds of both sexes) women are

not free to think and act outside the limited role given to them
in the broader society. We are allowed to speak but our thoughts
are not given serious attention until expressed by a male. We
are allowed sexual freedom but are (a) still faced with a loss
of respect on the part of many males if we take advantage of
that freedom, or (b) still expected to designate our "man" as
our first priority. (How many times have you heard a man express the sentiment that a woman in the movement is taking a
particular political position because that is what her "man"
thinks?)

As some of us women have become more aware of our intellectual and political powers we experience a loss of emotional
identity in our personal lives. Men seem to find it difficult to relate
to a person who combines both roles, i.e., "masculine" intellec-
tualism *and* "feminine" emotionalism. They insist we be one or
the other.

If we refuse to be relegated to a womanly, wifely emotional
role and insist on being accepted in the realm of the mind—
theoretical, strategic, and analytical work—most men will eventually accept us there (on a tenuous basis waiting for our first
big slip). However, we find *then* that we are no longer "feminine"
women to them and must look for emotional involvements outside the left environment. Some women react to this by revert-
ing to the physically feminine and intellectually passive role.
Hardly aware of it, they opt for the easier way—to have their
emotional and sexual needs fulfilled (by men they respect) at
the expense of their chance for intellectual development.

It is our contention that until the male chauvinists of the
movement (North American and world-wide) understand the
concept of Liberation in relation to us, the most exploited members of *any* society, the Women, they will be voicing political
lies.

Some Movement women are ready for revolution. We are thinking for ourselves. We are doing the necessary reading, writing,
and conversing to find the analysis and theory for the task. We
have the background of experience to do this. We have the
frustration of being excluded to force us to do this. We are real-
izing that we have brains—that we can be political. It is the

liberating feeling that black folk have when they discover that being black is beautiful and therefore they are beautiful. It is a feeling of beauty and power. We are getting these kinds of feelings. We have rejected many of the traditional leaders as irrelevant.

We are going to be the typers of letters and distributors of leaflets (hewers of wood and drawers of water) NO LONGER. We are recognizing our own existential position and know the exploitations that affect us. At some time the men of the Movement will have to understand our position. We are going to fight to change the atmosphere that forbids participation. We hope that those men who are excluded will join us in the fight.

S.D.S. National Resolution on Women

This resolution was passed at the December 1968 S.D.S. National Council meeting. The language of the resolution is an unfortunate example of the pompous jargon employed in S.D.S. literature since it has taken a strong Marxist-Leninist line. Even the defensive feminists here seem trapped by their self-imposed terminology.

WOMEN FORM the oldest and largest continually oppressed group in the family of human-kind, their subjugation dating from the downfall of primitive communal society and the rise of private property.

Pamphlet (Boston, New England Free Press, 1968).

The inability of the "most advanced, technologically developed" etc., capitalist society to provide equality to half its citizens not only exposes the thorough hypocrisy of all that society's words about "justice" and "equality." It also shows that the struggle for equality of women is a revolutionary task—that is, one which cannot be completed under the present system of private property and the exploitation of the majority of people by a social class which is defined by its ownership of the means of producing wealth.

Male supremacy in the movement mirrors male supremacy in capitalist society. The fact that male supremacy persists in the movement today, raises the issue that although no people's liberation can happen without a socialist revolution in this country, a socialist revolution could take place which maintains the secondary position of women in society. Therefore the liberation of women must become a conscious part of our struggle for people's liberation.

Women are not oppressed as a class but they are oppressed as women within each class. We emphasize that oppression of women through male supremacy, like racism which oppresses black people, is not merely a quantitative increase in the class exploitation which women experience but also a qualitatively different kind of oppression which they experience as women in addition to the exploitation of all working people.

Before discussing the material basis of the oppression of women, we must emphasize here that not only is the oppression of women most severe in the working class, but that black working-class women are the most oppressed group in the society. Black women are a uniquely oppressed group because as blacks, as workers, and as women, they experience the most compound forms of oppression capitalism-imperialism has devised.

The material basis of women's oppression can be listed under three main headings:

1. Women are a reserve army of labor to bring down wages; for instance, (a) they have been used in the past to take the place of male workers needed by the military in wartime; (b) at times women are used against collectively organized groups

of workers, since their condition forces them to work for lower
pay.

2. Women fulfill the function of saving enormous costs for the
bourgeoisie in that they perform free services (housekeeping),
providing the necessities of life for the working-class man at the
lowest possible costs.

3. Another objective function of the oppression of women in
capitalist society is to help obscure the class nature of that society.
The nature of women's material condition places them in a relationship which acts as a lightning rod for men's justified frustration, anger, and shame at their inability to control their natural and social environment. This means, for example, that the
potentially revolutionary violence of exploited and oppressed
people against the original forces of their exploitation and oppression are transformed and diverted into oppressive violence
towards those who have even less power than they do (e.g.,
women).

Again the analogy with racism is relevant: White workers
carry out the racist oppression of black workers in the shops.
While racism may serve to perpetuate the relative privilege of
white workers, this is in no way to say that white workers *ultimately* profit by dominating black workers, or that men *ultimately*
profit by dominating women, but rather to say that women (or
black workers) suffer their immediate oppression at the hands
of men (or white workers) who maintain a dominant position
for themselves, and as supremacists, try to perpetuate that position of dominance. . . .

In the process of this exploitation and oppression, women themselves have come to *act* by necessity according to the function
a class society has given them, hence *believe* in that function,
and, in turn, through the total internalization of the necessity
and value of that function, women themselves actively *contributed* to the perpetuation of their material exploitation. Thus
they have helped to maintain that entire ideologizing which has
"justified" these conditions.

It is incorrect to see this aspect of maintaining these conditions as "their fault" as it is incorrect to see it as the men's fault

when they accept their own lack of control in all institutions they work in and thereby support and further the interests of the ruling class. This perversion of consciousness has to be viewed as a direct result of and integral aspect of the totality of people's victimization. . . .

For clarification, we return to the much-loved and by now endearingly familiar terminology of this convention. Of course the basic-fundamental-primary contradiction is that between the working class and the bourgeoisie. At the same time the *sharpest* or most immediate contradictions may be what the convention likes to call "secondary." But whatever historical legitimacy that phrase may convey, it obscures the fact that a so-called secondary contradiction may in fact be the sharpest contradiction at a given time because people experience it most acutely in their lives. We emphasize that the sharpest contradiction can form the basis for the most immediate struggle against oppression which in turn leads to greater, more effective participation in the total struggle. Hence we do not believe that the struggle for women's liberation is a detraction from the worker-capitalist struggle. Rather, the fight for women's liberation is a concretization of the struggle for the liberation of all people from oppression. It doesn't stand apart from the fight against capitalism in our society, but rather is an integral part of that fight.

Program

In order for women to become full political people in S.D.S. and in order for the oppression of women to be taken on as a struggle by S.D.S., male supremacy must be eliminated within the organization itself. S.D.S. people must battle two beliefs. First, women in S.D.S. must battle the belief that struggling for their own liberation is not important. Second, S.D.S. must battle the belief that the fight for equality of women is solely the business of women, and that only women have the right and responsibility to oppose male domination.

Whatever forms within S.D.S. are decided upon to organize this campaign, they should be such that the chapter as a whole has charge and responsibility, with women taking the main responsibility to organize women for their liberation, and men taking the main responsibility to attack male supremacy and to win the support of other men.

We propose that S.D.S. take up the fight for women's rights on campus by raising several specific demands which will expose the way women are specially oppressed within the university set-up and rally students to fight against that oppression.

1. We should launch a campaign to bring the wages of women employees of the university up to the level of men's. This must definitely not be subordinated in a general struggle to raise wages of all employees, nor should it be postponed on the ground that it would divert attention from the just demands of all employees, male and female. The central question is oppression—the general oppression of all employees and the special harsh oppression of women employees. In some cases, tackling the especially low level of women's wages may prove to be the key to solidifying all the employees and winning improvements for all. In general, it would be better to raise the two questions side by side, with equal emphasis; but in no case should S.D.S. challenge the low wages and bad conditions generally without especially challenging the especially low wages and bad conditions for women.

2. It is necessary to begin the struggle for women's equality in educational institutions where working-class women are trained and socialized. Within the context of work in the high schools, state schools, teachers colleges, junior colleges, and trade schools, emphasis should be placed on beauty schools, secretarial, nursing, and other job training schools for women.

3. We should relate the struggle for women's rights in the schools to the struggle of women generally, and especially working class women, against the institutions that repress them, for example, juvenile court, girls' homes, women's detention centers and prisons, family court, welfare, labor battles such as Lévi-Strauss, and others.

4. Launch fights around curriculum and organize in classrooms to expose how the schools reinforce the male supremacist definition of "woman's role." Challenge the counseling practice of steering women into auxiliary occupations. Demand the teaching

of the history of women's struggles for liberation. This should be carried out in the context of on-going programs which challenge course content and direction.

The campaign for specific demands should be accompanied by research, internal education, and propaganda by S.D.S. explaining why women are still subjugated by men, why they cannot achieve equality under the present system, and why all men and women should fight for women's liberation.

The WITCH Manifesto

On Halloween 1968 women guerrillas dressed as witches descended on the New York Stock Exchange heaping curses and spells upon high finance and singing a song especially written for the occasion, "Up Against the Wall Street." The WITCH Manifesto is another expression of this vociferous and theatrical group—or should we say coven?

WITCH is in all women, everything.
It's theatre, revolution,
Magic, terror and joy.
It's an awareness that witches and gypsies
Were the first guerrilla and resistance fighters
Against oppression—the oppression of women,

From *Women's International Terrorist Conspiracy from Hell*, New York, 1968.

Down through the ages.
Witches have always been women who dared
To be groovy, courageous, aggressive,
Intelligent, non-conformist, explorative,
Independent, sexually liberated, and revolutionary.
(This may explain why nine million women
Have been burned as witches.)

Witches were the first friendly heads
    and dealers,
The first birth-control practitioners,
    and abortionists,
The first alchemists.
They bowed to no man,
Being the last living remnants
Of the oldest culture of all—
One in which men and women were equal
Sharers in a truly cooperative society,
Before the death-dealing sexual,
Economic, and spiritual repression
Of the "Imperialist Phallic Society"
Took over and began to shit all over nature,
And human life.

A witch lives and laughs in every woman.
She is the free part of each of us,
Beneath the shy smiles,
The acquiescence to absurd male domination,
The make-up or flesh-suffocating clothing
Our sick society demands.
There is no joining WITCH.
If you are a woman, and dare to look within yourself,
You are a witch.
You make your own rules.
You are free and beautiful.
You can be invisible or evident,
In how you choose to make your witch self known.

You can form your own Coven of sister witches,
Do your own actions.
Whatever is repressive,
Solely male-oriented,
Greedy, puritanical, authoritarian,
Those are your targets.
Your weapons are theatre,
Magic, satire, explosions, herbs,
Music, costumes, masks, stickers,
Paint, brooms, voodoo dolls,
Cats, candles, bells,
Your boundless beautiful imagination.
Your power comes from your own self,
As a woman.
From sharing, rapping, and acting
In concert with your sisters.
You are pledged to free our brothers
From oppression and stereotyped sexual roles,
As well as ourselves.
You are a witch by being female,
Untamed, angry, joyous and immortal.
You are a witch by saying aloud
"I am a witch"
And thinking about that.

Valerie Solanas / *The SCUM Manifesto*

The Society for Cutting Up Men—as far as the editors know—
has never had more than one member: its founder and theorist,
Valerie Solanas. Can the SCUM manifesto, therefore, be considered a *true* manifesto? Perhaps not. Yet that is what its author
intended it to be; and so we place it here. Had Solanas not let
her ideology steer her toward an attempt on the life of pop-
artist Andy Warhol in 1968, one might be tempted to regard
her exercise in misanthropic extremism as satire in the vein
of Swift's "Modest Proposal." As it is, one cannot be sure.
Perhaps she anticipated a following, knowing she had given
voice to a vindictive rage few of us, men or women, want to
admit exists in the female heart. Her diatribe takes its place
beside the intemperance of Nietzsche and Weininger as one of
the most savage assaults of the sex war.

LIFE IN this society being, at best, an utter bore and no aspect
of society being at all relevant to women, there remains to civic-
minded, responsible, thrill-seeking females only to overthrow the
government, eliminate the money system, institute complete automation, and destroy the male sex.

It is now technically possible to reproduce without the aid of
males (or, for that matter, females) and to produce only females.

From *SCUM (Society for Cutting Up Men)* Manifesto, New York, Olympia
Press, 1968. Excerpts from pp. 31–50; 52–57; 60–62; 71–73; 77–79; 83–84.
Reprinted by permission of the publishers.

We must begin immediately to do so. . . . To be male is to be deficient, emotionally limited; maleness is a deficiency disease and males are emotional cripples.

The male is completely egocentric, trapped inside himself, incapable of empathizing or identifying with others, of love, friendship, affection, or tenderness. He is a completely isolated unit, incapable of rapport with anyone. His responses are entirely visceral, not cerebral; his intelligence is a mere tool in the service of his drives and needs; he is incapable of mental passion, mental interaction; he can't relate to anything other than his own physical sensations. He is a half-dead, unresponsive lump, incapable of giving or receiving pleasure or happiness; consequently, he is at best an utter bore, an inoffensive blob, since only those capable of absorption in others can be charming. He is trapped in a twilight zone halfway between humans and apes, and is far worse off than the apes, because unlike the apes he is capable of a large array of negative feelings—hate, jealousy, contempt, disgust, guilt, shame, doubt—and moreover he is *aware* of what he is and isn't.

Although completely physical, the male is unfit even for stud service. Even assuming mechanical proficiency, which few men have, he is, first of all, incapable of zestfully, lustfully, tearing off a piece, but is instead eaten up with guilt, shame, fear and insecurity, feelings rooted in male nature, which the most enlightened training can only minimize; second, the physical feeling he attains is next to nothing; and, third, he is not empathizing with his partner, but is obsessed with how he's doing, turning in an A performance, doing a good plumbing job. . . .

The male, because of his obsession to compensate for not being female combined with his inability to relate and to feel compassion, has made of the world a shit-pile. He is responsible for: WAR. The male's normal method of compensation for not being female, namely, getting his Big Gun off, is grossly inadequate, as he can get it off only a very limited number of times; so he gets it off on a really massive scale, and proves to the entire world that he's a "Man." . . .

Every man, deep down, knows he's a worthless piece of shit. Overwhelmed by a sense of animalism and deeply ashamed of it; wanting, not to express himself, but to hide from others his total physicality, total egocentricity, the hate and contempt he feels for other men, and to hide from himself the hate and contempt he suspects other men feel for him; having a crudely constructed nervous system that is easily upset by the least display of emotion or feeling, the male tries to enforce a "social" code that ensures a perfect blandness, unsullied by the slightest trace of feeling or upsetting opinion. . . .

Although he wants to be an individual, the male is scared of anything about him that is the slightest bit different from other men; it causes him to suspect he's not really a "Man," that he's passive and totally sexual, a highly upsetting suspicion. . . . The male dares to be different to the degree that he accepts his passivity and his desire to be female, his fagginess. The farthest-out male is the drag queen, but he, although different from most men, is exactly like all other drag queens; like the functionalist, he has an identity—he is a female. He tries to define all his troubles away—but still no individuality. Not completely convinced that he's a woman, highly insecure about being sufficiently female, he conforms compulsively to the man-made feminine stereotype, ending up as nothing but a bundle of stilted mannerisms.

To be sure he's a "Man," the male must see to it that the female be clearly a "Woman," the opposite of a "Man," that is, the female must act like a faggot. And Daddy's Girl, all of whose female instincts were wrenched out of her when little, easily and obligingly adapts herself to the role.

Having no sense of right or wrong, no conscience, which can only stem from an ability to empathize with others . . . having no faith in his non-existent self, being necessarily competitive and, by nature, unable to cooperate, the male feels a need for external guidance and control. So he created authorities—priests, experts, bosses, leaders, etc.—and government. Wanting the female (Mama) to guide him, but unable to accept this fact . . . wanting to play Woman, to usurp her function as Guider and Protector, he sees to it that all authorities are male.

There's no reason why a society consisting of rational beings capable of empathizing with each other, complete and having no natural reason to compete, should have a government, laws or leaders.

The male's inability to relate to anybody or anything makes his life pointless and meaningless (the ultimate male insight is that life is absurd), so he invented philosophy and religion. Being empty, he looks outward, not only for guidance and control, but for salvation and for the meaning of life. Happiness being for him impossible on earth, he invented Heaven. . . .

Religion not only provides the male with a goal (Heaven) and helps keep women tied to men, but offers rituals through which he can try to expiate the guilt and shame he feels at not defending himself enough against his sexual impulses; in essence, that guilt and shame he feels at being a male.

Most men, utterly cowardly, project their inherent weaknesses onto women, label them female weaknesses and believe themselves to have female strengths; most philosophers, not quite so cowardly, face the fact that male lacks exist in men, but still can't face the fact that they exist in men only. So they label the male condition the Human Condition, pose their nothingness problem, which horrifies them, as a philosophical dilemma, thereby giving stature to their animalism, grandiloquently label their nothingness their "Identity Problem," and proceed to prattle on pompously about the "Crisis of the Individual," the "Essence of Being," "Existence Preceding Essence," "Existential Modes of Being," etc., etc.

A woman not only takes her identity and individuality for granted, but knows instinctively that the only wrong is to hurt others, and that the meaning of life is love. . . .

Being completely self-centered and unable to relate to anything outside himself, the male's "conversation," when not about himself, is an impersonal droning on, removed from anything of human value. Male "intellectual conversation" is a strained, compulsive attempt to impress the female.

Daddy's Girl, passive, adaptable, respectful of and in awe of the male, allows him to impose his hideously dull chatter on her. This is not too difficult for her, as the tension and anxiety, the lack of cool . . . the unsureness of her own feelings and sensations that Daddy instilled in her make her perceptions superficial

and render her unable to see that the male's babble is a babble;
like the aesthete "appreciating" the blob that's labeled "Great
Art," she believes she's grooving on what bores the shit out of
her. Not only does she permit his babble to dominate, she adapts
her own "conversation" accordingly.

Trained from early childhood in niceness, politeness, and "dignity," in pandering to the male need to disguise his animalism,
she obligingly reduces her "conversation" to small talk, a bland,
insipid avoidance of any topic beyond the utterly trivial—or, if
"educated," to "intellectual" discussion, that is, impersonal dis-
coursing on irrelevant abstractions—the Gross National Product,
the Common Market, the influence of Rimbaud on symbolist
painting. So adept is she at pandering that it eventually becomes
second nature and she continues to pander to men even when
in the company of other females only. . . .

Niceness, politeness, "dignity," insecurity and self-absorption
are hardly conducive to intensity and wit, qualities a conversation must have to be worthy of the name. Such conversation is
hardly rampant, as only completely self-confident, arrogant, out-
going, proud, tough-minded females are capable of intense,
bitchy, witty conversation.

Men have contempt for themselves, for all other men and for
all women who respect and pander to them; the insecure, approval-seeking, pandering male females have contempt for themselves and for all women like them; the self-confident, swinging,
thrill-seeking female females have contempt for men and for the
pandering male females. In short, contempt is the order of the
day.

Love is not dependency or sex, but friendship, and, therefore,
love can't exist between two males, between a male and a female
or between two females, one or both of whom is a mindless,
insecure, pandering male; like conversation, love can exist only
between two secure, free-wheeling, independent, groovy female
females, since friendship is based on respect, not contempt.

Even among groovy females deep friendships seldom occur in
adulthood, as almost all of them are either tied up with men in
order to survive economically, or bogged down in hacking their
way through the jungle and in trying to keep their heads above

the amorphous mass. Love can't flourish in a society based on money and meaningless work; it requires complete economic as well as personal freedom, leisure time, and the opportunity to engage in intensely absorbing, emotionally satisfying activities, which, when shared with those you respect, lead to deep friendship. Our "society" provides practically no opportunity to engage in such activities. . . .

Sex is not part of a relationship; on the contrary, it is a solitary experience, noncreative, a gross waste of time. The female can easily—far more easily than she may think—condition away her sex drive, leaving her completely cool and cerebral and free to pursue truly worthy relationships and activities; but the male, who seems to dig women sexually and who seeks constantly to arouse them, stimulates the highly-sexed female to frenzies of lust, throwing her into a sex bag from which few women ever escape. The lecherous male excites the lustful female; he *has* to—when the female transcends her body, rises above animalism, the male, whose ego consists of his cock, will disappear.

Sex is the refuge of the mindless. And the more mindless the woman, the more deeply embedded in the male "culture," in short, the nicer she is, the more sexual she is. . . .

On the other hand those females least embedded in the male "culture," the least nice, those crass and simple souls who reduce fucking to fucking, who are too childish for the grown-up world of suburbs, mortgages, mops and baby shit, too selfish to raise kids and husbands, too uncivilized to give a shit for anyone's opinion of them, too arrogant to respect Daddy, the "Greats" or the deep wisdom of the Ancients, who trust only their own animal, gutter instincts, who equate Culture with chicks, whose sole diversion is prowling for emotional thrills and excitement, who are given to disgusting, nasty, upsetting "scenes," hateful, violent bitches, given to slamming those who unduly irritate them in the teeth, who'd sink a shiv into a man's chest or ram an icepick up his asshole as soon as look at him if they knew they could get away with it; in short, those who, by the standards of our "culture," are SCUM . . . these females are cool and relatively cerebral and skirting asexuality. . . .

If all women simply left men, refused to have anything to do with any of them, ever, all men, the government and the national economy would collapse completely. Even without leaving men, women who are aware of the extent of their superiority to and power over men, could acquire complete control over everything within a few weeks, could effect a total submission of males to females. . . . The male . . . wants desperately to be led by females, wants Mama in charge, wants to abandon himself to her care. But this is not a sane society, and most women are not even dimly aware of where they're at in relation to men.

The conflict, therefore, is not between females and males, but between SCUM—dominant, secure, self-confident, nasty, violent, selfish, independent, proud, thrill-seeking, free-wheeling, arrogant females, who consider themselves fit to rule the universe, who have free-wheeled to the limits of this "society" and are ready to wheel on to something far beyond what it has to offer—and nice, passive, accepting, "cultivated," polite, dignified, subdued, dependent . . . insecure, approval-seeking Daddy's Girls, who can't cope with the unknown . . . who feel secure only with Big Daddy standing by, with a big, strong man to lean on and with a fat, hairy face in the White House, who are too cowardly to face up to the hideous reality of what a man is. . . .

But SCUM is too impatient to hope and wait for the debrainwashing of millions of assholes. Why should the swinging females continue to plod dismally along with the dull male ones? Why should the fates of the groovy and the creepy be intertwined? Why should the active and imaginative consult the passive and dull on social policy? Why should the independent be confined to the sewer along with the dependent who need Daddy to cling to? . . .

SCUM will become members of the un-work force, the fuck-up force; they will get jobs of various kinds and unwork. For example, SCUM salesgirls will not charge for merchandise; SCUM telephone operators will not charge for calls; SCUM office and factory workers, in addition to fucking up their work, will secretly destroy equipment. SCUM will unwork at a job until fired, then get a new job to unwork at. . . .

Dropping out is not the answer; fucking-up is. Most women are already dropped out; they were never in. Dropping out gives control to those few who don't drop out; dropping out is exactly what the establishment leaders want; it plays into the hands of the enemy; it strengthens the system instead of undermining it, since it is based entirely on the non-participation, passivity, apathy, and non-involvement of the mass of women. . . .

SCUM is against the entire system, the very idea of law and government. SCUM is out to destroy the system, not attain certain rights within it. Also, SCUM—always selfish, always cool—will always aim to avoid detection and punishment. SCUM will always be furtive, sneaky, underhanded (although SCUM murders will always be known to be such). . . .

The sick, irrational men, those who attempt to defend themselves against their disgustingness, when they see SCUM barreling down on them, will cling in terror to Big Mama with her Big Bouncy Boobies, but Boobies won't protect them against SCUM; Big Mama will be clinging to Big Daddy, who will be in the corner shitting in his forceful, dynamic pants. Men who are rational, however, won't kick or struggle or raise a distressing fuss, but will just sit back, relax, enjoy the show and ride the waves to their demise.

Women's Liberation Collective / *Towards a Woman's Revolutionary Manifesto*

The following are the recommendations for action and organization of the Palo Alto Women's Liberation Collective, a socialist group which takes the dissolution of American capitalism to be a precondition of women's emancipation. The mani-

Women's Liberation Collective, Palo Alto, California, 1969.

festo states that women's "participation in the revolutionary
movement must be twofold, (1) To expose the nature of the
capitalist control of the society: ruling class oppression of male
and female, white, black, and brown; (2) To expose the nature
of the oppression of women over the centuries, and continuing unabated under political systems of feudalism, capitalism
and imperialism." While convinced that socialist societies have
made "great advances" toward liberating women, the group
warns that women need independent political organization,
lest "after the people have achieved power over the State . . .
the 'people' will turn out to mean 'men.' "

1. LET US join together in groups (fifteen or less) to discuss
all aspects of womanhood. To understand the nature and extent
of our oppression, we must discuss everything from diapers to
orgasms, from political economy to the woman's page, from the
desire to have children to the desire to be married to the desire
to own a home. We must analyze everything we talk about. We
must encourage women from various classes and minorities to
meet in groups and talk about our real problems on an honest
basis, to interchange ideas evolved in all groups and learn from
each other. . . .

2. We must question every advertisement to find out how we
are being sold something and why. Observe how the advertisement portrays women. WE all know each other from the media;
we have ceased to know each other in actuality. What we see
portrayed in the media will tell men what to expect us to be
and what we ourselves will come to believe we are. Do we ap-
prove of this? If not, we must inform the advertisers that we
expect them to project what we believe ourselves to be. If no
compliance, WE MUST NOT BUY THE PRODUCT. . . . We
must subject magazine stories, articles and editorials, newspapers,
novels, theater, television programs, and sports to the same test.
We must write our own and tell the world what we really are.
We must cease to be defined by men—we must define ourselves.

3. We must learn to cooperate with and assist each other. For
example, we must join together to form nurseries, child-care

facilities and car pools, cooperatives and communes. We must take care of each other where employment, housing, medical, welfare, parole, and emotional needs arise; we must share clothes, toys, money, etc.

4. We must learn not to view ourselves as commodities and to correct those who do.

5. We must debunk myths on the nature of sexuality, inferiority-superiority, domination-subjugation, mental and physical capability. The truth will become evident through the interchange of ideas in all groups and by research and study.

6. We must oppose the educational institutions which serve the interests of capitalist society by emphasizing competition, possessiveness, greed and fear.

7. We must learn to respect ourselves and each other; to demand this respect from men, and implement this respect by explanation, not bargaining and concessions.

8. We must not adopt the values of men. Their values are as misshapen as our own at the present time. Protest the imposition of their values on ourselves and our children.

9. We must cherish each other.

REVOLUTIONARY DEMANDS

1. Full employment at equal pay for women. Paid time off when it is devoted to raising young children. Paid time off for maternity.

2. Free, nondiscriminatory education from kindergarten to the highest level. We will cease being channeled into a "service role" mentality, and will be trained to participate in all areas of intellectual activity and technical skills equally with men.

3. Complete control of our own bodies and reproductive functions, including birth control, abortion, and pregnancy.

4. Legal and social discrimination against non-married relationships should cease.

5. Free medical care for child-bearing, babies, young children, abortion and birth control.

6. Assumption of responsibility by the State for the socially necessary function of child-bearing. Reimbursement by the State

for the bearing and raising of children. Provision of nurseries, schools and child-care facilities as required by women.

7. Responsibility for the home should be assumed by all family members. Communal family members will share equally in the maintenance of the home and household duties. Single family units will do likewise.

8. Abolition of sex as a commodity. Sex is in no case to be sold; neither for money, services, nor for security, prestige, etc.

Redstockings Manifesto

Redstockings is the most outspoken radical women's group in New York. The name appears to be an allusion to the Victorian feminist, Harriet Grote, who used to sit with her feet up displaying bright red stockings.

I. AFTER CENTURIES of individual and preliminary political struggle, women are uniting to achieve their final liberation from male supremacy. Redstockings is dedicated to building this unity and winning our freedom.

II. Women are an oppressed class. Our oppression is total, affecting every facet of our lives. We are exploited as sex objects, breeders, domestic servants, and cheap labor. We are considered inferior beings, whose only purpose is to enhance men's lives. Our humanity is denied. Our prescribed behavior is enforced by the threat of physical violence.

Mimeographed; New York, July 7, 1969.

Because we have lived so intimately with our oppressors, in isolation from each other, we have been kept from seeing our personal suffering as a political condition. This creates the illusion that a woman's relationship with her man is a matter of interplay between two unique personalities, and can be worked out individually. In reality, every such relationship is a *class* relationship, and the conflicts between individual men and women are *political* conflicts that can only be solved collectively.

III. We identify the agents of our oppression as men. Male supremacy is the oldest, most basic form of domination. All other forms of exploitation and oppression (racism, capitalism, imperialism, etc.) are extensions of male supremacy: men dominate women, a few men dominate the rest. All power structures throughout history have been male-dominated and male-oriented. Men have controlled all political, economic and cultural institutions and backed up this control with physical force. They have used their power to keep women in an inferior position. *All men* receive economic, sexual, and psychological benefits from male supremacy. *All men* have oppressed women.

IV. Attempts have been made to shift the burden of responsibility from men to institutions or to women themselves. We condemn these arguments as evasions. Institutions alone do not oppress; they are merely tools of the oppressor. To blame institutions implies that men and women are equally victimized, obscures the fact that men benefit from the subordination of women, and gives men the excuse that they are forced to be oppressors. On the contrary, any man is free to renounce his superior position provided that he is willing to be treated like a woman by other men.

We also reject the idea that women consent to or are to blame for their own oppression. Women's submission is not the result of brainwashing, stupidity, or mental illness but of continual, daily pressure from men. We do not need to change ourselves, but to change men.

The most slanderous evasion of all is that women can oppress men. The basis for this illusion is the isolation of individual relationships from their political context and the tendency of men to see any legitimate challenge to their privileges as persecution.

V. We regard our personal experience, and our feelings about that experience, as the basis for an analysis of our common situation. We cannot rely on existing ideologies as they are all products of male supremacist culture. We question every generalization and accept none that are not confirmed by our experience.

Our chief task at present is to develop female class consciousness through sharing experience and publicly exposing the sexist foundation of all our institutions. Consciousness-raising is not "therapy," which implies the existence of individual solutions and falsely assumes that the male-female relationship is purely personal, but the only method by which we can ensure that our program for liberation is based on the concrete realities of our lives.

The first requirement for raising class consciousness is honesty, in private and in public, with ourselves and other women.

VI. We identify with all women. We define our best interest as that of the poorest, most brutally exploited woman.

We repudiate all economic, racial, educational, or status privileges that divide us from other women. We are determined to recognize and eliminate any prejudices we may hold against other women.

We are committed to achieving internal democracy. We will do whatever is necessary to ensure that every woman in our movement has an equal chance to participate, assume responsibility, and develop her political potential.

VII. We call on all our sisters to unite with us in struggle.

We call on all men to give up their male privileges and support women's liberation in the interest of our humanity and their own.

In fighting for our liberation we will always take the side of women against their oppressors. We will not ask what is "revolutionary" or "reformist," only what is good for women.

The time for individual skirmishes has passed. This time we are going all the way.

Joreen / *The BITCH Manifesto*

The BITCH Manifesto attempts to speak for the forgotten woman—the woman who doesn't fit in, who despises and utterly rejects the feminine stereotype, and who proudly proclaims that "bitch is beautiful."

BITCH is an organization which does not yet exist. The name is not an acronym. It stands for exactly what it sounds like.

BITCH is composed of Bitches. There are many definitions of a bitch. The most complimentary definition is a female dog. Those definitions of bitches who are also *Homo sapiens* are rarely as objective. They vary from person to person and depend strongly on how much of a bitch the definer considers herself. However, everyone agrees that a bitch is always a female, dog or otherwise.

It is also generally agreed that a Bitch is aggressive, and therefore unfeminine (ahem). She may be sexy, in which case she becomes a Bitch Goddess, a special case which will not concern us here. But she is never a "true woman."

Bitches have some or all of the following characteristics.

1) *Personality.* Bitches are aggressive, assertive, domineering, overbearing, strong-minded, spiteful, hostile, direct, blunt, candid, obnoxious, thick-skinned, hard-headed, vicious, dogmatic, competent, competitive, pushy, loud-mouthed, independent, stubborn, demanding, manipulative, egoistic, driven, achieving, overwhelm-

---

Unpublished manuscript, 1969. Printed by permission of the author.

ing, threatening, scary, ambitious, tough, brassy, masculine, bois-
terous, and turbulent. Among other things. A Bitch occupies a lot
of psychological space. You always know she is around. A Bitch
takes shit from no one. You may not like her, but you cannot
ignore her.

2) *Physical.* Bitches are big, tall, strong, large, loud, brash,
harsh, awkward, clumsy, sprawling, strident, ugly. Bitches move
their bodies freely rather than restrain, refine, and confine their
motions in the proper feminine manner. They clomp up stairs,
stride when they walk and don't worry about where they put
their legs when they sit. They have loud voices and often use
them. Bitches are not pretty.

3) *Orientation.* Bitches seek their identity strictly through
themselves and what they do. They are subjects, not objects.
They may have a relationship with a person or organization,
but they never *marry* anyone or anything: man, mansion, or
movement. Thus Bitches prefer to plan their own lives rather
than live from day to day, action to action, or person to person.
They are independent cusses and believe they are capable of
doing anything they damn well want to. If something gets in
their way, well, that's why they become Bitches. If they are
professionally inclined, they will seek careers and have no fear
of competing with anyone. If not professionally inclined, they
still seek self-expression and self-actualization. Whatever they
do, they want an active role and are frequently perceived as
domineering. Often they do dominate other people when roles
are not available to them which more creatively sublimate their
energies and utilize their capabilities. More often they are ac-
cused of domineering when doing what would be considered
natural by a man.

A true Bitch is self-determined, but the term "bitch" is usually
applied with less discrimination. It is a popular derogation to
put down uppity women that was created by men and adopted
by women. Like the term "nigger," "bitch" serves the social
function of isolating and discrediting a class of people who do
not conform to the socially accepted patterns of behavior.

BITCH does not use this word in the negative sense. A
woman should be proud to declare she is a Bitch, because
Bitch is Beautiful. It should be an act of affirmation by self and

not negation by others. Not everyone can qualify as a Bitch. One does not have to have *all* of the above three qualities, but should be well possessed of at least two of them to be considered a Bitch. If a woman qualifies in all three, at least partially, she is a Bitch's Bitch. Only Superbitches qualify totally in all three categories, and there are very few of those. Most don't last long in this society.

The most prominent characteristic of all Bitches is that they rudely violate conceptions of proper sex role behavior. They violate them in different ways, but they all violate them. Their attitudes towards themselves and other people, their goal orientations, their personal style, their appearance and way of handling their bodies, all jar people and make them feel uneasy. Sometimes it's conscious and sometimes it's not, but people generally feel uncomfortable around Bitches. They consider them aberrations. They find their style disturbing. So they create a dumping ground for all whom they deplore as bitchy and call them "frustrated women." Frustrated they may be, but the cause is social not sexual.

What is disturbing about a Bitch is that she is androgynous. She incorporates within herself qualities traditionally defined as "masculine" as well as "feminine." A Bitch is blunt, direct, arrogant, at times egoistic. She has no liking for the indirect, subtle, mysterious ways of the "eternal feminine." She disdains the vicarious life deemed natural to women because she wants to live a life of her own.

Our society has defined humanity as male, and female as something other than male. In this way, females could be human only by living vicariously through a male. To be able to live, a woman has to agree to serve, honor and obey a man and what she gets in exchange is at best a shadow life. Bitches refuse to serve, honor, or obey anyone. They demand to be fully functioning human beings, not just shadows. They want to be both female and human. This makes them social contradictions. The mere existence of Bitches negates the idea that a woman's reality must come through her relationship to a man and defies the belief that women are perpetual children who must always be under the guidance of another.

Therefore, if taken seriously, a Bitch is a threat to the social structures which enslave women and the social values which justify keeping them in their place. She is living testimony that woman's oppression does not have to be, and as such raises doubts about the validity of the whole social system. Because she is a threat she is not taken seriously. Instead, she is dismissed as a deviant. Men create a special category for her in which she is accounted at least partially human, but not really a woman. To the extent to which they relate to her as a human being, they refuse to relate to her as a sexual being. Women are even more threatened because they cannot forget she is a woman. They are afraid they will identify with her too closely. She has a freedom and an independence which they envy and challenges them to forsake the security of their chains. Neither men nor women can face the reality of a Bitch because to do so would force them to face the corrupt reality of themselves. She is dangerous. So they dismiss her as a freak.

This is the root of her own oppression as a woman. Bitches are not only oppressed as women, they are oppressed for not being like women. Because she has insisted on being human before being feminine, on being true to herself before kowtowing to social pressures, a Bitch grows up an outsider. Even as girls, Bitches violated the limits of accepted sex role behavior. They did not identify with other women and few were lucky enough to have an adult Bitch serve as a role model. They had to make their own way, and the pitfalls this uncharted course posed contributed to both their uncertainty and their independence.

Bitches are good examples of how women can be strong enough to survive even the rigid, punitive socialization of our society. As young girls it never quite penetrated their consciousness that women were supposed to be inferior to men in any but the mother/helpmate role. They asserted themselves as children and never really internalized the slave style of wheedling and cajolery which is called feminine. Some Bitches were oblivious to the usual social pressures and some stubbornly resisted them. Some developed a superficial feminine style and some remained tomboys long past the time when such behavior is tolerated. All Bitches refused, in mind and spirit, to conform to the idea that there were limits on what they could be and do. They placed no bounds on their aspirations or their conduct.

For this resistance they were roundly condemned. They were put down, snubbed, sneered at, talked about, laughed at, and ostracized. Our society made women into slaves and then condemned them for acting like slaves. Those who refused to act like slaves they disparaged for not being true women.

It was all done very subtly. Few people were so direct as to say that they did not like Bitches because they did not play the sex role game. In fact, few were sure why they did not like Bitches. They did not realize that their violation of the reality structure endangered the structure. Somehow, from early childhood on, some girls didn't fit in and were good objects to make fun of. But few people consciously recognized the root of their dislike. The issue was never confronted. If it was talked about at all, it was done with snide remarks behind the young girl's back. Bitches were made to feel that there was something wrong with them; something personally wrong.

Teen-age girls are particularly vicious in the scapegoat game. This is the time of life when women are told they must compete the hardest for the spoils (i.e., men) which society allows. They must assert their femininity or see it denied. They are very unsure of themselves and adopt the rigidity that goes with uncertainty. They are hard on their competitors and even harder on those who decline to compete. Those of their peers who do not share their concerns and practice the arts of charming men are excluded from most social groupings. If she didn't know it before, a Bitch learns during these years that she is different.

As she gets older she learns more about why she is different. As Bitches begin to take jobs, or participate in organizations, they are rarely content to sit quietly and do what they are told. A Bitch has a mind of her own and wants to use it. She wants to rise high, be creative, assume responsibility. She knows she is capable and wants to use her capabilities. This, not pleasing the men she works for, is her primary goal.

When she meets the hard brick wall of sex prejudice she is not compliant. She will knock herself out batting her head against the wall because she will not accept her defined role as

an auxiliary. Occasionally she crashes her way through. Or
she uses her ingenuity to find a loophole, or creates one. Or she
is ten times better than anyone else competing with her. She
also accepts less than her due. Like other women her ambitions
have often been dulled for she has not totally escaped the badge
of inferiority placed upon the "weaker sex." She will often
espouse contentment with being the power behind the throne—
provided that she does have real power—while rationalizing that
she really does not want the recognition that comes with also
having the throne. Because she has been put down most of her
life, both for being a woman and for not being a true woman,
a Bitch will not always recognize that what she has achieved
is not attainable by the typical woman. A highly competent
Bitch often deprecates herself by refusing to recognize her
own superiority. She is wont to say that she is average or less
so; if she can do it, anyone can.

As adults, Bitches may have learned the feminine role, at
least the outward style, but they are rarely comfortable in it.
This is particularly true of those women who are physical
Bitches. They want to free their bodies as well as their minds
and deplore the effort they must waste confining their physical
motions or dressing the role in order not to turn people off. Too,
because they violate sex role expectations physically, they are
not as free to violate them psychologically or intellectually. A
few deviations from the norm can be tolerated but too many
are too threatening. It's bad enough not to think like a woman,
sound like a woman, or do the kinds of things women are supposed to do. To also not look like a woman, move like a woman,
or act like a woman is to go way beyond the pale. Ours is a
rigid society with narrow limits placed on the extent of human
diversity. Women in particular are defined by their physical
characteristics. Bitches who do not violate these limits are freer
to violate others. Bitches who do violate them in style or size
can be somewhat envious of those who do not have to so
severely restrain the expansiveness of their personalities and
behavior. Often these Bitches are tortured more because their
deviancy is always evident. But they do have a compensation
in that large Bitches have a good deal less difficulty being taken

seriously than small women. One of the sources of their suffering as women is also a source of their strength.

The trial by fire which most Bitches go through while growing up either makes them or breaks them. They are strung tautly between the two poles of being true to their own nature or being accepted as a social being. This makes them very sensitive people, but it is a sensitivity the rest of the world is unaware of. For on the outside they have frequently grown a thick, defensive callus which can make them seem hard and bitter at times. This is particularly true of those Bitches who have been forced to become isolates in order to avoid being remade and destroyed by their peers. Those who are fortunate enough to have grown up with some similar companions, understanding parents, a good role model or two, and a very strong will, can avoid some of the worse aspects of being a Bitch. Having endured less psychological punishment for being what they were, they can accept their differentness with the ease that comes from self-confidence.

Those who had to make their way entirely on their own have an uncertain path. Some finally realize that their pain comes not just because they do not conform but because they do not *want* to conform. With this comes the recognition that there is nothing particularly wrong with *them*—they just don't fit into this kind of society. Many eventually learn to insulate themselves from the harsh social environment. However, this too has its price. Unless they are cautious and conscious, the confidence gained in this painful manner—with no support from their sisters—is more often a kind of arrogance. Bitches can become so hard and calloused that the last vestiges of humanity become buried deep within and almost destroyed.

Not all Bitches make it. Instead of calluses, they develop open sores. Instead of confidence they develop an unhealthy sensitivity to rejection. Seemingly tough on the outside, on the inside they are a bloody pulp, raw from the lifelong verbal whipping they have had to endure. These are Bitches who have gone Bad. They often go around with a chip on their shoulders and use their strength for unproductive retaliation when someone accepts their dare to knock it off. These Bitches can be very

obnoxious because they never really trust people. They have
not learned to use their strength constructively.

Bitches who have been mutilated as human beings often turn
their fury on other people—particularly other women. This is
one example of how women are trained to keep themselves
and other women in their place. Bitches are no less guilty than
non-Bitches of self-hatred and group-hatred and those who
have gone Bad suffer the worst of both these afflictions. All
Bitches are scapegoats and those who have not survived the
psychological gauntlet are the butt of everyone's disdain. As a
group, Bitches are treated by other women much as women in
general are treated by society—all right in their place, good to
exploit and gossip about, but otherwise to be ignored or put
down. They are threats to the traditional woman's position and
they are also an outgroup to which she can feel superior. Most
women feel both better than and jealous of Bitches. While
comforting themselves that they are not like these aggressive,
masculine freaks, they have a sneaking suspicion that perhaps
men, the most important thing in their lives, do find the freer,
more assertive, independent Bitch preferable as a woman.

Bitches, likewise, don't care too much for other women. They
grow up disliking other women. They can't relate to them, they
don't identify with them, they have nothing in common with
them. Other women have been the norm into which they have
not fit. They reject those who have rejected them. This is one
of the reasons Bitches who are successful in hurdling the obstacles society places before women scorn those women who
are not. They tend to feel those who can take it will make it.
Most women have been the direct agents of much of the shit
Bitches have had to endure and few of either group has had
the political consciousness to realize why this is. Bitches have
been oppressed by other women as much if not more than by
men, and their hatred for them is usually greater.

Bitches are also uncomfortable around other women because
frequently women are less their psychological peers than are
men. Bitches don't particularly like passive people. They are
always slightly afraid they will crush the fragile things. Women
are trained to be passive and have learned to act that way even
when they are not. A Bitch is not very passive and is not com-

fortable acting that role. But she usually does not like to be domineering either—whether this is from natural distaste at dominating others or fear of seeming too masculine. Thus a Bitch can relax and be her natural non-passive self without worrying about lacerating someone only in the company of those who are as strong as she. This is more frequently in the company of men than of women, but those Bitches who have not succumbed totally to self-hatred are most comfortable of all only in the company of fellow Bitches. These are her true peers and the only ones with whom she does not have to play some sort of role. Only with other Bitches can a Bitch be truly free.

These moments come rarely. Most of the time Bitches must remain psychologically isolated. Women and men are so threatened by them and react so adversely that Bitches guard their true selves carefully. They are suspicious of those few whom they think they might be able to trust because so often it turns out to be a sham. But in this loneliness there is a strength and from their isolation and their bitterness come contributions that other women do not make. Bitches are among the most unsung of the unsung heroes of this society. They are the pioneers, the vanguard, the spearhead. Whether they want to be or not, this is the role they serve just by their very being. Many would not choose to be the groundbreakers for the mass of women for whom they have no sisterly feelings, but they cannot avoid it. Those who violate the limits, extend them; or cause the system to break.

Bitches were the first women to go to college, the first to break through the Invisible Bar of the professions, the first social revolutionaries, the first labor leaders, the first to organize other women. Because they were not passive beings and acted on their resentment at being kept down, they dared to do what other women would not. They took the flak and the shit that society dishes out to those who would change it and opened up portions of the world to women that they would otherwise not have known. They have lived on the fringes. And alone or with the support of their sisters they have changed the world we live in.

By definition Bitches are marginal beings in this society. They have no proper place and wouldn't stay in it if they did. They are women but not true women. They are human, but they are not male. Some don't even know they are women because they cannot relate to other women. They may play the feminine game at times, but they know it is a game they are playing. Their major psychological oppression is not a belief that they are inferior but a belief that they are not. Thus, all their lives they have been told they were freaks. More polite terms were used of course, but the message got through. Like most women they were taught to hate themselves as well as all women. In different ways and for different reasons, perhaps, but the effect was similar. Internalization of a derogatory self-concept always results in a good deal of bitterness and resentment. This anger is usually either turned in on the self—making one an unpleasant person—or on other women—reinforcing the social clichés about them. Only with political consciousness is it directed at the source—the social system.

The bulk of this Manifesto has been about Bitches. The remainder will be about BITCH. The organization does not yet exist and perhaps it never can. Bitches are so damned independent and they have learned so well not to trust other women that it will be difficult for them to learn to even trust each other. This is what BITCH must teach them to do. Bitches have to learn to accept themselves as Bitches and to give their sisters the support they need to be creative Bitches. Bitches must learn to be proud of their strength and proud of themselves. They must move away from the isolation which has been their protection and help their younger sisters avoid its perils. They must recognize that women are often less tolerant of other women than are men because they have been taught to view all women as their enemies. And Bitches must form together in a movement to deal with their problems in a political manner. They must organize for their own liberation as all women must organize for theirs. We must be strong, we must be militant, we must be dangerous. We must realize that Bitch is Beautiful and that we have nothing to lose. Nothing whatsoever.

This manifesto was written and revised with the help of several of my sisters, to whom it is dedicated.

San Francisco Redstockings/
Our Politics Begin with Our Feelings

This is an important recent statement because in it we can see radical women beginning to break away from New Left socialist dogma and to criticize the treatment of women under socialism as well as capitalism. They are rejecting the rhetoric of male radicalism and are searching for new, nonauthoritarian modes of organization and activity.

I

1. OUR POLITICS begin with our feelings: Feelings are a direct response to the events and relationships that we experience; that's how we know what's really going on. For centuries women's information has been categorized as magic, instinct, intuition, witchcraft, and more recently, projections, distortions, personal hang-ups, and other variations on a theme designed to render our knowledge meaningless and empty. Women who have insisted on communicating and acting on their knowledge have traditionally been punished according to the customs of the times. Three hundred years ago we were burned; now we are locked up in punitive institutions and labeled mentally ill, threatened with rape, isolation, and death. Information derived from our feelings is our only reliable information; and our politi-

Unpublished statement presented at a San Francisco meeting on women's liberation by the San Francisco Redstockings, March 21, 1970.

cal analysis can be trusted only so long as it does not contradict our feelings.

Our first task is to develop our capacity to be aware of our feelings and to pinpoint the events or interactions to which they are valid responses. This method has taught us that we do not oppress ourselves and that our pain is not the result of masochism, self-hate, or inferiority, but is a response to some behavior that was in fact designed to humiliate, hurt, and oppress us.

2. The political unit in which we can discover, share, and explore our feelings is the small group. Raising our collective consciousness is not a process that begins and ends, but is continuous and necessary given the enormous pressure placed on us everywhere to deny our own perceptions or feelings. By facing our pain together we can begin to imagine the absence of that pain and develop an idea of our needs or our vision. In our groups we ask what stands between us and that vision and in each particular case we see the enemy is men and their interests: male supremacy.

3. Male supremacy is neither a psychological set nor a meaningless abstraction that we feel, but cannot touch. Male supremacy is that total system which oppresses us in every aspect of our lives. Male supremacy as an economic system is that in which every individual man has greater access to scarce goods and resources than any individual woman. All women must perform some kind of labor for a man or men in order to survive. The kind of labor in each particular case depends on the economic relationship of the man to other men. Male supremacy is expressed in every encounter between a man and a woman, beginning with the most subtle gesture, which if not successful escalates in intensity until physical violence occurs. Male chauvinism is the system of beliefs or ideology by which men have rationalized their position of power and dominance and reduced the need for resorting to violence by defining the oppressed class in such a manner as to make the system appear to be an immutable law of nature.

Historically male supremacy has gone through distinct stages. In most of these, such as slavery, feudalism, and capitalism, a few men have dominated other men in some aspects of their lives as well as all men totally dominating women. Monopoly capitalism-imperialism is the current stage of male supremacy in our society; and socialism in, for example, Cuba, China, and the Soviet Union, is a more advanced stage of male supremacy in which the means of production and reproduction are owned by all men collectively. Both bourgeois and Marxist social scientists have failed to produce any meaningful analysis of society because they have excluded over half the world's population and focused only on the fluctuating patterns of dominance and exploitation between men, rather than on the basic economic system which has remained remarkably stable for centuries.

In each historical stage of the system women have been exploited as labor and objects owned by men and thus divided. Women controlled directly by "working class men" have been labeled "working class women," and women controlled directly by "ruling class men" have been labeled "ruling class women" when in fact they have had nothing whatsoever to do with controlling the means of production. These women's real class interests lie entirely with the women who are controlled directly by "working class" men. Dominance hierarchies between women have reflected the hierarchies of their controllers thus facilitating the smooth working of the system.

The technological changes that put women in the mills early in the industrial revolution broke the chain of total dependency on the private male controller, or the family. Thus, the short-range interests of capitalist profits planted the seeds that will ultimately destroy the system.

4. The economic system of male supremacy lies at the core of our oppression, and until it has been destroyed we will never be free. Equality and justice will be meaningless until we have equal access to scarce goods and resources so that we do not need to work and put out for men in order to survive. Because men benefit in every way from the system in which they reap all the rewards, they will not hand us our liberation. In order to be free we must seize power from men in all aspects of our lives.

II

1. Our movement is under pressure from the media, the New Left, and the Old Left, all of which are run by men, and, consequently, interested in destroying us. They are using old well-

tested techniques: pushing individual opportunism, appealing to our guilt, to our oppression. Their real intentions are most often hidden behind deviously supportive rhetoric designed to co-opt us. Our only protection is in our method of sharing our real feelings regardless of how unacceptable we fear they are. Each one of us has a secret wish to be rich and famous or a *Life* magazine revolutionary hero because the alternative has been invisibility. Each one of us longs for respect and warmth because we have been totally deprived and starved, while somehow giving all to males. A tendency to opportunism lives in each of us, and is dangerous only when we hide it from one another. We can withstand the efforts to co-opt us if we honestly share the feelings such efforts evoke and deal with their causes by real support. In this sense we are entering a new era in which we are really being treated as a collectivity and responding as a collectivity and our consciousness-raising must intensify and direct itself to the collective issues at hand.

2. Within our movement there is a strong tendency towards idealism which is dangerous because it obscures real motivations with fancy rhetoric about morals and ethics which makes us afraid or ashamed to express our true feelings and blocks the communication of information necessary for successful evaluation of real conditions. We cannot rely on the moral principle of a sisterhood which does not exist. It is as absurd as its power counterpart, the Mafia, or brotherhood. What we can rely on is a real understanding of the necessity of the collectivity in order to achieve the ends of the self-interests of each one of us. Good and bad is not at issue. Our success depends on a realistic appraisal of the conditions of every situation, not on our wishes, and idealistic thinking hinders such an appraisal.

3. We identify with all women. We define our best interest as that of the poorest, ugliest, most brutally exploited woman. We repudiate all economic, racial, educational, religious, or status differentiations that divide us from other women.

4. We are often criticized for not doing anything. While there is a truth to that criticism and it's very hard for us to take ourselves seriously enough to stick with endeavors outside of our small groups, the solution is not to jump into superficial pseudo-

activities but to carefully analyze the prevailing conditions that have made it difficult for us to carry through projects and actions. The success of a project depends on the commitment to oneself and one another. The initiative and responsibility taken by each woman involved and the analysis of why a project fails must refer back to the small group in which each woman identifies the feelings associated with that aspect of her work which will provide the necessary clues for analysis. For example, if we want to understand why our abortion workshop stopped functioning, each woman involved has to reconstruct what really went down that inhibited her initiative. Piecing each story together will give us a realistic idea of what happened and why, and perhaps make the next project more successful.

5. Our bodies are male-occupied territory. The point about power is that what the lord can give, the lord can take away; women are still forced into the ultimate oppression—the total schizophrenia of being completely intimate, yet completely not ourselves. When the lord can take away personhood, it is total state power vested in one individual; and the other is in solitary.

We are not allowed to love any woman's body including our own. In addition to being considered unlovable, women are considered incomplete human beings, and therefore any bond existing between two women must always by its nature remain an inadequate alternative to bondage to a man. The fear of "lesbianism" is an effective male device to keep us from relating freely to ourselves and each other. Nor, as is often forgotten, can we relate freely to men since slavery is our condition and is designed to fulfill their needs, never ours.

6. Many of us entered the women's movement while still involved with various left-wing organizations. We expected to be able to work in both movements and were surprised by the speed with which our so-called "comrades" on the left threw us out as we began to make our demands. Painful as such experiences were to us, they served the purpose of clarifying the distinctions between friends and enemies. Quite naturally, the men used the women under their control as henchmen, a tactic which worked quite nicely in creating a division between us. They dug it as voyeurs watching a catfight. Now we are openly slandered as

"bourgeois feminists," "cultural Kotex," "honky mothers," "white bitches," "lesbians," etc. Woman is again a dirty word not to be mentioned in public. While we clearly cannot allow the women controlled by movement men to disrupt our meetings or plans, we should not fall for the enemy's tactics and consider ourselves permanently divided from those women many of whom will choose to leave the stagnant (male-dominated) movement, and become feminists as the women's movement becomes a strong and visible revolutionary alternative for them and one that better serves their own self-interests.

7. Some of us feel that it is time to begin to define ourselves as a membership organization or party of revolutionary feminists consisting of our small groups, intergroup council, or council if we become national. In other words, things would be as they are now, but our identity would be strengthened and clarified in terms of what we stand for instead of what we are against. We would work both inside and outside of our party and join other women in their particular struggles against male supremacy trying wherever possible to bring them into small groups. Our party would be neither the traditional mass party nor a centralist party, but a flexible organization of a non-hierarchical, non-authoritarian nature in which forms would evolve from rather than direct the needs of the members. The openly stated long-range revolutionary goal of such an organization would in no way hinder its members from working on particular short-range goals which the counterleft has often called reformist but which in fact are necessary steps in the overthrow of male supremacy.

No "Chicks," "Broads," or "Niggers" for Old Mole

As a final portent of things to come, we offer the following statement from a leading underground newspaper in the Boston area, *The Old Mole*, which announces a change in policy that could very well change the face of all publishing—aboveground or underground. We heartily commend this policy stand and hope that other publications and writers will quickly follow suit.

THE *Old Mole* announces that it will no longer accept manuscripts or letters that use language such as emasculation, castration, balls to mean courage, letters addressed "Dear Sir" or "Gentlemen" or other examples of male supremacist language.

Use of this language reflects values and patterns of thought that are oppressive to half the people in the world and harmful to all. To use the word balls to mean courage implies that (1) balls have something to do with courage and that (2) women, because they don't have balls, don't have courage. Similarly, the words castration and emasculation imply acceptance of the myth that man is superior to woman because of the strength that having a penis gives him.

These words reflect a power structure (men having power over women) that we want to change. One way we can work to change this is to challenge the use, conscious or unconscious, of

Reprinted from the *Nickel Review,* Syracuse, New York, April 13, 1970, p. 3.

words and phrases that go along with this power structure. In other words, we will not print letters that call women "broads" just as we would not print letters that call blacks "niggers."

From now on if we receive a letter that uses male supremacist language, we will return it to the sender. We will answer the letter, and we will explain why we are sending it back and why we thought the language was oppressive, since we realize these oppressive thought patterns and values are not always conscious and deliberate. But we will not print this language in the paper.

People have asked us to explain our policy of rejecting advertising which exploits women. These are ads everyone is familiar with: a movie ad illustrated with a picture of a girl in a bathing suit; a car, cigarette or record ad which implies that women will sleep with a guy if he buys the product; a cosmetics or deodorant ad which tries to make women feel inadequate or ugly without the "right" look; a classified ad in which men advertise for "chicks." These are all ads which use women as sex objects and play on stereotypes.

We recognize that all advertising misleads, manipulates, and tries to get people to allow themselves to be exploited. That's what it's for. We hate to accept *any* advertising, but we can't figure out how else to survive financially. Hardly any newspaper in America, even straight ones, gets enough money just from selling the paper. The sources of left-liberal wealth are drying up as things get heavier.

But we know that everybody else knows advertising is a hype. We will not destroy capitalism by refusing to accept their ads. We *can* help build the movement that will destroy capitalism by continuing to publish, and taking their money.

So why do we refuse ads that specifically exploit women? Most people, especially men, still view women as secondary, different, mysterious, weak, stupid, decorative, sex objects—something less than real people (men). Those attitudes go so deep that even if they are not as blatant as in advertising they are still present to some degree in all of us. If we have any influence, as a newspaper, with anyone, we want to use it to say: male chauvinism is so intolerable to us that we refuse to print it for money.

People take it for granted that women are used this way in

advertising. We are saying it is no longer something that people should take for granted. The use of women in advertising is one of the hammers beating against women's minds to keep them down.

People often say this attitude is puritanical—that the underground press is part of a revolutionary new culture that rejects the repression of sex, and celebrates bodies, free love, sensuality. But the cultural revolution, like any revolution, is phony if it's only for half the people. The "sexual revolution" can be just a new way for men to use and exploit women. There's a lot of difference between being sexually free and being a better object for someone else's sexual feelings, a groovy decoration for a "hip" life style, a symbol of sex or the earth or beauty or anything. Ads which encourage these attitudes toward women are no different, no less exploitative, than ads in which straight women are offered to men as objects to own in their straight lives. The culture will always be repressed if it represses the active humanity of half the people.

A Last Word

Betty Roszak / *The Human Continuum*

RECENT YEARS have seen a resurgence of feminism that has taken mainstream America by surprise. It began with the discontent of lonely middle-class suburban housewives, whose malady was given a name by Betty Friedan in her immensely influential book, *The Feminine Mystique*. But it didn't become what we know as a "women's liberation movement" until the growth of the New Left from the civil rights and peace movements of the early 1960's. It wasn't until then that hundreds of young women, many of whom were seasoned veterans of antiwar and antisegregationist activities, began to realize the anomaly of their situation. Here they were, radical women involved in a struggle for human equality and an end to oppression, willing to dedicate years of effort to effecting political change, and what were they being allowed to do? Typing, mimeographing, addressing envelopes, sweeping, providing coffee and sexual diversion for the vigorous young men who were making all the decisions. Far from going forward together to change the world, men and women were once more stuck (and this time with a vengeance) with their time-honored roles: the men to think and act; the women to serve and drudge. The last equality—that between women and men—was never even mentioned. In fact, movement women found that they were even worse off than apolitical women, because they were aware of and extremely sensitive to the hypocrisies of their male colleagues who talked idealistically of equality, but who acted scornful of women in their everyday lives. The rhetoric of equality was directed at black, brown, and Third World *men* only. The New Left of the late sixties had begun to take on a tough, aggressively male tone, born of the idolization of Ché Guevara, guerrilla warfare, and admiration for the exaggerated, overcompensating manliness of the Black Panthers. As nonviolence, exemplified by Martin Luther King, Jr., became discredited by revolutionary and black militancy, so the tough style became a political requirement. In deference to this new brutalism men found it easy to take the necessary traditional he-man attitude toward women, the attitude of dominance and power. This left women in a bewildering dilemma. Were they to remain in a movement which allowed them to exist only as lackeys and silently submissive bedmates, or would they refuse to accept a subordinate status?

As this dilemma is being resolved today, there sounds in the background the laughter of contemptuous radical men: "Crazy feminist bitches!" The words merely echo a shared male ridicule that knows no class lines. Women find themselves of necessity beginning to re-examine the traditions of misogyny that even radical men have unknowingly inherited.

In our cultural past "Woman" was the symbol of sex; and sex, though necessary, was at the same time known to be an abhorrent evil, a degrading passion. In the Middle Ages, the masculine world view of the church dared not make light of women. Church authorities of the fifteenth century, ever on the alert for the malevolence of the devil, used a popular handbook on the identification and treatment of witches, the *Malleus Maleficarum*, in searching out evil in the form of women. "What else is woman," says this medieval antisubversive activities manual, "but a foe to friendship, an unescapable punishment, a necessary evil, a natural temptation, a desirable calamity, a domestic danger, a delectable detriment, an evil of nature painted with fair colors?" By the eighteenth century, Rousseau, one of France's most prolific proponents of democratic equality, could write with impunity, "Women have in general no love of any art; they have no proper knowledge of any; and they have no genius," thus curtly dismissing half of humanity to a status of hopeless inferiority. By mid-nineteenth century, the "evil of nature" had turned into an object of scorn, and Schopenhauer's indictment of women as "that undersized, narrow-shouldered, broad-hipped, and short-legged race," denied women even their beauty, their "fair colors," along with their intellectual capacity.

Today's predominantly male society no longer sees women as evil, at least on the surface. The ambivalent fear and attraction of the Middle Ages has changed along with the prevailing attitude toward sex. Now that sexuality has lost its mystery, the once dangerous and seductive female can be safely ignored and denied her power. The fear has turned to ridicule. One cannot ignore evil, but one can pretend that the ridiculous does not exist. Men irritably ask the rhetorical question (echoing Freud), "What do women want?" meaning, of course, that anything women want is absurd. The question is asked not of individual women but of the world, and in an exasperated tone, as if women were dumb and couldn't answer. The false barrier continues to be built: "We" cannot understand "Them." Why are "They" so restive? Further communication between the sexes seems useless. Always it is men talking to men about women.

The fact of ridicule is constantly with us. When it was proposed in 1969 in the British House of Commons that attention be paid to developing a contraceptive pill for men, "the idea provoked hearty laughter," according to Paul Vaughan in the London *Observer*. Moreover, he tells us, the British government has rejected outright any allocation of funds for research on a pill for men. When the question was under discussion in the House of Lords, one Labour peer advised the government to ignore " 'these do-gooders who take all the fun out of life' (laughter)." Researchers explain their reluctance to tamper with the male germ cells. Yet the same researchers have not hesitated to tamper with the female germ cells in developing the pill for women. Nor have unpleasant side effects or hazards to women's health deterred them, while they quickly stopped research on a substance being tested on men because it was noted that when men drank alcohol while taking it, their eyes became reddened! Doctors have been known to laugh at the mention of labor pains during childbirth and in the not too distant past have been willing to stand by, calmly withholding anesthetics while women underwent great agonies in labor. So, too, male legislators have laughed at the idea of the legalization of abortion, hinting at unprecedented promiscuity (on the part of women, not men) if such a thing were allowed. Meanwhile, thousands of desperate women die each year as the direct result of male laws making abortion illegal.

Women are learning the meaning of this male laughter and indifference in the face of the most hazardous and serious biological enterprise women undertake, willingly or not. And in cultural enterprises, whenever women attempt to enter any of the male-dominated professions (who ever heard of a woman chairman of the board, a woman orchestra conductor, a woman Chief Justice, a woman President or a woman getting equal pay for equal work?), we again hear the familiar laughter of male ridicule. If we look at the image of woman men present to us in novels, drama, or advertising, we see a scatterbrained, helpless flunky, or a comical sex-pot, or a dumb beast of burden. Is this what they mean when they exhort us in popular song to "enjoy being a girl"? But women are beginning to relearn the old lesson: in this male-dominated world, it is a misfortune to be born female.

From the very moment of birth a higher value is placed by his society on the male infant, a value which accumulates and accelerates into his adult life. By the time the female infant has grown into adulthood, however, if she has learned society's lessons well, she will have come to acquiesce in her second-class status—to accept unconsciously the burden of her inferiority. No matter what honors she wins, what her exploits, what her achievements or talents, she will always be considered a woman first, and thus inferior to the least honored, talented and worthy male of that society—foremost a sexual being, still fair game for his aggressive sexual fantasies. As Albert Memmi puts it, ". . . every man, no matter how low he may be, holds women in contempt and judges masculinity to be an inestimable good."

Male society's disparagement of women has all the force of an unconscious conspiracy. It is even more subtle than the racist and colonial oppressions to which it is so closely allied, because it is softened and hidden by the silken padding of eroticism. We women grow to think that because we are wanted as lovers, wives, and mothers, it might be because we are wanted as human beings. But if by chance or natural inclination we attempt to move outside these male-defined and male-dependent roles, we find that they are, in reality, barriers.

For many women this is the first inkling of the fact of oppression. Pressed from birth into the mold of an exclusively sexual being, the growing girl soon develops what Sartre calls the "phantom personality"; she comes to feel that she is what "they" tell her she is. This other self envelops her like a second skin. When she begins to experience a natural sense of constriction (which is growth), her real feelings clash with what "they" say she should feel. The more forceful and vital she is, the more she will have to repress her real feelings, because girls are to be passive and manipulatable. She becomes frightened, suspicious, anxious about herself. A sense of malaise overcomes her. She must obey the social prohibitions which force her back into the mold of the sexual being. She is not to desire or act, but to *be* desired and acted upon. Many women give up the struggle right there and dully force themselves to remain stunted human beings. The butterfly must not be allowed to come forth from its chrysalis: her vitality is only allowed guilty expression in certain private moments or is turned into sullen resentment which smolders during all her unfulfilled life.

Family and home, which look like a refuge and a sanctuary, turn out to be the same kind of trap. Beyond the marriage ghetto there is outright rejection and exclusion. In the work world there are lower wages, union and employer discrimination, the prohibitive cost of child care. In the professions mere tokenism takes the place of acceptance and equality. The same is true in government and political activity. The single woman knows only too well the psychological exclusionism practiced by male society. She is suspect, or comic, if over a certain age. All men assume she would be married if she could—there must be something psychologically wrong with her if she isn't. And single women have the added burden of not being socially acceptable without an "escort"—a man, any man.

Further, women are the nonexistent people in the very life of the nation itself—now more so even than the blacks who have at last forced themselves into the nation's consciousness. The invisible man has become the invisible *woman.* William James called it a "fiendish punishment" that "one should be turned loose on society and remain absolutely unnoticed by all the members thereof." Yet that is the treatment male society metes out to those women who wish to escape from the male-defined erotic roles. Left out of the history books, not credited with a past worth mentioning in the masculine chronicles of state, women of today remain ignorant of women's movements of the past and the important role individual women have played in the history of the human race. Male historical scholarship sees the suffragists and feminists of the nineteenth century as figures of fun, worthy of only a paragraph here and there, as footnotes on the by-ways of social customs, far from the main roads of masculine endeavor: the wars, political intrigues, and diplomatic maneuverings which make up the history of power.

With the blacks and other oppressed minorities, women can say, "How can we hope to shape the future without some knowledge of our past?" If the historic heroines of feminism are ignored or treated trivially, today's women are hindered from dealing with their own repression. This undermining of self-confidence is common to all oppressed peoples, along with the doubts of the reality of one's own perceptions. Women's self-rejection as worthwhile human beings thus becomes an inevitable extension of the cycle of oppression.

But radical women have begun to rebel against the false, exclusively sexual image men have created for them. And in rebelling, many women are seeing the need for bypassing the marriage ghetto altogether. They are recognizing the true nature of the institution of marriage as an economic bargain glossed over by misty sentimentalizing. Wash off the romantic love ideal, and underneath we see the true face of the marriage contract. It is grimly epitomized by the immortal slogan found chalked on innumerable honeymoon getaway cars: "She got him today; he'll get her tonight." Or, as put more sophisticatedly by Robert Briffault, "Whether she aims at freedom or a home a woman is thrown back on the defense of her own interests; she must defend herself against man's attempt to bind her, or sell herself to advantage. Woman is to man a sexual prey; man is to woman an economic prey." And this kind of oppression cuts across all economic class lines, even though there may be social differences between streetwalker Jane X, housewife Joan Y, and debutante Jacqueline Z. One may sell her body for a few dollars to the likeliest passerby; one for a four-bedroomed house in the suburbs; and one for rubies and yachts. But all must sell their bodies in order to participate in the bargain. Yet if women were to refuse to enter into the sexual bargain, they not only would refute the masculine idea of women as property, but they also would make it possible to free men from the equally self-destructive role of sole breadwinner. Thus there would be a chance to break the predatory cycle.

Beyond marriage and the old, outmoded roles, radical women are seeking new ways of dealing with the oppressive institutions of society. No longer will they acquiesce in the pattern of dominance and submission. They are beginning to take control of their own lives, building new relationships, developing new modes of work, political activity, child rearing and education. Rejection of male exploitation must start with psychic as well as economic independence. The new female consciousness is going to develop cooperative forms of child care; women's centers as sanctuaries for talk, planning, and action; all-female communes where women can escape for a while from the all-pervading male influence; the sharing of domestic drudgery with men in cooperative living arrangements; the building up of competence and self-confidence in such previously male-dependent endeavors as general mechanical repair work, carpentry, and construction.

By rejecting the false self for so long imposed upon us and in which we have participated unwittingly, we women can forge the self-respect necessary in order to discover our own true values. Only when we refuse to be made use of by those who despise and ridicule us, can we throw off our heavy burden of resentment. We must take our lives in our own hands. This is what liberation means. Out of a common oppression women can break the stereotypes of masculine-feminine and enter once more into the freedom of the human continuum.

Women's liberation will thus inevitably bring with it, as a concomitant, men's liberation. Men, no less than women, are imprisoned by the heavy carapace of their sexual stereotype. The fact that they gain more advantages and privileges from women's oppression has blinded them to their own bondage which is the bondage of an artificial duality. This is the male problem: the positing of a difference, the establishment of a dichotomy emphasizing oppositeness. Men are to behave in this way; women in that; women do this; men do the other. And it just so happens that the way men behave and act is important and valuable, while what women do is unimportant and trivial. Instead of identifying both the sexes as part of humanity, there is a false separation which is to the advantage of men. Masculine society has insisted on seeing in sexuality that same sense of conflict and competition that it has imposed upon its relation to the planet as a whole. From the bedroom to the board room to the international conference table, separateness, differentiation, opposition, exclusion, antithesis have been the cause and goal of the male politics of power. Human characteristics belonging to the entire species have been crystallized out of the living flow of human experience and made into either/or categories. This male habit of setting up boundary lines between imagined polarities has been the impetus for untold hatred and destruction. Masculine/feminine is just one of such polarities among many, including body/mind, organism/environment, plant/animal, good/evil, black/white, feeling/intellect, passive/active, sane/insane, living/dead. Such language hardens what is in reality a continuum and a unity into separate mental images always in opposition to one another.

If we think of ourselves as "a woman" or "a man," we are already participating in a fantasy of language. People become preoccupied with images of one another—surely the deepest and most desperate alienation there is. The very process of conceptualization warps our primary, unitary feelings of what we are. Mental images take the place of the primary stimuli of sex which involve the entire organism. Instead of a sense of identification, we have pornographic sex with its restrictive emphasis on genital stimulation. This "short circuiting between genitals and cortex" as William E. Galt calls it (in a brilliant article, "The Male-Female Dichotomy," in *Psychiatry*, 1943) is a peculiarly modern distortion of the original, instinctual nature of sex. We are suffering from D. H. Lawrence's "sex in the head." In childhood we know sexuality as a generalized body response; the body is an erotic organ of sensation. To this Freud gave the nasty name of polymorphous perversity. But it is actually the restriction to localized genitality of the so-called "normal" adult that is perverted, in the sense of a twisting away from the original and primary body eroticism. Biological evidence indicates that the sex response is a primitive, gross sensory stimulation—diffused and nonlocalizable. Phallic man, however, wishes to assert the primacy of his aggressive organ. The ego of phallic man divides him off from the rest of the world, and in this symbolic division he maintains the deep-seated tradition of man *against* woman, wresting his sexual pleasure *from* her, like the spoils of war. The total body response must be repressed in order to satisfy the sharpness of his genital cravings.

But in the primary sexual response of the body, there is no differentiation between man or woman; there is no "man," there is no "woman" (mental images), just a shared organism responding to touch, smell, taste, sound. The sexual response can then be seen as one part of the species' total response to and participation in, the environment. We sense the world with our sensitive bodies as an ever-changing flow of relationships in which we move and partake. Phallic man sees the world as a collection of things from which he is sharply differentiated. If we consider the phenomenon of the orgasm in this light, we can see that its basic qualities are the same for male and female. There can be no real distinction between the feminine and masculine *self*-abandonment in a sexual climax. The self, or controlling power, simply vanishes. All talk of masculine or feminine orgasm misses this point entirely, because this is a surrender which goes beyond masculine or feminine. Yet how many men are there who are willing to see their own sexual vitality as exactly this self-surrender?

When men want desperately to preserve that which they deem masculine—the controlling power—then they insist on the necessity of the feminine as that which must be controlled and mastered. Men force themselves into the role of phallic man and seek always to be hard, to be tough, to be competitive, to assert their "manhood." Alan Watts wisely sees this masculine striving for rigidity as "nothing more than an emotional paralysis" which causes men to misunderstand the bisexuality of their own nature, to force a necessarily unsatisfactory sexual response, and to be exploitative in their relations with women and the world.

According to Plato's myth, the ancients thought of men and women as originally a single being cut asunder into male and female by an angry god. There is a good biological basis to this myth; although the sexes are externally differentiated, they are still structurally homologous. Psychologically, too, the speculations of George Groddeck are apt:

Personal sex cuts right across the fundamental qualities of human nature; the very word suggests the violent splitting asunder of humanity into male and female. *Sexus* is derived from *secare*, to cut, from which we also get *segmentum*, a part cut from a circle. It conveys the idea that man and woman once formed a unity, that together they make a complete whole, the perfect circle of the individuum and that both sections share the properties of this individuum. These suggestions are of course in harmony with the ancient Hebrew legend, which told how God first created a human being who was both male and female, Adam-Lilith, and later sawed this asunder.[1]

The dichotomizing of human qualities can thus be seen as a basic error in men's understanding of nature. Biologically, both sexes are always present in each. Perhaps with the overcoming of women's oppression, the woman in man will be allowed to emerge. If, as Coleridge said, great minds are androgynous, there can be no feminine or masculine ideal, but only as the poet realizes,

> . . . what is true is human,
> homosexuality, heterosexuality
> There is something more important:
>
> to be human
> in which kind
> is kind.[2]

1. *The World of Man* (New York, Vision Press, 1951).
2. Clayton Eshleman, from "Holding Duncan's Hand."

Selected Bibliography

1. Articles and Pamphlets

BROPHY, BRIGID. "Women" in *Don't Never Forget; Collected Views and Reviews*. New York, Holt, Rinehart and Winston, 1966, pp. 38–44. (Originally published in the *Saturday Evening Post*, November 1963.) Writing in her usual astringent style, Brigid Brophy takes on modern society's treatment of women.

BUCK, PEARL S. "The Education of Women" in *To My Daughters, With Love*. New York, John Day, 1967, pp. 157–175. Pearl Buck says, "Woman is still living in the age of man's vengeance."

COMFORT, ALEX. "The Naked Lady" in *Darwin and the Naked Lady; Discursive Essays on Biology and Art*. New York, Braziller, 1962, pp. 100–118. On art and eroticism seen from an exclusively male viewpoint; women considered as art objects, sexual objects, passive receivers of erotic pleasure—never as viewers or doers. The artist is always considered as a man. A good example of unconscious sexual stereotyping.

DeCROW, KAREN. "Women and Politics" in *Mademoiselle*, vol. 70, no. 4, February 1970, pp. 34–36. The story of what happened when a militant feminist ran for mayor of Syracuse, New York.

FREEMAN, JO. "The Building of the Gilded Cage," unpublished paper, 1969. A sharp assessment of the socialization and social control of women, and of the agents of that social control; legal, sociological viewpoint and references.

FRISOF, JAMIE KELEM. "Textbooks and Channeling," in *Women: A Journal of Liberation*, vol. 1, no. 1, Fall 1969, pp. 26–28. An analysis of five social studies textbooks and their presentation of women in contemporary life.

GAGNON, JOHN, and WILLIAM SIMON. "Is a Women's Revolution Really Possible?" in *McCall's*, October 1969, pp. 76 ff. If women were to be truly liberated our society would have to change so radically in work, family, and sex, we would hardly recognize it. Are men or women ready or capable of such change?

GALT, WILLIAM E. "The Male-Female Dichotomy in Human Behavior: A Phylobiological Evaluation," in *Psychiatry*, vol. 6, 1943, pp. 1–14. Galt was assistant to Trigant Burrow, a pioneer in group psychiatry. He sees "normal" sex life as a restriction of the organism's response. For a discussion of the ideas in this article see Betty Roszak's "The Human Continuum" in this anthology.

GINOTT, HAIM. "Sexual Role and Social Function" in *Between Parent and Child*. New York, Macmillan, 1965, chapter 10. This influential manual of child psychology preaches the traditional sexual virtues: boys must be raised to be he-men and breadwinners; girls to be shy maidens and homebodies. A continuing best seller, the book is a striking example of how popular psychology can be used to legitimize the oppression of women.

LIMPUS, LAUREL. "Liberation of Women: Sexual Repression and the Family," a reprint from *This Magazine Is About Schools*. Boston, New England Free Press, Spring 1969. An attack on woman's role as defined by the family.

"Little Mommy, You Have a Long Way to Go," *Association of American University Women Journal*, vol. 63, no. 2, January 1970, pp. 57–61. A panel discussion of women's liberation.

McCARTHY, MARY. "The Tyranny of the Orgasm," in *On the Contrary*. New York, Farrar, Straus and Cudahy, 1951, pp. 167–173. Review of Lundberg and Farnham's *Modern Woman, the Lost Sex*. Good in its opposition to the "anatomy is destiny" school of thought.

MASLOW, ABRAHAM H. "Self-Esteem (Dominance-Feeling) and Sexuality in Women," in *Journal of Social Psychology*, vol. XVI, 1942; reprinted in Ruitenbeek, Hendrik M., ed., *Psychoanalysis and Female Sexuality*. New Haven, Conn., College and University Press, 1966, pp. 161–197. Women's sexual attitudes are more the "functions of personality and social and cultural relationships than of sheer biological endowment." Maslow finds that women with a high sense of self-esteem are sexually aggressive and more responsive than those with low self-esteem.

MASLOW, ABRAHAM, H. RAND, and S. NEWMAN. "Some Parallels Between Sexual and Dominant Behavior of Infra-Human Primates and the Fantasies of Patients in Psychotherapy," from *Journal of Nervous and Mental Disease,* vol. 131, 1960, pp. 202–212. Dr. Maslow and his associates conclude that the dominance/submission sex relationship is a sign of immature development and leads to a diminution of human sexuality.

MORGAN, ROBIN. "Women's Liberation," in *WIN Magazine,* Feb. 15, 1969, pp. 10–12. An excellent review of the movement.

O'NEILL, WILLIAM L. "Feminism as a Radical Ideology," in *Dissent; Explorations in the History of American Radicalism,* ed. by Alfred F. Young. De Kalb, Ill., Northern Illinois University Press, 1968, pp. 273–300. Good historical study of why the first wave of feminist activity failed.

PHELAN, LANA CLARKE. "Abortion Laws: The Cruel Fraud," speech delivered at the California Conference on Abortion, Santa Barbara, Calif., February 10, 1968. Reprinted by the Society for Humane Abortion.

PIERCY, MARGE. "The Grand Coolie Dam" in *Leviathan,* vol. 1, no. 6, Oct./Nov. 1969, pp. 16–22. Things are getting worse, not better, for women in the movement. The double standard reigns in radical male behavior.

PRIESTLEY, J. B. "Women Don't Run the Country," in *Essays of Five Decades.* Boston, Little, Brown, 1968, pp. 239–243. (Originally published in *Saturday Evening Post,* December 12, 1964.) Contrary to prevailing views, there is no "matriarchy" in the U.S., according to Priestley. Rather *Logos,* or masculinity, dominates, and we need the healing power of *Eros,* or femininity.

REEVES, NANCY. *Stereotypes of Woman's Place,* pamphlet. Los Angeles, University of California, 1969. A witty, stylish assessment of women in our society. Used as a text in Reeves's course at U.C.L.A.

RICHIE, JEANNE. "Church, Caste and Women" in *Christian Century,* vol. LXXXVII, no. 3, January 21, 1970, pp. 73–77. Clergymen are unconcerned while women demand more responsibility, less "volunteerism" in the church, as well as recruitment to the ministry.

RIEFF, PHILIP. "Sexuality and Domination," parts IV and V in *Freud: The Mind of the Moralist.* New York, Anchor Books, 1961, pp. 191–204. Shrewd analysis of the significance of Freud's misogyny. Rieff shows how Freud's hostility to women underlies his psychoanalytic theory.

SHAW, GEORGE BERNARD. "Woman-Man in Petticoats," in *Platform and Pulpit,* ed. by Dan H. Laurence. New York, Hill and Wang,

1961, pp. 172–178. In this speech delivered in 1927 Shaw argues away all the stereotyped differences between male and female.

SIMON, WILLIAM, and JOHN GAGNON. "Psychosexual Development," in *Trans-action*, vol. 6, March 1969, pp. 9–17. "We see sexual behavior . . . as scripted behavior, not the masked expression of a primordial drive."

THOMAS, KEITH. "The Double Standard," in *Journal of the History of Ideas*, April, 1959, pp. 195–216. Relates the mystique of female chastity to property rights.

UNWIN, HARRIET. "In a Man's World; the Best of Both Worlds," in *Anarchy* (London), vol. 5, no. 56, October 1965, pp. 302–310. Discussion of Betty Friedan's book and its implications for British women.

WILLIS, ELLEN. "Whatever Happened to Women?—Nothing, That's the Trouble," in *Mademoiselle*, vol. 69, no. 5, September 1969, pp. 150 ff. Pop-critic for *The New Yorker* and member of N.Y. Redstockings glares at the master-slave relationship.

ZILBOORG, GREGORY. "Male and Female," in *Psychiatry*, VII, 1944, pp. 257–296. Fascinating review of "phallocentric" psychoanalysis; discusses the work of Lester F. Ward, a late nineteenth-century sociologist who attacked male supremacy.

2. Books

BIRD, CAROLINE. *Born Female: The High Cost of Keeping Women Down*. New York, David McKay, 1968. Especially good on the economic facts of life for women.

BRIFFAULT, ROBERT. *The Mothers: The Matriarchal Theory of Social Origins,* abridged ed. by Gordon Rattray Taylor. New York, Universal Library, Grosset and Dunlap, 1963. First published in several volumes in 1927. A study of the matriarchal nature of primitive society. Briffault sees monogamy as a late development of the patriarchy.

CARSON, JOSEPHINE. *Silent Voices: The Southern Negro Woman Today*. New York, Delacorte Press, 1969. Deals movingly with the overwhelming poverty, drudgery, and struggle of the Southern Negro woman.

FERGUSON, CHARLES W. *The Male Attitude*. Boston, Little, Brown, 1966. Demonstrates how masculine thinking has dominated the course of American history; examines development of the gun, slavery, and the machine as male institutions. A much neglected work.

FIGES, EVA. *Patriarchal Attitudes: Women in Society.* London, Faber and Faber, 1970. An English novelist examines historical attitudes toward women; especially good for the selection of quotations from Rousseau, Freud, and Otto Weininger.

FLEXNER, ELEANOR. *Century of Struggle.* Belknap Press of Harvard University, 1959. History of American feminism.

FRIEDAN, BETTY. *The Feminine Mystique.* New York, Norton, 1963. The book that started it all.

JEANNIERE, ABEL. *The Anthropology of Sex.* Foreword by Dan Sullivan. New York, Harper, 1967. French Catholic anthropologist looks at the stereotypes of male and female; Sullivan's excellent foreword discusses De Beauvoir, love, sexuality, and the Christian tradition.

KANOWITZ, LEO. *Women and the Law: The Unfinished Revolution.* Albuquerque, University of New Mexico Press, 1969. Carefully documented scrutiny of legal discrimination on the basis of sex in the U.S.

KRADITOR, AILEEN S. *Ideas of the Woman Suffrage Movement, 1890–1920.* New York, Columbia University Press, 1965. A study of both profeminist and antifeminist thought in America.

———. *Up From the Pedestal: Selected Writings in the History of American Feminism.* Chicago, Quadrangle Books, 1968.

LAWRENCE, D. H. *Assorted Articles.* New York, Knopf, 1930. A collection of brief essays, several of which deal petulantly with the "cocksure" women of the day. Classic statements of defensive masculinity by the author of *Lady Chatterley's Lover.*

LEFORT, GERTRUDE VON. *The Eternal Woman: The Woman in Time, Timeless Woman.* Milwaukee, Bruce, 1954. Woman as bearer of salvation; Catholic viewpoint on the veil, mystery, and chastity.

LIFTON, ROBERT JAY, ed. *The Woman in America* (The Daedalus Library). Boston, Houghton, Mifflin, 1964. Contains a number of good articles, including Alice Rossi's "Equality Between the Sexes: An Immodest Proposal."

LUNDBERG, FERDINAND, and MARYNIA F. FARNHAM. *Modern Woman: The Lost Sex.* New York, Harper, 1947. Women seen as passive sufferers. This is the book refuted by Mary McCarthy in her article "The Tyranny of the Orgasm."

MARDER, HERBERT. *Feminism and Art; A Study of Virginia Woolf.* Chicago, University of Chicago Press, 1968. See especially his chapter, "Feminism and Art" for a perceptive study of V. Woolf's feminist ideas.

MASTERS, R. E. L., and EDUARD LEA. *The Anti-Sex: The Belief in the Natural Inferiority of Women: Studies in Male Frustration and Sexual Conflict.* New York, Julian Press, 1964. Hate-filled selections by misogynists through the ages, including Aristophanes, Juvenal, Schopenhauer, Jonathan Swift, and Otto Weininger among others.

MEMMI, ALBERT. *Dominated Man: Notes Toward a Portrait.* New York, Orion Press, 1968. Chapter on women deals mainly with Simone de Beauvoir. Illuminating on the psychology of oppressed and oppressor with a definition of racism that would apply just as well to sexism.

MERRIAM, EVE. *After Nora Slammed the Door: American Women in the 1960's: The Unfinished Revolution.* Cleveland, World Publishing Co., 1964. Cleverly written indictment of women's role.

O'NEILL, WILLIAM L. *Everyone Was Brave: The Rise and Fall of Feminism.* Chicago, Quadrangle Books, 1969. Scholarly account of early American feminism and its demise.

PARTURIER, FRANÇOISE. *Open Letter to Men.* New York, Heinemann, 1968. Reply to previously published *Open Letter to a Woman of Today,* by André Soubiran (Heinemann); French feminist viewpoint, dedicated to Simone de Beauvoir; light, whimsical, but filled with a sense of outrage.

PHELAN, LANA CLARKE, and PATRICIA MAGINNIS. *The Abortion Handbook for Responsible Women.* North Hollywood, Calif., Contact Books, 1969. Down-to-earth discussion of all phases of abortion, including what to do and what not to do. Hypocrisy of the medical profession exposed.

SCHMALHAUSEN, SAMUEL D., and V. F. CALVERTON. *Woman's Coming of Age: A Symposium.* New York, Liveright, 1931. Essays by Charlotte Perkins Gilman, Havelock Ellis, Dora Russell, Rebecca West, and others.

STERN, KARL. *The Flight from Woman.* New York, Farrar, Straus and Giroux, 1965. Idea of woman as muse and closer to nature than men. Stern is a believer in sexual polarities: "masculine rationalism" versus "feminine intuitiveness."

STOLLER, ROBERT J. *Sex and Gender: On the Development of Masculinity and Femininity.* New York, Science House, 1968. Refutes "innate differences" theory of masculine-feminine behavior: ". . . insofar as the development of gender identity is concerned in almost all humans, by far the most powerful effect comes from postnatal psychodynamic factors. . . ."

WATTS, ALAN. *Nature, Man and Woman.* New York, Pantheon, 1958. Sex as cosmic union; opposed to grasping, power-play aspects of Western attitude toward nature and sex.

WEININGER, OTTO. *Sex and Character.* London, Heinemann, 1906. Rabidly antifeminist tirade.

WOOLF, VIRGINIA. *A Room of One's Own.* New York, Harcourt, Brace, 1929; and *Three Guineas*, London, Hogarth Press, 1938. Imaginative treatments of the intellectual and economic exploitation of women.

WRIGHT, SIR ALMROTH. *The Unexpurgated Case Against Woman's Suffrage.* New York, Paul B. Hoeber, 1913. Well-known antifeminist book of the prevote era.

3. *Fiction and Drama*

This is obviously only a small, personal selection from the vast number of works of literature which deal with woman's struggle for sanity and social equality.

DRABBLE, MARGARET. *The Millstone.* New York, Morrow, 1965. Adventures of a young unmarried woman who decides to have her baby on her own in London. Harrowing and beautifully written.

GILMAN, CHARLOTTE PERKINS. "The Yellow Wall-Paper" in *Ghostly Tales to Be Told,* ed. by Basil Davenport. New York, Dodd, Mead, 1950. Anthologized widely as a horror story, it is in fact the real experience of Mrs. Gilman. The woman in the wallpaper trying to get out is . . . herself, trying to become real. She states in her autobiography, *The Living of Charlotte Perkins Gilman,* that she wrote the story in 1890 after a nervous breakdown, following which she became subject to fits of depression all of her life.

GELLHORN, MARTHA. *Two by Two.* New York, Simon and Schuster, 1958. Bitter-sweet collection of short stories on modern marriage and love.

GODARD, JEAN-LUC. *La Femme Mariée.* Film about the life of a married woman who is deeply alienated; she has the same empty relationship with both her lover and her husband. When she finds she is pregnant and asks the doctor for an abortion, he refuses to advise her. She is the epitome of woman as exploited by the advertising image.

GRANVILLE-BARKER, HARLEY. *The Madras House,* in *Edwardian Plays,* ed. by Gerald Weales. Mermaid Dramabook, New York,

Hill and Wang, 1962. Drawing-room melodrama which mirrors Edwardian preoccupation with women's place.

KAUFMAN, SUE. *Diary of a Mad Housewife.* New York. Random House, 1967. Bitter, but hilarious account of an urban wife's marital tribulations.

LAWRENCE, D. H. *The Daughter-In-Law,* in *Complete Plays* (Phoenix ed.). London, Heinemann, 1965. Play about a brutish coal-miner, his wife, who has cultural aspirations, and his mother, who seeks to dominate them both. The scenes of marital conflict are as bitter and powerful as any of Strindberg's.

LESSING, DORIS. *The Golden Notebook.* New York, Simon and Schuster, 1962. Fictional life of a woman struggling to be free and herself in contemporary London.

PAVITT, DAWN, and TERRY WALE. *The Bond.* A B.B.C. Television Play. A young woman gradually becomes aware of her marriage as bondage. Excellent for use as an introduction to all problems of women's liberation. Should be screened on as many educational TV outlets as possible.

PLATH, SYLVIA. *The Bell Jar.* London, Faber and Faber, 1966. Novel about a girl who doesn't, can't, and won't fit in, and her horrifying experiences of psychosis in a mental hospital.

SHAW, GEORGE BERNARD. *Getting Married,* in *Edwardian Plays,* ed. by Gerald Weales. Mermaid Dramabook, New York, Hill and Wang, 1962.

STRINDBERG, AUGUST. *Married: Stories of Married Life,* trans. by Ellie Schleussner. London, Frank Palmer, 1913.

WELLS, H. G. *Ann Veronica: A Modern Love Story.* New York, Harper, 1909. Ann Veronica, a spirited, intelligent girl, runs away from her repressive father to London, joins the suffragettes, gets arrested, and falls in love on her own terms. The epilogue—disappointingly—finds her a respectable married woman.

72 73   12 11 10 9 8 7 6 5 4

COLOPHON BOOKS ON SOCIOLOGY

Format by C. Linda Dingler
Set in Caledonia
Composed by Westcott & Thomson, Incorporated
Printed and bound by Murray Printing Company
HARPER & ROW, PUBLISHERS, INCORPORATED